THE GOOD, THE BAD, AND THE UGLY
MINNESTOTA TWINS

THE GOOD, THE BAD, AND THE UGLY
MINNESOTA TWINS

HEART-POUNDING, JAW-DROPPING, AND GUT-WRENCHING
MOMENTS FROM MINNESOTA TWINS HISTORY

Steve Aschburner

TRIUMPH
BOOKS

8/08

Library of Congress Cataloging-in-Publication Data

Aschburner, Steve.
    The good, the bad, and the ugly : Minnesota Twins : heart-pounding, jaw-dropping, and gut-wrenching moments from Minnesota Twins history / Steve Aschburner.
      p. cm.
    Includes bibliographical references.
    ISBN-13: 978-1-60078-076-9
    ISBN-10: 1-60078-076-8
    1. Minnesota Twins (Baseball team)—History. I. Title.

GV875.M55A78 2007
796.332'6409776579—dc22

                    2007041063

This book is available in quantity at special discounts for your group or organization. For further information, contact:

Triumph Books
542 South Dearborn Street
Suite 750
Chicago, Illinois 60605
(312) 939-3330
Fax (312) 663-3557

Printed in U.S.A.
ISBN: 978-1-60078-076-9
Design by Patricia Frey
Photos courtesy of Getty Images unless otherwise indicated.

For the Brookfield Boys, who were with baseball and me every step of the way, from lob games to APBA through those endless summers, from countless trips to Wrigley Field and Comiskey Park to the daring night we called up Johnny Bench.

And to Wendy, who still claims she is related somehow to Arch Ward.

CONTENTS

FOREWORD

Baseball fans familiar with my reputation for fun and games—okay, pranks and practical jokes, too—might not realize that I always took the rules of baseball very seriously. For instance, I learned very quickly, soon after making it to the big leagues as a 19-year-old with the Minnesota Twins, that there was a strict code of conduct for giving a proper hotfoot:

1. Timing is everything. You have to make sure you're ahead in the game.
2. You can't light up an everyday player. I couldn't get Kirby Puckett. You couldn't have him running out to center field with his shoes on fire.

C'mon, baseball has to be fun. This game is a roller-coaster ride with endless highs and lows, and having fun is the best way to release some of that pressure. A lot of the guys don't do the hotfoots or the gum on the hats or the messing around anymore because they don't want it in the newspapers, especially if they lose. You don't have many guys like Steve Lyons, Jay Johnstone, Jerry Reuss, Mickey Hatcher, or Willie Stargell even, guys who always came to the ballpark to have fun. They basically thought, *Who can I agitate today to get* them *so mad, it keeps everyone else loose?* You see it once in a while; with Cleveland, someone gets interviewed after the ballgame and they put a pie in his face. That's about the most fun I've seen in today's game.

That's what I think you'll find—some fun—in *The Good, the Bad, and the Ugly: Minnesota Twins*. The book's author, Steve Aschburner, looks at many of the happiest and most entertaining episodes in the team's history. He takes readers back to some of the Twins' proudest moments and greatest achievements, while recalling the club's most colorful characters, some regrettable or forgettable tales, and a few embarrassing-then, amusing-now stories. And when I see that Ron Davis is featured in the "Ugly" chapter...wow, I know he is pulling no punches.

I was fortunate to have two tours with the Twins: called up as a teenager in the spring of 1970 for six-plus seasons and 99 victories (before a trade to Texas with Danny Thompson in 1976), then brought back at age 34 for another three-plus seasons and 50 more victories. In that decade or so of pitching for Minnesota, stretched across 19 seasons, I had the opportunity to play alongside both Harmon Killebrew and Puck, the two greatest guys ever for the franchise. I learned how to work at my craft from veterans such as Jim Perry, Jim Kaat, Dave Boswell, and Ron Perranoski, and how to keep my personality (even through hard times) from a guy like Luis Tiant, who never let his frustrations over a sore arm spoil his fun. So when Frank Viola was facing big expectations to win when I got back to the Twin Cities in the mid-1980s, I was able to share some of my experiences to help him mature: like never call out a teammate for a play that wasn't made or a hit that didn't come.

My dad [Johannes] taught me to have fun—every night, he had a joke at the dinner table—and all about hard work, determination, and stubbornness. He and my mom came from Holland with $72 in their pockets. My dad worked his butt off his whole life—he was a bumper straightener when he came to the United States, a big strong man until his back went out.

That's one of the reasons I appreciate the fans. The true fan is the guy who sits here every game, you see him, you wave to him, and it's his six-month life. In Minnesota, I don't care what sport it is—Twins, Vikings, Timberwolves, Wild, Gophers—they're great fans. We saw it in the way they packed the Metrodome late at night after we beat Detroit in the 1987 ALCS, a moment that brought tears to players' eyes and had us fired up to face St. Louis in pursuit of the first World Series championship in franchise history. We see it now through the winter caravan, how many fans have followed the Twins from 1961 to today.

So from my signing with the organization in 1969, through my pitching career and another dozen seasons as a team broadcaster, I have been with the Twins for more than half of their existence. Steve's book will take you through those years, as well as the ones I wasn't around for, and stir memories of our best teams, our MVPs, our Cy Young winners, our Hall of Famers (and a few more who ought to belong), and our unsung heroes, along with some of our flops, fistfights, and contract hassles. Fans will get to relive their favorite moments, just like I get to "pitch" every night now from the broadcast booth.

That's how I know, for example, that in giving up 16 home runs in his first 61 innings in 2007, Twins rookie right-hander Kevin Slowey was on pace to shatter my major league record of 50 home runs allowed (in 271⅔ innings in 1986). I hope that's in this book.

—Bert Blyleven

ACKNOWLEDGMENTS

hanks to all those in the Minnesota Twins organization who helped, especially those from the communications department who provided direct assistance: Mike Herman, Molly Gallatin, and Dustin Morse. They didn't blink when they heard the title, taking the good-bad-ugly stuff in the spirit of the project. And they gave me freedom and time to dig through stacks of team files—a trip down the ballclub's memory lane that was invaluable.

Thanks, too, to those within the Twins (past or present) who influenced the crafting of this book unknowingly, with the excitement, memories, and great stories provided by the 1987 and 1991 teams particularly. Kirby Puckett, Andy MacPhail, Bert Blyleven, Frank Viola, Al Newman, Dan Gladden, Terry Ryan, Jeff Reardon, Dick Such, Kent Hrbek, Gary Gaetti, Tom Brunansky, Dave Winfield, Brian Harper, Kevin Tapani, Mark Guthrie, Rick Stelmaszek, Rick Aguilera, Carl Willis, Roy Smalley, Gene Larkin, Randy Bush, Jim Kaat, Tony Oliva, Harmon Killebrew, Joe Niekro, Chili Davis, Don Baylor, and even snarly Jack Morris were interesting, helpful, and willing interview subjects over the years, along with dozens of others. (Tom Herr, John Smiley, and Steve Carlton...eh, not so much.)

Special thanks to Blyleven for his assistance with the book's foreword and instant credibility. The same goes for Tom Mee, the Twins' former media relations director who always has been gracious and generous with his time and institutional knowledge of the franchise and its people. From the first day I stepped in the Metrodome press box as a Minneapolis sportswriter in 1986 through our last phone conversation in September 2007 about the tragedy of Danny Thompson and the underratedness of Greg Gagne, Tom was never less than stubbornly determined to help.

Thanks to Patrick Reusse of the *Minneapolis Star Tribune,* one of the great baseball writers, whose love of the game and appreciation of its characters hasn't gotten wrung out of him by the requirements of his job. Reusse is the walking encyclopedia of Twins history, and in doing this book, I needed him to open a vein and bleed a few hours of insight. Then there is Charley Walters of the *St. Paul Pioneer Press,* the Big Shooter who made the amazing transition from hard-throwing pitcher to always amusing and informative sports columnist. He is the classiest sportswriter in the Twin Cities, and he knows exactly why I feel that way.

This book wouldn't have happened, either, without all the other Twin Cities and national scribes through the years whose work captured the deeds, sights, sounds, and personalities of the various Twins teams. More than any of the others, baseball is a beat writer's sport, with daily newspaper clippings revealing, little by little, the story of a season and an organization. Kind of like those fancy mosaic pictures that are made up of thousands of smaller pictures.

During my research, I got bleary-eyed from reading so many clips and looking at so many microfilm reels and computer screens. I also read all or parts of the following books: *Cool of the Evening: The 1965 Minnesota Twins,* by Jim Thielman; *Twins Pride: For the Love of Kirby, Kent, and Killebrew,* by Alan Ross; *Talkin' Baseball: An Oral History of Baseball in the 1970s,* by Phil Pepe; *The New Biographical History of Baseball,* by Donald Dewey, Nicholas Acocella, and Jerome Holtzman; *Baseball in Minnesota,* by Stew Thornley; *75 Memorable Moments in Minnesota Sports,* by Joel Rippel; *The Baseball Timeline,* by Burt Solomon; *Magic! The 1987 Twins' Enchanted Season,* by the *Minneapolis Star Tribune* sports staff; *Total Baseball, Fourth Edition,* edited by John Thorn and Pete

Palmer; *The Bill James Historical Baseball Abstract,* by Bill James; and *I Love This Game! My Life in Baseball,* by Kirby Puckett.

I have to thank the folks at www.baseball-reference.com, whose incredible website transported me all the way back to innings and pitch counts and dugout decisions made three, four, or five decades ago.

I'd better not forget Erik Meints and Lindsey McCabe, who shared with me the Twins fan's perspective that I didn't have in Chicago, where I rooted for a Twins rival (the White Sox) some of the time and another heartbreaking team (the Cubs) the rest of the time.

Finally, I need to thank Mary Schmitt, a colleague for many years and a pal for even longer, for her encouragement with this project.

THE GOOD

KIRBY PUCKETT

There has been, among some of the baseball purists and the numbers crunchers and, always, the crowds on both coasts, a mild backlash in the past couple of years regarding Kirby Puckett's rightful place in baseball's Hall of Fame.

Some of the second-guessers aren't sure he belongs at all, given lifetime statistics that stopped as abruptly as Puckett's magnificent career did when he lost the sight in his right eye days before the 1996 season. Others accept Puckett's enshrinement, but think sentiment swept him in prematurely in his first year of eligibility in 2001. These folks acknowledge that Puckett put together a Hall of Fame résumé but act as if he should have been scheduled for a second or third interview.

To which we can say here: hogwash.

Puckett didn't reach 3,000 hits. He didn't hit .400, slug 500 home runs, win a Most Valuable Player award, or hit safely in 57 consecutive games. But he did one thing over the span of his career better than anyone else in the game, maybe better than anyone since (and this will give it away) Ernie Banks.

Puckett epitomized the joy of baseball.

He played the way most fans like to think they would play, if they had the chance and were good enough and, naturally, didn't let the pressure get to them or get waylaid by the nicks and the bruises or start to treat a game like a job.

Puckett brought joy with him to the ballpark early each day and usually wouldn't let it go home much before midnight. He toted it along in each inning, into the field and to the plate. It was obvious in the easy, accessible way he made fans and friends out of strangers or bonded with rival players, deftly separating the fraternization from the competition.

And fortunately, before he left the game and long before he left the Earth so suddenly, too young, in March 2006, Puckett understood fully what his greatest asset was.

On an invitation-only trip to Cooperstown, New York, in May 2001, to get acquainted with the Hall of Fame a few months before his induction ceremony, Puckett took a few minutes to talk with local reporters. He told them he sometimes thought about how great it would be to possess Lou Brock's speed, Henry Aaron's power, and Roberto Clemente's arm. In other words, the absolute best pieces from the parts bins, most likely for a chassis slightly taller than 5'8".

"But personality," Puckett said, "I get to have my personality."

Puckett became, during his career with the Minnesota Twins and for at least the first five years afterward, the most popular athlete in the state's sporting history. He did it with his accomplishments, sure; as an anchor of the 1987 World Series team that brought Minnesota its first major championship since the old George Mikan Lakers, Puckett's value was undeniable. But he also did it by bringing and keeping the fans close, smiling without selling out, even failing at times in ways they could appreciate.

"In so many ways, professional athletes are living the dream of the average guy," former Twins general manager Andy MacPhail said after learning of Puckett's Hall election. "Yet so many athletes today seem to approach everything they do as if it is a terrible imposition. As if every day is a battle. Kirby conveyed just the opposite. He let everybody know that he was having fun playing the game. He was the beacon for baseball at a time when the game needed it."

Said Puckett: "I just played baseball like every game was my last. Some days, I came to work and [Kent] Hrbek and Lauds [Tim Laudner] and Molly [Paul Molitor] can tell you: I didn't feel like working, just like anybody else. But I'd take a couple aspirin, take batting practice and start sweating, and, when the bell rang, whether it was 1:05 or 7:05 or whatever time it was, I was ready to play."

Harmon Killebrew, "Mr. Twin" in the franchise's pre-Puckett era, once said of the round center fielder, "He's just a down-to-earth nice guy. The old ballplayers, we'd use the term that he's a throwback to the olden days.... He's never too busy to talk to people and say 'Hello.'"

Kirby Puckett's infectious smile helped make him one of the most popular athletes in baseball history.

The story of Puckett's career has been told often and well, to the point that some surely know its highlights by heart:

There was his start in Chicago's grim Robert Taylor Homes project on the city's South Side, one of nine kids. They were raised and steered away from most of the mayhem by Catherine and William, two strong parents whose values and lessons trumped the neighborhood's harsh economics or any easy excuses. "Sixteen-story buildings with 10 apartments per floor and two elevators," Puckett once shared. "The elevators would go out, and what floor were we on? The 14th. My mother would go get the groceries, and then she would put together an assembly line with us, the nine kids, to get the groceries up all those floors to our apartment."

Growing up so close to old Comiskey Park, with the National League Cubs a subway ride away on the North Side, Puckett gravitated to baseball and some of the local teams' stars. That meant Banks, Billy Williams, and, from the 1920s and '30s, short, squatty Hack Wilson. "I found out Hack was only 5'6", 5'7", and he hit 56 home runs and 190 RBIs [later changed to 191]," said Puckett, who kept a photo of Wilson in his clubhouse stall for years. "He was a little guy who did big things."

Puckett played some college baseball, initially at Bradley in Peoria, then at Triton College outside of Chicago. Drafted by Minnesota in 1982, Puckett was a quick study for a needy team, so on May 7, 1984, he flew from Portland, Maine, through Atlanta, to join the Twins in Anaheim. That produced Puckett's famous empty-wallet cab ride from LAX to the Angels' ballpark in Orange County. He owed a $60 or $85 tab (the amount keeps changing), so Puckett left one of his suitcases as collateral with the cabbie while he bummed the money in the visitors' clubhouse.

At some point, some Twins wondered about this Puckett kid they had heard so much about. "This was the phenom we've been waiting for?" Randy Bush said after getting his first glimpse.

Well, uh, yes. And Puckett showed it the next night, rapping four hits to become only the ninth player to do that in his big-league debut. Eventually, he would become the first player in baseball's modern era to get 2,000 hits in his first 10 full seasons.

Always a free-swinger at the plate but far from a finished product when he arrived, Puckett added a distinctive leg kick to his batting stance as a timing and weight-shifting mechanism, a technique taught to him by Twins great Tony Oliva. It triggered a surge in power, too, with Puckett soaring from no home runs in 1984 to 31 two years later.

Rather quickly from that point, as both the team and its center fielder improved, so did Puckett's achievements, such as 10 All-Star selections, six Gold Gloves, and the 1989 AL batting title. He piled up five seasons with at least 200 hits, three in which he scored 100 runs or more, three in which he drove in at least 100, and six seasons hitting 20 homers or more. And on the last weekend in August 1987, Puckett single-handedly tore up Milwaukee, going 10-for-11, including a line shot off ace reliever Dan Plesac that came at him out of a shadow and still ended up about six rows beyond the outfield fence. "I was unconscious," Puckett said.

Defensively, Puckett was robbing wannabe home runs at the Metrodome long before Torii Hunter made it his trademark. Playing deep to begin with, he would churn his sturdy legs back to the warning track, then leap in front of the wall or the Plexiglas. That's exactly what he did, in fact, to take an extra-base hit away from Ron Gant in Game 6 of the 1991 World Series. That's the day, in the hours prior to first pitch, he famously told his Twins teammates to "jump on my back."

A couple of years later, Puckett said, "If I had written it up myself, it couldn't have turned out any better. I was just instigating something when I said it, because everyone was so tight, and as soon as I said it, I could see people give a sigh of relief. 'Oh, Puck's going to take care of things.' We relaxed and played ball."

Part of Puckett's appeal, beyond his personality, was his shape, which always looked (deceptively so) more cuddly than coiled. Children were drawn to him because he was built like a mascot. And let's face it, he had a great sports name, especially as bellowed by longtime Twins P.A. announcer Bob Casey. Somehow, had Puckett been christened "Joe Jones," none of this would have been as much fun.

NICE COMPANY

During the years of Kirby Puckett's career, only Wade Boggs (.333) and Tony Gwynn (.337) posted higher batting averages than Puckett's .318.

In 1993 Minnesota slipped below .500 and stayed there for Puckett's final three seasons. The core of the two World Series teams broke apart bit by bit until he was the last one left. In 1995, at age 35, Puckett batted .314 with 23 home runs and 99 RBIs, missing his shot at 100 when Dennis Martinez hit him in the face with a pitch, ending his season a few games early.

The following March, he got two hits off Atlanta's Greg Maddux in the final spring training game, then woke up the next morning with a big dark spot in his right eye. The diagnosis: glaucoma. After tests, treatment, and surgery, Puckett was told that his playing days were over.

The bad news sparked sadness, anger, suspicions that Martinez's beanball might have contributed to Puckett's ailment, and much gnashing of teeth all around. Others cried. Puckett, as far as anyone ever knew, did not.

"My god, you have a guy struck down in his prime, and never once have I read or heard him exhibit any self-pity," MacPhail said. "There was no 'what-could-have-been' from him. Kirby has always learned to live in the moment."

Said manager Tom Kelly: "He handled it better than anybody. We're all dying here, and he's laughing and joking and trying to make everybody feel okay. The guy lost his eyesight and he's cheering us up."

Said Puckett: "What else am I supposed to do? It's like playing poker. You get dealt a hand. You've got a choice to either hold 'em or fold 'em. I'm not a folder."

Puckett went to work as a vice president with the Twins. Five years flew by and the baseball writers elected him into the Cooperstown shrine. He was one of the most popular inductees in recent memory, with both fans and fellow Hall of Famers.

The next, and last, five years of Puckett's life flew by, too. But they weren't nearly as happy. His marriage to wife Tonya failed. He was accused of repeated infidelities by both his ex-wife and an ex-mistress. Puckett also got snared in an embarrassing, demeaning sexual assault trial after an alleged incident at a nightclub. A jury acquitted him but couldn't erase all the bad publicity the charges had generated.

The Twins carefully, corporately, distanced themselves from the greatest player in their history. That was followed soon enough by Puckett's self-imposed exile down to Scottsdale, Arizona. His weight ballooned, and those friends who didn't lose contact with him worried about his health.

He never opened that car wash he had talked so excitedly about early in his career, a simple plan for a meaningful post-baseball existence. But he did have a new fiancée, a plan to shed some pounds, and a chance at a fresh start.

On March 5, 2006, Kirby Puckett suffered a massive stroke at his Arizona home. He died the next day, a week before his 46th birthday.

"Baseball owes me nothing," the Twins' former center fielder said several years before his death. "I owe everything to baseball. My whole life as a kid, it's what I saw and what I wanted to play, and I did it every day. And when it was over, I missed it just for a little bit. Then I went home and looked in the mirror and said, 'Puck, you couldn't have done any better than you did.'"

1987 WORLD CHAMPIONS

With Texas in town for a weekend series in mid-August, deep into the 2007 schedule, the Twins celebrated the 20th anniversary of their first World Series championship team. In many ways, it was a remix of the 10-year anniversary celebrated back in 1997, with the same sort of nostalgia, fond memories, and renewed friendships, with a few additional harmless jokes about waistlines, wrinkles, and receding hairlines.

In other ways, it was completely different: Kirby Puckett wasn't around for this latest reunion, having died in March 2006 after suffering a massive stroke at the age of 45. Joe Niekro, a pitcher on that '87 team, had died seven months after Puckett, at age 61, from a brain aneurysm. Bullpen closer Jeff Reardon and his family had suffered serious setbacks—the loss of son Shane, a battle with mental illness for Jeff—and only recently were finding ways to be happy again. Real life and time were intruding on all of them, in ways large and small that they hadn't back in 1997.

And then, in at least one way, the anniversaries in both 2007 and 1997 were misnomers entirely, a little false advertising to those who remembered best what unfolded back in 1987.

That is to say, when the Minnesota Twins won their first World Series title, they didn't really have a championship *season*. They had more of a championship run. Or a championship stretch drive.

In reality, the most memorable "season" in franchise history lasted less than two months. On August 28, after Milwaukee's Chris Bosio beat them 1–0 for their ninth loss in 10 games, the Twins' lead in the AL West dwindled from a high of five games (August 18) to, well, none; Oakland (66–62) was in a virtual tie with Minnesota (67–63). But by October 25, this unlikely champion had done enough, at precisely the right times, to win its first division title since 1970, beat the heavily favored Detroit Tigers in five games in the AL Championship Series, and turn the most maligned ballpark in the major leagues into the game's greatest home-field advantage.

After a largely ordinary 85–77 regular season, the Twins beat the more postseason-savvy St. Louis Cardinals, four games to three, by winning four times at the Metrodome. No champion in Series history, to that point, had ever finished more poorly over 162 games (in 2006, the Cardinals went 83–78 before winning it all). And just like that, a raucous bunch of fun-loving players, bonded at the core through several years of losing, earned a special place in the state's sports history.

More special than the old Minneapolis Lakers' five NBA titles more than a generation earlier. More special than the Vikings' four (unsuccessful) trips to the Super Bowl. More special, too, than when the Twins did it all over again in 1991.

"I talk more about '87, I think, than I do '91," said Kent Hrbek, the hometown guy from Bloomington who played first base for both World Series teams. "I guess because it was the first one. People always ask me which one I had more fun in, which one I liked best. It's not that I liked the '87 one best, it's just that we kind of all grew up together in the minor leagues, the '87 team, and went through the rough spots together in the early '80s when we were terrible and lost 100 ballgames."

That core included the likes of Hrbek, third baseman Gary Gaetti, catcher Tim Laudner, outfielder Randy Bush, and pitcher Frank Viola. Puckett arrived in 1984, and fellows such as Greg Gagne, Steve Lombardozzi, and Sal Butera had taken their share of lumps.

"The management has stuck with us for a long time," Viola said in spring training, calling it a put-up or shut-up season. "How many years are they going to go with Bruno, Herbie, G-Man, and myself if we don't win?"

The Twins had a 33-year-old general manager, Andy MacPhail, and a 37-year-old field manager, Tom Kelly, working in tandem for their first full season. Other pieces were added that were just as valuable: on February 3, MacPhail completed a deal that had been in the works for months, acquiring Reardon and catcher Tom Nieto from Montreal for pitcher Neal Heaton, catcher Jeff Reed, and two minor leaguers. On March 31, a week before the season opener, the Twins sent three minor leaguers to San Francisco for outfielder Dan Gladden.

With the scrappy, aggressive Gladden leading off the batting order and the glowering, hard-throwing Reardon closing out games from the bullpen, the Twins for once were in a position to seize control of their games' beginnings and endings.

The timing was right for Minnesota in another way: by the time they faced St. Louis in October, the Twins were the seventh different franchise in seven seasons to win the AL pennant. Whatever the fears had been about free agency tilting the playing field toward a few major markets, and however that would play out in the next decade or so, there was a certain randomness at work, a parity, through most of the 1980s.

Make no mistake, the first four or five months of the regular season had their share of highlights: Hrbek's bases-loaded single in the tenth inning to win the opener and spark a sweep of Oakland. Gaetti's single in the ninth to beat California 8–7 on April 25, the first sellout in the Metrodome's five years of existence. A doubleheader sweep at Detroit on a blistering May 31, outscoring the Tigers 20–8 that day.

There was a 4–3 victory in 10 innings on June 10 that completed a sweep of Kansas City, the rival that led the AL West when the month began; the Twins were never worse than tied for the division lead after that. "They won, they're in first. Fine," Royals outfielder Danny Tartabull said. "We'll see them in October."

Late in July, Seattle's Mark Langston limited the Twins to two hits through eight innings, but Lombardozzi's three-run homer in the ninth tied the score, and Gaetti's solo shot two batters later won it. Desperate for starting pitching over a 20-game stretch in July—

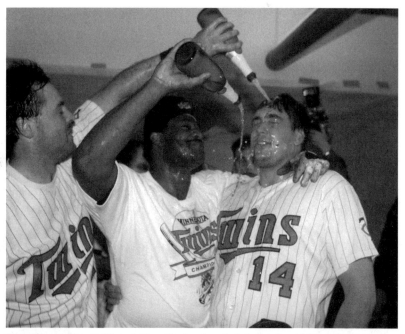

Tom Brunansky (left) and Don Baylor (center) douse Kent Hrbek in champagne after the Twins captured the 1987 World Series.

Twins starters were 2–8—MacPhail added Hall of Fame–bound but by then broken-down left-hander Steve Carlton. He joined Joe Niekro as the staff's second 42-year-old starting pitcher.

August provided a pair of games that immediately were etched into franchise lore. On August 3, in the fourth inning at California, umpire Tim Tschida tossed Niekro after finding an emery board and a piece of sandpaper in his pocket; the umps and the Angels were convinced that Niekro had been illegally scuffing the ball. Four weeks later, Puckett capped an electric weekend in Milwaukee with a 6-for-6 performance, including two doubles and two home runs. On the heels of his 4-for-5 game the day before, the center fielder set an AL record and tied the big-league mark for most hits in consecutive nine-inning games. On August 31, though failing to acquire any pitching help, MacPhail added designated hitter Don Baylor.

Only in September did the vision of what was possible come into focus. A four-game winning streak including three straight 2–1 victories—two of them in extra innings—put the Twins in front by three games. A six-game streak two weeks later pushed that lead to six with nine to play. But Tartabull was right; Minnesota still had two series remaining against the Royals, including one in the first weekend of October.

The Twins lost the first two meetings, both at their beloved Metrodome. Only one home game remained, followed by six on the road; anything could happen. Skeptics worried, worriers fretted, and fretters curled up in the fetal position. Even the normally unflappable Kelly, who could be laconic with his hair on fire, gave in a little to the urgency of the situation: he started veteran right-hander Bert Blyleven, 36, on just three days' rest.

Small problem: Blyleven didn't start sharp. "I couldn't wait to get out there," he said, reflecting years later. "And then I walked the first batter, Willie Wilson, and [Kevin] Seitzer hit one off the baggie [right-field wall] in right. There were runners on first and third with no outs, and George Brett was batting. Nice way to start."

But a completely unexpected and unorthodox play by utility infielder Al Newman at second base—taking Gaetti's throw after

Brett's short-hop grounder to force Seitzer, then throwing home to nail Wilson from third—snuffed the Royals' early hopes and fired up the Twins. There was something else at play, too. In the team's 81st home game, the Metrodome stands were filled, alive, and making noise like never before. The players noticed, Kelly noticed, and the fans themselves noticed, as they basically carried the Twins on a wave of sound and high hopes to an 8–1 victory.

The next night in Arlington, Texas, the crowd dropped from 53,106 to 9,986. But the Twins won 5–3, clinching the division. Mission accomplished? Apparently. They went out and dropped their last five regular-season games.

Next up: Detroit. As solid as some of Minnesota's offensive numbers were during the season—a combined 125 home runs by Hrbek, Gaetti, Tom Brunansky, and Puckett; Puckett's .332 average and 207 hits; Gaetti's 109 RBIs—its pitching rotation was a 2½ hurler operation. Viola won 17, Blyleven 15, and no other starter topped eight victories. The staff ERA was 4.63, and it gave up 210 home runs. And the Tigers were more formidable on both sides of the ball, leading the majors with 98 victories and surviving a tense division race with Toronto into the final weekend.

"Even if we had won those last five games of the season, it wouldn't have mattered," Reardon said. "Everybody cuts down the American League West."

And yet the underdogs thoroughly outplayed the Tigers, taking the best-of-seven ALCS in five games. With a four-run rally in the bottom of the eighth, the Twins went up 8–5 in Game 1 and beat Detroit's Doyle Alexander, a pitcher acquired at the cost of some prospect named John Smoltz but seemingly worth it when he posted a 9–0 mark down the stretch for the Tigers.

The next night, they faced Jack Morris—Detroit's ace, a St. Paul native who had never lost a game in Minnesota and who would pitch the game of his lifetime four years later at the Metrodome—and they beat him 6–3. In Motown for the weekend, the Twins lost Game 3 when Pat Sheridan got Reardon for a two-run homer in the eighth inning of a 7–6 Tigers victory. But Viola and Blyleven both won on short rest, the Twins taking Game 4, 5–3, with strong relief work (three guys, four innings, two hits) and a pivotal pickoff at third base of Darrell Evans. A day later, Minnesota hung four runs on the board in the second inning, three more for cushion in the top of the ninth, and batted around Alexander and three others for 15 hits in a 9–5 victory. For the team's "Class of '82," another dream had just come true.

"It is, isn't it?" Bush said, choking with emotion after the ALCS clincher. "It is everybody's dream from the time they are five years old. You're in the backyard and you're pretending you're in the World Series."

Little did the Twins know that the best was yet to come. Beating St. Louis in seven games over the next two weeks for the championship? Well, that too. But just as special, maybe even more remarkable, was what they experienced upon their return from Detroit as October 12 turned into October 13.

An unexpected throng of well-wishers at the airport, waiting for the Twins when they landed back in the Twin Cities, offered no clue of what was in store for them at the Metrodome. There, late at night with no events, no tickets, and no security, fans spontaneously filled the football-first stadium to welcome home the 1987 AL champs. The team's buses pulled into the Dome and...bedlam!

"I remember saying, 'What are all these cars on the street?'" bullpen coach Rick Stelmaszek recalled. "And they bused us into the Dome and lifted that door about three-quarters of the way up. The power wasn't on entirely, and there were 50,000 people in there. And it was, like, goose bumps. Amazing."

Players and their families cried. Gaetti, whose team in 1983 needed 14 home dates to draw 83,000 fans in September, raised his ALCS Most Valuable Player trophy high before the packed stands. Juan Berenguer, already a crowd favorite for his "El Gasolino" antics on the mound whenever he got hitters out, stepped off the bus in a trenchcoat and Panama hat, carrying a briefcase and instantly becoming a comic folk hero of the title run.

Minnesota's first World Series since 1965, back in the days of Harmon Killebrew, Bob Allison, and Mudcat Grant, proved a little more challenging for the home team. It proved challenging to a nation's baseball fans, too, experiencing the Fall Classic for the first time under a roof. The noise generated by the capacity crowds for Games 1, 2, 6, and 7 seemed more like what you might hear at a Duke–North Carolina hoops game, with a killer roller coaster in one corner. At its peak, the clamor reached 118 decibels, said to rival an airline jet taking off.

"[The thing] that I remember most from the '87 season was the way most of the people here were screaming, the fans," Puckett said. "When the guys from St. Louis kept telling me, 'I can't hear! I can't hear!' well, I couldn't hear either. Nobody could hear. The fans were screaming like crazy. I mean, my ears actually rung, I'm telling you, for, like, a week."

Minnesota outscored the Cardinals 18–5 in the first two games, and St. Louis players grumbled from the start about bad bounces and tracking fly balls under the Teflon roof.

"We're on a mission," Gaetti said as his club headed and to St. Louis with a 2–0 lead. "At least in the Dome, anyway."

Uh, exactly. The turf at Busch Stadium might as well have been Kryptonite carpeting, the way the Twins' superpowers vanished on the road. They looked as mortal as the 29–52 team they had been all season in other clubs' ballparks, getting a total of 18 hits in three games after rapping 21 in Games 1 and 2. They dropped the three midweek games 3–1, 7–2, and 4–2 while turning weak-hitting Tom Lawless into a home-run hero (Game 4) and succumbing to real Cardinals baseball (five stolen bases in Game 5). They even earned derision from famed L.A. sportswriter Jim Murray, who accused the Twins, in their struggles away from home, of being "like a guy who only sings good in the shower."

Fortunately for the Twins, they were headed back to their acoustically friendly ballpark, where they went from pipsqueaks to Pavarottis. "We never feel down in this place," Gaetti said after an 11–5 victory in Game 6. "Either we play well [here] or other teams just don't pitch well."

St. Louis's John Tudor was doing fine until the Twins reached him for four runs in the sixth, going up 6–5. In the seventh Hrbek ended a 1-for-14 drought against left-handers, greeting reliever Ken Dayley for a game-icing grand slam.

All that left was Game 7, one last chance for the Cardinals and Twins, one more chance for the record 55,376 who packed the Dome and brought the noise. This one was basic baseball, with a couple of bad umpire calls mixed in, including one that let Gagne reach safely in the fifth and eventually tie it 2–2. An inning later the Twins shortstop beat out an infield hit as Brunansky scored. Frank Viola, in earning the Series MVP honors, settled down after a shaky second inning, and Reardon, the confidence changer from seasons past, mowed down the Cards 1-2-3 in the ninth.

For the first time in 84 World Series, the home team won every game. And for the first time in 26 years, the Twins won their rings and earned a parade.

"I remember catching the throw from Gary at the end to clinch it up," Hrbek said recently, nearly 20 years removed from that moment. "And then riding in the parade. To hold your finger up and say you're number one and actually be the best. To get to ride in the parade down the street and have people throw things at you and holler at you, that's something I really remember."

Said Viola: "I was trying to get to the pile after the last out of Game 7. I was just hoping my legs would get me to the pile. That's such a special moment, when you win. You want to be in there with all your teammates and coaches. That's what you play sports for—to be the best. And on that day, we were the best."

1991 WORLD CHAMPIONS

The Twins' World Series title in 1987 played mostly to the heart. That team won unexpectedly, shrugging off embarrassment over a mediocre regular-season record (85–77) and wisecracks about its overreliance on a freaky home ballpark. The core of that team had grown up together the hard way in the big leagues, taking lumps (102 of them in 1982), then finally coming together, growing together, at just the right time.

The Twins' title team four years later, though, was all about the head. And guts.

When the Twins beat the Atlanta Braves in seven games in 1991, they did it by outmaneuvering, outstrategizing, and outplaying the

National League pennant winners. But they also did it by outlasting them, in a white-knuckle World Series that featured five games decided by a single run, three that went into extra innings, and two more that were tied into or through the eighth.

They called it the Worst-to-First World Series, because both the Twins and the Braves had finished at the bottoms of their respective divisions in 1990. But it just as easily could have been dubbed the Milk of Magnesia Series or the Gnawed Nails Series, given how tense and nerve-racking the games were.

It was a Series that made daily newspapers feel obsolete, given their inability to hit deadlines with final stories and box scores. It was a Series for Bad Screenwriting 101 as well, since only in a cheesy B-picture would some hack scriptwriter dare to cram in so many twists and turns, moments of comic relief, clutch plays, bad

Dan Gladden scores the winning run in Game 7 of the 1991 World Series.
Photo courtesy of AP/Wide World Photos.

decisions, fundamentally precise baseball, and examples of true heroism (or as close as anything sporting can ever get to that), all in a period of seven games over nine days.

Either that, or you just settled in with your popcorn and Milk Duds and got Hitchcock, Shelton, the Coen brothers, Tarantino, Apatow, and Spielberg, all rolled into one.

Before the start of Game 7 at the Hubert H. Humphrey Metrodome, as Atlanta leadoff hitter Lonnie Smith stepped to the plate, he shook hands with Twins catcher Brian Harper. The two had been involved in a bone-jarring collision in one of the Braves' victories down south, but this wasn't any sort of peace offering. It was a bonding of sorts, a moment in which the two men nodded to the enormity and fun of what they were doing.

It was, in its way, Pete Rose shouting to Carlton Fisk during Game 6 of the classic 1975 Series: "Isn't this the greatest game?"

In this case, though, Smith and Harper still had nine...wait, 10...innings to go. Few would have believed it at that moment, what with all the tension and fatigue and dramatics already, but those guys hadn't seen nothin' yet.

"After Game 6, people started telling me this is one of the greatest World Series ever played," Twins manager Tom Kelly said. "Then you start thinking about what you've gone through in the dugout and you think maybe they're right."

Wait a minute. This is starting to sound like "heart" stuff all over again. Truth is, the roller-coaster ride that Minnesota went on with its baseball team from the first Dome-dominated Series to the second was all part of a carefully designed plan. Surprisingly well-executed and serendipitously punctuated, but carefully designed all the same.

It wasn't that general manager Andy MacPhail, Kelly, and his staff wanted to go from the top to the bottom and back to the top again, exactly. But they knew things had to change, that there was more fluke and magic in the 1987 championship than some were willing to admit, and that a rebuilding wasn't just preferable but necessary.

So when the Twins' second-place finish in 1988 was followed by a drop to fifth in 1989, then to gnarly ol' seventh in 1990, no one panicked. "I think it's ridiculous for us to be judged as incompetent last season and then as geniuses now just because the team is playing better," MacPhail said midway through the 1991 season, as his vision was turning tangible.

To get there-from-here, MacPhail stuck with a core of holdover players, sure. There were seven: Kent Hrbek and Greg Gagne in the infield, Kirby Puckett and Dan Gladden in the outfield, and Randy Bush, Gene Larkin, and Al Newman off the bench. Half of the starting position players and the entire pitching staff, however, were new.

The pitchers of the '91 team came from inside and out, harvested from the farm system that MacPhail always made a priority and acquired, most notably, in a big 1989 trade that sent Frank Viola to the Mets for a handful of hurlers. Among them: Rick Aguilera, who would fill Jeff Reardon's role as lockdown closer, and Kevin Tapani, an innings-eating starter.

With Juan Berenguer gone as a free agent, MacPhail had Kelly plug the middle innings with the likes of Mark Guthrie, Steve Bedrosian, Terry Leach, and Carl Willis. He used a newbie, Chuck Knoblauch, at second base and got a Rookie of the Year performance out of him. To fill the void at third left by Gaetti, another free-agent loss, MacPhail went for a retread, former Yankee Mike Pagliarulo. Then he backed up Pagliarulo with little-known farmhand Scott Leius.

Harper in 1991 was about a 100-point upgrade, in batting average, from Tim Laudner of that '87 club and only a slight drop-off defensively. Chili Davis was another flyer of sorts, hobbled by a back problem in 1990 with California. With Minnesota, he went from 12 home runs, 58 RBIs, and a .265 average to 29, 93, and .277, respectively, as the AL's top designated hitter.

Last but not least (which is the way he eventually would send everyone home in October), the Twins brought in Jack Morris, the St. Paul native who had shopped his services in Minneapolis—remember the fur coat tour?—before the club's previous championship season. That was in baseball's funky collusion era of the 1980s, when quality free agents such as Morris mysteriously couldn't attract contract offers, not even from a spender like

Kirby Puckett and the Twins celebrate after winning one of the most memorable Game 7s in baseball history.

George Steinbrenner. But this time, with Morris out for maximum bucks and willing to gamble on an incentive-laden deal, the 36-year-old came home.

So it was a mix of old and new, established and driven, young and old, homegrown and store-bought, that meshed in a chemistry nearly equal to the '87 team's and a day-in, day-out performance that was far superior. The 1991 Twins won 95 games, 21 more than the season before and 10 up on the first bunch of October heroes. The Twins in 1987 were built for power (four hitters combined for 125 home runs), defense, a money closer, and as much mileage as they could get out of Viola, Bert Blyleven, Les Straker, and the equivalent of fantasy campers fleshing out the starting rotation. In 1991 Minnesota's top four HR hitters totaled only 82. Defensively, though, this group was even tighter than the first, and the pitching, from Morris to the 10th or 11th man, was much deeper. This staff shaved nearly a full run off its ERA, from 4.63 to 3.69, while walking almost 100 fewer batters and giving up 139 home runs versus 210 in 1987.

These Twins won the AL West by a comfy eight games over second-place Chicago, and then worked their way through the Toronto Blue Jays in the ALCS. And while that best-of-seven series, on paper, seemed worthy of the one that would follow—the first three games were decided by one run, and the Twins finally lost a postseason game (Game 2) in their beloved Metrodome—it never seemed in doubt. While the teams split the first two in Minneapolis, the winner of each never trailed or was tied. The third game, at Skydome, had tension that was released on Pagliarulo's pinch-hit homer in the tenth. But in Games 4 and 5, Minnesota outscored their East Division counterparts 17–8. And breaking a 5–5 tie in the eighth inning of the deciding game isn't all that exciting when the winning team had two home games to spare.

The most impressive aspects? Kirby Puckett's .429 average and five RBIs to be named MVP of this round, Aguilera near-flawless

CALL HIM "MISTER LOGO"

Legend has it that Harmon Killebrew was the unknowing model for the Major League Baseball logo. We're talking about the silhouette of the batter, from his arms up, bat high, poised for a pitch. It is similar to the one used by the NBA, which never hid the fact that it used Lakers great Jerry West as its iconic basketball dribbler.

Baseball long has denied that it based the design on any specific individual. But the logo was created in 1969, when Killebrew had his best, and baseball's best, individual season with 49 home runs, 140 RBIs, and 145 walks.

Besides, it could have been worse. Baseball could have used Denny McLain or Pete Rose.

in three saves, and the Twins becoming the first road team to win three times in a playoff series.

"We had a much better ballclub this year [than in 1990]," Puckett said after Game 5. "I can't lie to you and say I knew we were going to be in the World Series, but I knew we weren't going to come in last again. With the changes we made, we knew we had a winning combination."

As they had just proved again, the 1991 Twins weren't as dependent on a home-field advantage as the '87 crew, going 44–37 on the road compared to 29–52. Still, the Series was set up according to alternating years, not All-Star Game outcomes, and the Twins knew they had the first two and, if needed, the last two at the Dome.

In broad strokes, that's exactly how it played out again. The Dome was just as loud as the first time, fans again were showing up with hankies, and the Braves looked only slightly more comfortable in the prefab ballpark than the Cardinals had four years earlier. But this Series, make no mistake, was not decided by plastic grass, a Teflon roof, or the oversized Hefty bag draping the wall beyond right field. This was all players, coaches, managers, luck, and guts.

The opening game was about as conventional as this Series was going to get, except for maybe Braves manager Bobby Cox's decision to start Charlie Leibrandt ahead of Tom Glavine. Greg Gagne, Minnesota's defensive ace at shortstop but a light hitter, poked a three-run homer in the 5–2 victory. The next most significant thing might have been Leibrandt striking out Puckett twice, something Cox remembered to his eternal second-guessing regret five games later.

In Game 2, the Twins' hitting star was Leius, breaking a 2–2 tie with a homer in the bottom of the eighth. Gagne? Leius? It was almost as if the guys at the bottom of Minnesota's batting order were throwing down a gauntlet to Atlanta's versions, guys like Mark Lemke and Greg Olson. Something else filed for future reference. Hrbek seemed to throw his weight around at Ron Gant to nail the Braves outfielder with a half-lift, half-tag that earned him death threats from Braves fans. As for Glavine, he allowed only four hits, went the distance, and lost.

After a day to travel, to purge the DH rule for a few days, and to shift the intensity into a higher gear, Game 3—the first World Series game ever played in Atlanta—made its own claims to all-time status. *Washington Post* baseball writer Thomas Boswell, for instance, called it "perhaps the most complex World Series game ever played." The managers used 12 pinch hitters and 42 players, both single-game records. Cox got criticized royally for removing starter Steve Avery in the eighth inning with a 4–2 lead—and only 84 pitches thrown on his chart—because Chili Davis promptly lashed a two-run homer off reliever Alejandro Pena to tie it. Then Kelly took some of the heat off the Braves' manager by having only Aguilera left to bat with the bases loaded in the twelfth inning and the Twins one swing away from a 3–1 Series lead.

In the bottom of the twelfth, Atlanta's David Justice, bogged down in a miserable postseason until this night, singled with one out. Another out, then Justice stole second. Then Lemke, the Braves' bespectacled second baseman, knocked a single over the shortstop, sending Justice around and home. The onetime Mr. Halle Berry flopped headfirst toward the plate, snagged it with one hand, and evaded a tag by Harper to win it 5–4. It had taken a mere 4 hours, 4 minutes.

"So many things happened," said Ray Knight, the former New York Met working the Series as a broadcaster for ESPN. "You saw things go from darkness to light in one inning."

The next night, the teams shaved more than an hour off Game 4, without dialing down the competitiveness one bit. Morris battled John Smoltz, but neither starter was around after Pagliarulo and Smith matched solo shots in the seventh inning to keep it tied at 2–2. Hrbek assured his continued safety at Atlanta–Fulton County Stadium by stranding two runners in scoring position and going to 1-for-10 in the Braves' park. In the bottom of the ninth Lemke tripled to left with one out, and then scored on pinch-hitter Jerry Willard's fly to right.

The last of the three games in Atlanta slipped away early, and then got out of hand late, ending in a 14–5 Braves rout that allowed everyone to exhale for a night. The Twins went Bizarro, with Davis playing right field—wow, he really did own a glove!—Shane Mack benched, and five pitchers sharing in the 17-hit abuse. David West went the infinity route, facing four batters, retiring no one, throwing only four strikes, and giving up four runs.

Heading into the postseason's final two days, back in Minneapolis, it felt for a while like 1987 all over again: the Dome, the noise, the circumstances. Until, that is, Puckett grabbed Game 6 by the throat. He put the Twins up 2–0 in the first inning with an RBI triple and a run scored. In the third inning the hydrant-shaped center fielder leaped against the Plexiglas outfield window and grabbed Gant's blast with a man on, likely saving one run or more. He put the Twins up 3–2 with a sacrifice fly in the fifth, and then singled and stole a base in the eighth.

At 3–3 in the bottom of the eleventh, Cox went to that man again, Leibrandt. Puckett got a good look at three pitches from the veteran left-hander. Then, in a moment that seemed preordained, he swatted Leibrandt's fourth over the fence in left-center. As Puckett cranked his arm and punched it, a dozen jet airplanes took off, serenaded by 76 jackhammers, with a chorus of 100 thundering pachyderms. At least that's how it sounded in that joint.

"Ten, 30, 50 years from now, when I look at it, it might be different," Puckett said up in the home clubhouse afterward. "Right now? Unbelievable, man. Unbelievable."

By the evening of October 27, several players on both sides already were talking in hushed tones about the magnificence of the Series in which they were involved, offering up bunk about "what a shame that either team has to lose." Had Morris, the Twins' scheduled starter for Game 7, heard any of that coming from his guys, he would have a) smirked, b) spit, c) scratched himself, or d) all of the above. He would not have joined the choir.

"I'm a lousy loser," he had said earlier in the Series. "But I've learned to accept it."

An entire generation of Braves fans grew up hating a guy they never met, thanks to Game 7. It was the only reasonable response after Morris, inning after inning, stomped to the Metrodome mound and blanked their favorite team. The nasty right-hander, the AL's top starter through the 1980s, was in peak form two years into another decade. Morris gave up seven hits, struck out eight, issued one unintentional walk, and threw one wild pitch. Of the 10 Atlanta men who batted with runners in scoring position, Morris set down nine of them; the tenth was Smith's bunt single, moving Lemke from second to third in the fifth inning. So Morris stranded both of them, getting Terry Pendleton to pop up and striking out Gant.

In the eighth, the Twins wriggled out of a runners-on-second-and-third, nobody-out jam which was a break in itself, thanks to Knoblauch and Gagne faking lead runner Smith into a notorious brain cramp on Pendleton's double, preventing him from scoring. Morris got Gant again on a weak grounder and, after an intentional walk to Justice, coaxed exactly what he wanted—a double-play ball out of Sid Bream. But the Braves matched it in the bottom of that inning, Mike Stanton getting Hrbek to line into a double play with the bases loaded.

Morris sailed through the ninth, and then had his toughest confrontation of the night—fending off Kelly's attempt to call on his bullpen. Successfully persuading the manager that he was feeling fine (with or without the threat of doing bodily harm), Morris then sailed through the tenth.

Gladden doubled to center, the Twins' ninth hit of the night, in the bottom of the tenth. Knoblauch sacrificed him to third, so the Braves walked Puckett and Hrbek for options at any base. With Atlanta's outfielders creeping in, pinch-hitter Gene Larkin smacked the first pitch he saw from Pena past Brian Hunter, into left-center. Gladden bounded home, and the Twins who weren't already on the field streamed from the dugout, Morris among them. He was an easy choice for Series MVP after arguably the best Game 7 pitching performance in baseball history.

Hardly anyone left for a long time after Larkin's base hit, in the stands or beneath them. The champagne flowed, followed by other beverages of choice, in the Twins clubhouse. Crusty old guys and too-cool twentysomethings alike were wide-eyed, exhausted, and giddy. Pagliarulo got a lot of airplay for gushing like a fan.

"This was the greatest game," the third baseman said. "How could the TV guys describe it? They [the Braves] had a chance to win, but they didn't. We had a chance to win, but we didn't. Then we did."

Morris was more succinct. "Days like this," he said, "are what make all the rest of the [stuff] you endure in life worthwhile."

THE BAD

THE GREAT RACE OF 1967

In Boston, the 1967 American League season is known as "The Impossible Dream," one glorious summer in which the Red Sox unexpectedly ended a 21-year pennant drought and revived the city's enthusiasm for baseball in a way that hasn't waned since.

In Detroit, it was a tune-up year, a prelude to the Tigers' own memorable season, the Denny McLain carnival, and a World Series championship in 1968.

In Minnesota, though, 1967 is commonly remembered for the pennant that got away, wriggling out of the Twins' grasp like a walleye slipping back into one or another of the state's 10,000 lakes.

"There are a few things you can laugh at now, I guess, but we absolutely should have won that thing," pitcher Dean Chance, the ace of a strong Twins staff, told the *Minneapolis Star Tribune* years later. "We had a great, great ballteam."

But the American League was different then. Mickey Mantle was still playing for the Yankees, clubbing his 500th home run that May. The Athletics still called Kansas City home, their last season before moving to Oakland. And the major leagues were still two years away from another expansion and a realignment into divisions, with an extra round of postseason play.

That's how four surprising but deserving teams ended up in a dogpile for much of the summer, shifting atop the AL standings down the stretch as if tethered together.

The Twins were two years removed from their 1965 World Series experience and more than a little made-over with Chance, the 1964 Cy Young Award winner acquired the previous December, and a rookie second baseman named Rod Carew. Chance, Jim Kaat, and Dave Boswell each notched more than 200 strikeouts—the first time three pitchers on the same staff had done that—and a resilient group of eight hurlers ranked second in league ERA (3.14).

With Carew on his way to the AL Rookie of the Year Award, Harmon Killebrew near his peak with 44 home runs and 113 RBIs, Bob Allison chipping in 24 homers, and Tony Oliva good for 17 home runs and 83 RBIs, Minnesota had a potent attack and ranked third in average.

The competition was equally tough. Boston led the league in runs, hits, and home runs (158), with right-hander Jim Lonborg having his career year (22–9) at age 25. Led by Al Kaline's 25 home runs, the Tigers had four men hit at least 20, and four starting pitchers with at least 14 victories each. Chicago's lineup was toothless—no regular hitter batted higher than .241—but with Gary Peters, Joe Horlen, and Tommy John, its staff ERA of 2.45 was the AL's best by a wide margin.

Each of the clubs had its moments, good and bad. Chicago spent the longest time in first place (71 days) and at one point had the fattest lead (5½ games). Detroit called first place home for 32 days, though it never enjoyed more than a two-game cushion. The Red Sox were seven games out of first place on July 8 but had vaulted in front by 1½ games by late August. Boston had only 21 days atop the pack but, obviously, was there when it counted most. And the Baltimore Orioles, baseball's Series champs in 1966, made it all possible by plummeting from 97–63 to 76–85.

One of baseball's most tragic moments ever took place at Fenway Park on August 18, when a pitch from California's Jack Hamilton slammed into Tony Conigliaro's left eye, ending the young outfielder's season and curtailing his career. None of the other clubs, Twins included, faced anything so traumatic. But Minnesota's season wasn't without its hiccups: manager Sam Mele, good enough to get the team to the World Series in '65, had trouble keeping this Twins club focused and sharp. His fault or not, they dropped 10 of their first 15 games, were two games under .500 by the end of May, and, on June 8 against Cleveland, blew a 5–3 lead in the ninth inning with Mele allegedly too passive for owner Calvin Griffith's liking. The next day, Griffith fired him, promoting easygoing Cal Ermer from the minors.

"Sam had been around awhile, we'd had some success, and it seemed like he changed some the last couple of years," Kaat recalled. "There was a feeling in the clubhouse that he was taking too much credit for the good and none of the blame for the bad. There was a little discord starting to form. Cal Ermer was a great guy. I don't know if he ever had control over big-league players, but he was a different presence than Sam, and it worked for the rest of that season."

By September 6, the four teams were locked in a virtual tie for first place: Boston and Detroit at 79–62, Minnesota and Chicago at 78–61 and theoretically better off with one fewer loss. Heading into the final week, they were clumped within one game of each other, with the White Sox having the friendliest schedule; their final eight games were against Cleveland, Kansas City, and Washington, three of the AL's four scruffiest teams. But Chicago petered out, going 2–6 down the stretch.

That left three teams. On the morning of Saturday, September 30, the Twins were alone in first at 91–69 and facing a two-game series in Boston. The Red Sox were a game back at 90–70. Detroit, also one game back, was 89–69 but had two doubleheaders against California crammed into the season's final two days. Sweeping or even winning three was expecting a lot.

With Kaat and Chance rested and ready, the Twins' chances looked good. With Boston's Jose Santiago lugging a 4.52 ERA in 10 previous starts that season into Saturday and Lonborg dragging an 0–6 career mark against Minnesota into Sunday, those chances looked ever better. The visitors grabbed a 1–0 lead in the first inning, but when Kaat struck out Santiago to start the Boston third, he ruptured a tendon in his left elbow. Jim Perry hustled in to finish the inning and pitched a hitless fourth, but Boston went up 2–1 in the fifth. Its lead was 3–2 when left fielder

As the Red Sox celebrate, the Twins' Rich Rollins (left, with helmet) trots off the field after making the last out in Boston's 1967 pennant-clinching victory. Photo courtesy of AP/Wide World Photos.

Carl Yastrzemski greeted reliever Jim Merritt with a three-run homer in the seventh, and that was enough in a 6–4 victory. In Detroit, the Tigers and the Angels split the first doubleheader.

So it came down to Sunday. Detroit needed a sweep to force a playoff game with whoever won in Boston. Otherwise, the Twins or the Red Sox would take the pennant outright.

Minnesota got within 12 outs, but its 2–0 lead vanished in the sixth when Boston scored five runs, the rally started by Lonborg's bunt single. Yastrzemski drove in two to tie with a bases-loaded single, and Ken Harrelson's grounder scored Dalton Jones. Twins reliever Al Worthington threw two wild pitches while facing George Scott to allow another run, and an error by Killebrew on Reggie Smith's grounder scored another.

With two outs in the Twins' eighth, Killebrew and Oliva singled, and Allison pounded a ball off Fenway's Green Monster in left. Killebrew scored, but Yastrzemski nailed Allison trying to stretch his hit into a double. In the ninth, Ted Uhlaender led off with a base hit, but Carew grounded into a double play, and Rich Rollins popped out.

For the Red Sox, one bit of business remained. They huddled in their clubhouse, getting what was left of the Tigers–Angels doubleheader on the radio. Detroit won the first game 6–4 and had an early 3–1 lead with McLain on the mound in the nightcap. But McLain's sore ankle flared up, forcing him out in the third. Don Mincher—one of the Twins dealt away in the trade that delivered Chance—did what he could (too late) to help his old club by slamming a homer off reliever John Hiller for a 4–3 Angels lead.

California added three more in the fourth and one in the fifth, and led 8–5 when the Tigers got two men on with no outs in the ninth. But reliever George Brunet got Jim Price to fly out, and then caused Dick McAuliffe to hit into only his second double play of the entire season, ending it.

The Red Sox clubhouse erupted, the champagne finally uncorked. Boston, a 100-to-1 shot to win the World Series, wound up losing to St. Louis in seven games, almost a technicality after the excitement of the pennant race.

Yastrzemski's clutch weekend (7-for-8 with six RBIs and 11 total bases) capped a torrid September for him (.417, nine home runs, and 26 RBIs). His season totals (44, 121, .326) earned him the Triple Crown—though Killebrew actually tied him with 44 homers—and made the 27-year-old Boston star an easy MVP selection.

"I've never seen a perfect player," Red Sox manager Dick Williams gushed to Yaz on that final day, "but you were one for us. I've never seen anyone have a season like that."

Actually, it was the AL's second Triple Crown in as many seasons—the Orioles' Frank Robinson had done it in 1966. No one in either league has won one since.

For Minnesota, the final weekend was a heartbreaker. And it didn't help matters to realize that, over the full season, the Twins had outscored Boston 71–54 in 18 meetings. Worse, they had won or tied their season series with each of the other three contenders, going 11–7 against the Red Sox, 10–8 against the Tigers, and 9–9 with the White Sox.

The problem was beating the also-rans; Minnesota won a total of 30 games against Cleveland, Kansas City, and New York. Boston cleaned up by beating those teams 37 times, and Detroit won 32 of its 54.

THE HARD-LUCK KID

Picking on Terry Felton in "The Bad" chapter of any book on the Minnesota Twins isn't like shooting fish in a barrel; it's like draining the barrel of its water entirely, picking up the fish from the bottom, and then going all Michael Vick on the poor little critter.

Sure, Felton mostly is remembered in Twins annals for a pair of unsavory and unwanted major league records that he set while pitching with the club from 1979 to 1982. Frankly, that Felton's career in the big leagues lasted precisely three years—he made his debut on September 28, 1979, and bid adieu after working Minnesota's game on September 28, 1982—was the only perfect thing about his stay at baseball's highest level.

Everything else was 100 percent imperfect.

The blond-haired Felton gave fans, at least those who didn't blink, a glimpse of troubles to come with unsuccessful cameo appearances in 1979, 1980, and 1981. Across those three seasons, the right-hander from Texarkana, Arkansas, totaled 21 innings in seven games, striking out 16 and walking 11 while compiling an 0–3 record with an 8.57 earned run average. Not exactly a budding Dwight Gooden, but still promising enough and priced right for a Twins team determined to cut costs and force-feed kids to get a full look in 1982.

It wound up an avert-your-eyes train wreck for Felton. He lost 13 more times, setting the record for most consecutive defeats (16) at the start of a career. And since Felton never surfaced in the show after the '82 season ended, he holds the mark for most losses in a career without even a single victory.

In essence, Terry Felton became and, for some with long memories, remains the poster boy for pitching futility. His name gets invoked, to this day, whenever a pitcher starts a season with a shaky or bad-luck stretch or when some hurler is slow getting out of the gate in general. Twins pitcher Matt Guerrier, for instance, brought back visions of Felton when he started 0–4 in 2004 and 2005, before finally gaining a victory in 2006.

See, it can get kind of harsh. Felton, after all, didn't cost the Twins a postseason berth or spoil an Opening Day or scare small children with his work on the mound. The 1982 team lost 102 times, so he was hardly alone in his struggles. He never wreaked havoc on anyone else's staff after leaving the Twins, and most reports had him settling into a peaceful post-baseball existence, working for a while as a prison guard and as a detective in Baton Rouge, Louisiana.

And frankly, if you look closely enough, you can find some legitimate highlights in Felton's pitching career, particularly in what some have portrayed as his hellish 1982 season. Among them:

In Felton's major league debut, against Milwaukee, he entered in the eighth inning with the Twins hopelessly behind, 9–1. But Felton was flawless, retiring the Brewers' final six batters without allowing a hit or a run—okay, he gave up a sacrifice fly to Ben Oglivie that plated an inherited runner—and striking out one;

The next time he faced big leaguers in a game that counted, Felton worked seven innings, gave up six hits and three runs, and got no decision in a game at Anaheim that Minnesota won 5–3. He trailed 1–0 when he gave up a two-run blast to Bobby Grich with two down in the seventh;

Four days later, Felton struck out seven in 5⅓ innings at Seattle, giving up three runs. The Twins, alas, scored only two;

On April 28 of that season, in his fourth and final start, Felton got stuck with four unearned runs in the fourth inning against the Mariners, due to two Twins errors. (Of course, one was by Felton, who also walked four in 3⅔ innings.)

Felton spent most of the 1980 season in Toledo and got credit for beating the Columbus Clippers in the International League postseason. That stood for 25 years as the Mud Hens' last playoff victory. So did Felton's mark for most career victories by a Mud Hen hurler (33), until Shane Loux topped him in 2004. (Felton still holds a Toledo record for most metal lockers smashed to pieces with a bat [1], after one distressing outing.)

That horrible season of 1982? Look closely at how it started. Sure, he was 0–2 by the end of April, used as both a starter and a reliever, but in five of his appearances that month, he gave up a total of six hits and four runs in 17 innings—that's a 2.12 ERA with 12 strikeouts and two walks. It was just one appearance—an April 17 start at California when he got rocked for 10 hits, five runs, five walks, and two homers in 5⅓ innings—that bloated his statistics to that point.

Felton went 0–6 in May and June and was his own worst enemy by walking 37 in 60⅓ innings and yielding 10 home runs. But check this out: opposing batters hit just .235 against him those two months.

When Felton took another loss courtesy of the Angels on August 11, dropping to 0–11, he had left with a 3–2 lead but got victimized when reliever Ron Davis gave up a grand slam to Don Baylor. That got him one of the records: his 0–14 career mark was worse than Guy "Alabama Blossom" Morton's, who started 0–13 for Cleveland in 1914 but won his 14th decision. Morton lasted 11 seasons, going 98–88 with a 3.13 ERA. He even fathered a son who played one game with Boston in 1954.

So where's the highlight in that for Felton? Morton died tragically at age 41 on October 18, 1934. Felton breezed past 41 in 1998 and kept right on going.

From August 16 through the end of the season, Felton made nine appearances, gave up 11 runs, 17 hits, and 16 walks in 17 innings and lost only once more. Who said baseball was fair?

It wasn't as if Felton never experienced the thrill of contributing to a major league victory; he did pick up three saves in 1982. Of the games he played in that year, the Twins won five. (Okay, so they lost 43.)

Fans in the Twin Cities shouldn't have been so hard on Felton. In 22 appearances at Met Stadium and the Metrodome, he was a barely offensive 0–4. It was on the road (0–12) that the right-hander struggled most.

Twins batters gave Felton little help, providing run support of 2.29 per start. Compare that to the 5.20 runs per start that Johan Santana got during his 20–6 season in 2004. Or the 5.46 runs Frank Viola got when he went 24–7 in 1988. Or Scott Erickson's 5.53 runs en route to a 20–8 mark in 1991.

Opponents hit a collective .240 against Felton in his brief career. Not bad, when you consider the lifetime marks of Jack Morris (.247), Bert Blyleven (.248), Greg Maddux (.249), and Viola (.260). All of those guys, admittedly, kept opponents off the bases more consistently than Felton (.352). But Erickson lasted 15 years in the big leagues, compiled a 142–136 record, and earned millions of dollars while getting hit at a .282 pace, with an OBP of .348.

Here's another highlight for you: in the book *The Scouting Report: 1983*, Orioles Hall of Famer Brooks Robinson offered this analysis of Felton: "What can you say about a guy who has lost 16 in a row? He has to get better if his control improves. He has outstanding stuff, and there is just no way that he is as bad as his 1982 record indicates. Don't give up on him yet." Somebody obviously didn't take Robinson's advice.

Felton had not given up on himself, at least by that point. He made minor headlines, in fact, when he picked up a 5–2 victory at Pawtucket on June 15, 1983. He had dropped his first four decisions for Toledo that spring before finally ending his personal 18-game losing streak. It was his first victory since August 24, 1981, when he beat Columbus 2–1.

"Through the entire losing streak, I never got that far down," Felton said in the *Toledo Blade*. "I never felt like quitting. I love baseball too much to give it up. They'd have to run me out of this game before I'd ever quit."

A teammate all too aware of Felton's hard luck once tried to get him to treat the game the way ballplayers traditionally handle no-hit bids: by sitting in the same spot in the dugout each half inning, placing his glove in the same place, and so on. But Felton

THEIR JOBS TO LOSE

For all of the criticism Kent Hrbek took over the years for his rather casual approach to conditioning, fitness, and diet, he did pretty well on the team's longevity scale. Sure, Hrbek was known to occasionally gobble a Drumstick ice cream cone after a game or imbibe a beer—sometimes both at once—but the beefy first baseman still logged more years at his position than any other Twins position player at any other spot.

Hrbek was the regular first baseman from 1982 through 1994, a span of 13 seasons. Next in line, by number of years: Kirby Puckett, the team's center fielder from 1984 through 1995 (12 seasons).

By position, here are the other longest-serving Twins:
- Catcher: Earl Battey, 1961–1966
- Second base: Rod Carew, 1967–1969, 1971–1975
- Shortstop: Greg Gagne, 1985–1992
- Third base: Gary Gaetti, 1982–1990
- Outfield: Tony Oliva, 1964–1971
- Outfield: Bob Allison, 1961–1963, 1965–1969

shook him off. "I was 0–9 in the big leagues when I realized it didn't pay to be superstitious," he said. "I'd already gone through all the superstitions, and they didn't matter."

"Everybody really has been pulling for Terry," Mud Hens manager Cal Ermer said afterward. "He was more a pitcher tonight than a thrower, and that's what we've been trying to get him to do for a long time. One thing I have to say about Terry—he's not a quitter."

Felton owns another piece of baseball history that most folks know nothing about. On May 29, 1982, he gave up singles in the second inning to Yankees Bobby Murcer and Graig Nettles, and then struck out Roy Smalley. The runners were moving, and Sal Butera's throw to Gary Gaetti was so quick that Murcer stopped and retreated to second. Gaetti chased him over, saw Nettles racing back toward first, and fired the ball to Kent Hrbek, who tagged Nettles. Meanwhile, Murcer broke toward third, so Hrbek threw across to Felton, who was covering that bag, and the Yankees veteran was called out.

Thus, Felton became only the fourth pitcher in baseball's modern era to complete a triple play. The others were Ted Lewis, Jake Thielman, and Tommy John. After the game, Murcer cracked, "We need a second-base coach."

Finally, Terry Felton deserves some credit, inadvertently or not, for adding to the game's long history of bloopers and malapropisms. It happened when Fred White, an announcer of Kansas City Royals games, was tracking out-of-town scores one night and came across a wire-service summary that mistakenly showed Felton as both the starter and the reliever in a distant Twins game.

"Well, I see in the game in Minnesota," White said, "that Terry Felton has relieved himself on the mound in the second inning."

BACK TO THE FUTURE

First in war, first in peace, last in the American League.

That was the slogan attached to the Washington Senators for most of the team's 60 years in the nation's capital. Sometimes it was said affectionately, sometimes caustically, but most of the time, especially near the end, it was said with a sneer and very little respect.

Washington, of course, was the franchise that became the Twins, and there is no sugar-coating the reasons why that ballclub relocated to the prairies of the Upper Midwest. Unlike some of baseball's so-called lovable losers through the years—think Chicago Cubs or Brooklyn Dodgers at various times—the Senators were simply losers. Losers of ballgames and losers of money, first for owner and baseball legend Clark Griffith and later for his nephew Calvin.

How's *that* for a slogan?

The Senators were established at the same time as the American League itself, born out of a defunct Kansas City franchise from the Western League. A little-known fact is that, for most of their stay in Washington, the team was also known as the

Nationals. Not that it mattered much—the club frequently and accurately could be simply called "doormats." In the AL's first decade of competition, four of its teams won the pennant at least twice. The Senators helped make that possible by finishing sixth in their first two seasons, then dropping to seventh or eighth for the next nine years.

In 1910 a tradition was born when President William Howard Taft threw out the first pitch of the season from his box seat. In the local club's 64 home openers through 2007—three franchises, two leagues—a dozen presidents have tossed the ceremonial pitch a total of 45 times, some from the front row, others from the mound. One, Harry Truman, showed off his ambidexterity by throwing balls with both arms in 1950.

But it was a big right-hander who arrived on the scene as a teen in 1907 who finally offered the organization some hope. Walter Johnson, a strapping farm lad born in Humboldt, Kansas, threw the ball as hard as anyone who had played to that point and possibly anyone since. He took a while to gain command of his powerful arm, losing 25 games in 1909. But the Big Train, as he was soon known, won 25 in each of the next two seasons and, in the 10 years through 1919, totaled 265 victories with an ERA that only once rose above 1.90.

Griffith came aboard after the 1911 season. An outstanding pitcher for St. Louis, two Chicago clubs, and several other teams near the turn of the 20th century (a 237–146 record and seven 20-victory seasons), Griffith had organized the New York Highlanders—the team that would become the Yankees—while giving the new league some name recognition in New York. But he had his eye on the Senators' managerial post and finally got it, along with a 10 percent ownership stake in the franchise, in October 1911.

With the Old Fox at the helm, the Senators won 17 games in a row in 1912 and got their first real taste of a pennant race, finishing second to Boston. They were runners-up again in 1913—thank you, Walter Johnson, for those 36 victories, 11 shutouts, and 1.14 ERA—but soon slipped back into the pack in wins and losses.

In 1924 two changes in the dugout had dramatic results. First, Griffith stepped down as field manager and appointed his 27-year-old second baseman, Bucky Harris, to the job. Second, Griffith's nephew Calvin became a batboy. Okay, so the former had more to do with the Senators' first pennant and World Series championship than the latter. Johnson, at 36, was rejuvenated by the team's 92–62 season, went 23–7 with six shutouts, and was named the AL's Most Valuable Player. After waiting 18 big-league seasons to play in a Series, Johnson lost his two starts, including a 12-inning duel with Art Nehf in Game 1. But he made a relief appearance in Game 7 and was on first base when Earl McNeely doubled home Muddy Ruel with one out in the twelfth.

Johnson, by the way, was in the inaugural Hall of Fame class when the shrine in Cooperstown opened its doors in 1936. But Washington had a number of great and very good performers through the years who spent all or much of their careers with the club, including:

- Sam Rice, an outfielder who played 19 of his 20 seasons with the Senators, retiring from Cleveland at age 44 in 1934. Rice, who went into the Hall of Fame in 1963, finished with 2,987 hits and once said that, if he knew 3,000 was going to become such a big deal, he would have stuck around to get the last 13.
- Goose Goslin played nine-plus seasons in Washington, then came back briefly in 1933 and 1938 after stays with the St. Louis Browns and Detroit Tigers. A good all-around outfielder, Goslin batted .316, drove in 1,609 runs, banged 248 triples, and made it to Cooperstown in 1968.
- Outfielder Heinie Manush, a career .330 hitter, spent 5½ of his 17 seasons with Washington and finished third in MVP voting in 1932 and 1933. He, too, got into the Hall, courtesy of the Veterans Committee in 1964.
- Catcher Rick Ferrell had two tours with Washington, both after age 31. He was an eight-time All-Star and later a coach and executive mostly with Detroit. Curiously, Ferrell got into the Hall of Fame despite hitting .281 with 28 homers in his

career—10 fewer than his brother Wes, a pitcher who also had six 20-victory seasons and a 193–128 lifetime record.

- Pitcher Early Wynn, an eventual 300-game winner, spent his first eight seasons in Washington but was an early loser (72–87 with the Senators, 228–157 with the Indians and White Sox).
- Joe Judge, a 5'8" first baseman, hit better than .300 nine times, had 159 triples in 20 seasons, and roomed with Johnson for seven years.
- Emil "Dutch" Leonard won 191 games in the big leagues, spent the prime of his career in Washington (1938–1946), and was considered the top knuckleball pitcher of his era.
- Slick-fielding first baseman Mickey Vernon was a seven-time All-Star and two-time batting champ while playing most of his 20 seasons with the Senators. He returned to manage the expansion version from 1961 through 1963 after Griffith moved the original franchise to the Twin Cities.
- Shortstop Joe Cronin played for the Senators from 1928 through 1934, finished seventh or higher in MVP balloting three times, was picked for the first two AL All-Star teams, and ended up marrying Clark Griffith's niece Mildred. That last move still didn't prevent Griffith from trading Cronin to Boston for shortstop Lyn Lary and $225,000, as the Senators became more and more cash-strapped.

Cronin, as a player/manager, guided Washington to 99 victories in 1933, its final pennant, and a loss to the Giants in five games in the Series. The next season, he earned his trade out of town when the Senators won only 66 times and saw attendance fall by 25 percent. Griffith claimed that Cronin was dealt in part to spare him from nepotism charges and the awkwardness of some day firing his in-law. But that didn't stop the owner from employing plenty of other family members, including nephew Calvin and niece Thelma (both of whom were adopted by Griffith during a stretch of family struggles). Three of Calvin's and Thelma's brothers—Sherry, Billy, and Jimmy Robertson—all worked in the team's front office, too. And Thelma married a former Senators pitcher named Joe Haynes, who was given an executive position.

During World War II, as he had in the First World War, Griffith played a key role in persuading Congress to keep baseball active as an entertainment option during wartime efforts. He also fended off more than one attempt to unseat him as the team's controlling partner.

But over the Senators' final 25 seasons in the nation's capital, they finished within 17 games of first place only twice. And even one of the good seasons ended regrettably: in 1945, Griffith grew so pessimistic about the team's chances that he scheduled extra doubleheaders in September to keeps Sundays available for the football Redskins (the Griffith family owned the stadium, leased it out for NFL games and other events, and made money off the concessions and parking). In the end, though, the Senators finished only 1½ games behind Detroit, in part because their pitching staff had been worn down by all those doubleheaders.

In the early 1950s Calvin Griffith began handling more of the franchise's day-to-day operations. The poor on-field performance and resulting lack of drawing power attracted representatives from cities such as Los Angeles, San Francisco, Atlanta, Louisville, and Houston eager to purchase the team or lure the Griffith clan into a relocation.

Finally, Griffith settled on Minneapolis–St. Paul, forcing his fellow AL owners to avoid the possible wrath of an unhappy Congress by putting an expansion club in Washington. Rechristened the Twins, the team was a financial and competitive success, reaching the World Series in its fifth year in Minnesota and winning division titles in its ninth and 10th seasons there. As baseball's economics shifted significantly in the 1970s, though, the Twins' baseball-only ownership had trouble competing again, history repeating itself and ultimately forcing the Griffiths to sell.

THE LOST YEARS (1993–2000)

As unpopular as he is in the Twin Cities, maybe baseball commissioner Bud Selig really is owed a thank-you note, if not an outright apology, from the Minnesota Twins and their fans.

It was Selig, remember, who stunned, insulted, and frightened longtime Twins fans shortly after the 2001 World Series was complete, announcing that his sport would eliminate two of its sputtering franchises. The Montreal Expos were an easy choice, hemorrhaging money, struggling to develop and retain top talent, and playing in a miserable ballpark. The Twins were experiencing most of the same problems and, word soon leaked out, were volunteered for the gallows by their owner, Carl Pohlad.

But a funny thing happened.

The Twins started to win. A lot.

They took whatever momentum had been generated by their encouraging 85–77 finish in 2001, good for second place in the American League Central, and built on it. Over the next three seasons, the Twins won 94, 90, and 92 games, taking the division crown each year. They earned their way back into fans' hearts, boosting home attendance from dead-last in the league in 2000 (1,000,760) to three consecutive seasons from 2002 through 2004, flirting with 2 million. By 2005, Pohlad's ballclub had made the dingy and synthetic Metrodome an "in" place again, surpassing that 2 million mark in ticket sales in each of the next three years. And in 2006 they won the AL Central again.

So as bloodless and as ill-conceived as Pohlad's and Selig's back-room plan to extinguish the team might have been, it produced a rather impressive result. Putting the Twins on contraction notice in the winter of 2001 had the same effect that whispering the word "glue" in the ear of a disappointing racehorse might have.

Because, make no mistake about it, the Twins at that point had a lot more nag than thoroughbred in them.

It's easy for fans to recall the excitement from 1987 and 1991, the team's two world championship seasons. Their two afterglow seasons were memorable, too: in 1988 the Twins became the first AL team to draw 3 million fans, they won 91 games, Frank Viola (24–7, 2.64) won the league's Cy Young Award, and Kirby Puckett batted .356 with 121 RBIs. In 1992 nearly 2.5 million fans turned out, Puckett hit .329, Rick Aguilera saved 41 games, and the club won 90.

The run of three straight division titles, and four in five seasons, was an obvious highlight. So, too, was the emergence in those years of budding stars such as Johan Santana, Torii Hunter, Justin Morneau, Joe Nathan, and Joe Mauer.

But the years in between, from 1993 through 2000, those vague and fuzzy seasons that seem to blend together and slip from the imagination even when you really concentrate? Let's call that the Minnesota Twins' "lost" era. Not unlike Ray Milland's old *Lost Weekend*, except a lot longer.

Twins fans weren't shy about expressing their feelings about commissioner Bud Selig's rumored plans to contract the franchise. Photo courtesy of AP/Wide World Photos.

For those eight seasons, the Twins were more like Tom Hanks from his *Bosom Buddies* days than Tom Hanks from *Philadelphia* or *Saving Private Ryan*. The Metrodome had all the appeal of Guantanamo Bay. If Picasso thought he had a blue period, he should have tried sitting through a handful of Minnesota baseball games during that time.

From 1993 through 2000, the Twins were 171 games under .500, an average of more than 21 per season. They went 528–699, a .430 winning percentage, and won fewer games in eight seasons than the 2001 through 2006 Twins won in six. They finished fourth in their division four times, and finished fifth four times.

Granted, baseball in general was not helping. The players' strike that shortened the 1994 and 1995 seasons and wiped out a World Series seemed to get taken especially hard in Minnesota, where sports frequently are treated more like pleasant diversions than sources of civic pride, at least compared to some of the old-school rust belt markets like Chicago, Detroit, or Cleveland.

Also, Pohlad kept the clamps on the team's payroll at a time when spending, courtesy of teams in New York, Boston, and elsewhere, was skyrocketing. That doused enthusiasm even before Opening Day for a lot of fans. Local hero Kent Hrbek retired at the relatively young age of 34, his body breaking down before his hand-eye coordination. Then there was the rotten news from spring training in 1996: Puckett was forced to retire, glaucoma cutting short his Hall of Fame career.

But the Twins earned much of the failure and apathy on merit. The limited payroll meant more youth than experience on the roster, more potential than proven results. Some highly touted prospects, such as David McCarty, Derek Parks, Willie Banks, Pat Mahomes, and Todd Walker, never quite panned out, at least not as well as the scouting department had hoped.

Outfielder Marty Cordova, the AL Rookie of the Year in 1995, was derailed by a series of injuries. Veterans imported from elsewhere, such as Otis Nixon, Roberto Kelly, Terry Steinbach, and Bob Tewksbury, were stopgap solutions at best.

"It was trying," said general manager Terry Ryan, looking back from the relative calm of 2003, "because you started to question whether or not you were headed in the right direction, whether or not your decision-making was accurate, whether or not you had enough strength to stay the course. When you lose 90 to 100 games a year for a number of years in a row, there isn't anybody in the world that could have the mental capacity to say, 'Yeah, things are going great here.'"

As the 20th century ground toward its dreary end for the Minnesota franchise, the powers that be decided to make an even greater commitment to rebuilding. It traded away some of the last connections to the club's glory days, sending second baseman Chuck Knoblauch to the Yankees for a bundle of young players, and reliever Rick Aguilera to the Cubs. It slashed payroll at the big-league level even further, to an estimated $16 million for 1999, while continuing to fund the farm system. It kept its management team intact, from Pohlad to Ryan to field manager Tom Kelly and his coaches, considering that a key to the credibility and continuity of the plan.

As Ryan told the *Rocky Mountain News*, "You've got a credible manager down there running this operation, and players didn't have to look too far to see leadership and the mental strength that he had even going through the lean years."

Some of the new faces, in both the first and second waves of talent, began to click. Right-hander Brad Radke won 20 games in 1997 and became a workhorse and anchor for an ever-mutating pitching staff. Catcher A.J. Pierzynski, first baseman Doug Mientkiewicz, and outfielder Jacque Jones blossomed. Shortstop Cristian Guzman, acquired in the Knoblauch deal, made Pat Meares, a solid player, expendable. Hunter reached the big leagues to stay in 1999. Santana arrived a year later.

By 2001, after an encouraging 85–77 finish, the club was on course enough for Kelly to hand off the manager's job to coach Ron Gardenhire. Gardenhire, while coming across to the public as a little more personable than his predecessor, largely has been a surrogate of Kelly in baseball terms, preaching preparation, defense, and a minimum of mistakes.

"The goal on my watch, or whatever you want to call it, for myself and my staff is to maintain that level of respect that we have in the league," Gardenhire said. "I thought my biggest challenge as a manager was to maintain that, because I didn't want to come in here and change the whole system. It's a pretty darn good system."

That system has produced four postseason appearances since 2002 and, in 2006, the trifecta of AL Most Valuable Player Morneau, AL Cy Young winner Santana, and AL batting champion Mauer. The Twins became one of the most admired, envied, and copied organizations in the major leagues, not all that long after nearly being contracted out.

"There isn't a better feeling for us as a team [than] to watch other organizations want to do things the way the Twins do," Ryan said. "It wasn't too long ago that we weren't exactly the blueprint."

THE UGLY

FIGHTING MAD

Baseball fights generally aren't what you would consider "ugly," unless you happen to be scoring according to the Marquess of Queensberry's rules for pugilists. They are more likely to be silly, lazy, sloppy, halfhearted, and full of clinching, pushing, cussing, and glaring. Precipitated most commonly by a hit batsman, a message pitch, a collision at home plate, or an overly aggressive slide or tag, baseball brawls tend to simmer down almost as quickly as they flare up, with players on both sides looking for someone to grab and hang onto, out of harm's way.

That's how it frequently is, anyway, when it's team versus team. But when the fighting gets taken in-house and pits teammate against teammate or player against manager, things truly *can* get ugly.

It's impossible to know how many internal fights take place in the course of one major league season—the players and the teams have a rooting interest in keeping such reports out of the media—but it is fair to say they can be more dangerous, or at least more detrimental, to a ballclub's well-being.

For instance, when players from opposing teams fight, there is only a 50-50 chance your guy will get injured. But when it's a pair of teammates, the odds go up to 100 percent if someone ends up sidelined by the commotion. And that doesn't even begin to address the damage done to harmony, chemistry, trust, and other warm-and-fuzzies that can be important over 162 games.

The Oakland Athletics of the early 1970s seemed to thrive on physical confrontations, and a little bad blood didn't stop them from winning three consecutive World Series from 1972 to 1974. Los Angeles pitcher Don Sutton finally did what some teammates wanted to do, mixing it up with Steve Garvey after Garvey's Mr. Perfect act frayed a few too many nerves, and that didn't stop the Dodgers from winning three pennants during their time together.

The Twins have had at least three in-house skirmishes of varying degrees, each of which got its fair share of coverage. With the franchise well into its fifth decade since relocating to the Twin Cities, it is quite possible that unreported incidents of fraternal fisticuffs far outnumber these three. But for now, we'll stick with the public record and let you be the judge as to which combatant in each fight should be considered the "evil Twin."

Martin vs. Boswell

It wasn't just the circumstances or the participants that made this bout so legendary. It was the venue, too. The Lindell AC was a popular Detroit sports bar—a few blocks from old Tiger Stadium at Michigan and Cass—and as vital to the Motor City's sporting scene from the 1950s into the 1980s as Toots Shor's was in New York as a haunt for Joe DiMaggio and other legendary Yankees.

The bar-and-grill closed its doors in 2002 and was razed in 2006 to make way for the Rosa Parks Transit Center, but in its day, the Lindell AC—the AC was a smirking reference to "Athletic Club"—was a watering hole to, and crossroads of, major Detroit and out-of-town sports figures. It was the Lindell AC where Detroit Lions lineman Alex Karras got into trouble for gambling in 1963—NFL commissioner Pete Rozelle considered the saloon to be a center for illegal sports betting and ordered Karras to sell his financial stake in the establishment.

And it was the Lindell AC where Billy Martin, as Twins manager in 1969, punched out one of his own starting pitchers.

Dave Boswell had been a prize prospect for Minnesota, which bid on him as an 18-year-old free agent, signing him with a $15,000 bonus in 1963. He was brought up quickly, pitched in one game of the 1965 World Series against Los Angeles, and then went 12–5 in 1966. In 1969 he had his best season, going 20–12 while striking out 190 in 256⅓ innings. He also wrestled with his control at times—he walked 99, hit eight batters, and tossed 10 wild pitches that season—but in Game 2 of the 1969 ALCS, Boswell had a memorable duel with Baltimore left-hander Dave McNally. The 24-year-old pitched 10 scoreless innings before the Orioles beat him in the eleventh, 1–0.

It probably was more impressive, though, that Boswell's season wasn't KO'd by his run-in with Martin. In early August the Twins were in Detroit, and Martin showed up at his favorite postgame nightspot to find Boswell there. After several rounds of beverages, Martin reportedly told Boswell that he was aware the pitcher had failed to run the required number of sprints before the game.

Boswell figured that pitching coach Art Fowler, a good friend of Martin, had ratted him out to the skipper. He stormed out, suggesting he would "get" Fowler, and outfielder Bob Allison went after Boswell.

Here is where the reports get sketchy. Some state that Boswell had decked and possibly even kicked Allison in the alley behind the Lindell AC and that Martin, after he stepped outside, went after the pitcher for that. Other accounts claim that Martin got hit accidentally in a Boswell–Allison skirmish and went after Boswell. Yet another version said Boswell was wrapped up by Allison or others when Martin started to pummel him.

In its August 15, 1969, issue, *Time* magazine reported the incident and quoted the Twins manager: "I hit him five or six times in the stomach. Then I hit him in the head, and when he came off the wall I hit him again. He was out before he hit the ground." The result? Boswell required 20 stitches to close wounds on his face, and Martin reportedly needed seven.

Years later, Frank Quilici, a Twins infielder and Boswell's roommate, told the *Minneapolis Star Tribune*: "He [Boswell] was beat to a pulp."

Boswell flew the next day to Baltimore, his hometown and the Twins' next stop on their 15-game East Coast trip. But he didn't pitch again until August 18, a no-decision in Boston. Still, Boswell went 8–3 over the season's final six weeks, helping Minnesota to an easy division title over Oakland and the AL's second-best record (97–65).

Boswell reportedly came from a pretty combative family, but for Martin, fistfights were right after oxygen and alcohol as essential elements in life. In addition to numerous bar fights during his playing days, Martin gained notoriety for charging the mound and breaking the jaw of Cubs rookie Jim Brewer in 1960 after he thought the left-hander had thrown at him. Brewer was out for two months and won a $10,000 lawsuit against Martin, then with Cincinnati.

While coaching for the Twins under Sam Mele in 1966, the former second baseman hit Howard Fox, the team's traveling secretary. His busy fight card eventually included Reggie Jackson; a marshmallow salesman in Bloomington, Minnesota, in 1979; and Yankees pitcher Ed Whitson in a Baltimore hotel in 1985. In that one, Martin had an arm broken and accused Whitson of kicking him.

Battling friends, foes, and virtual strangers led to Martin's undoing from several jobs, and Minnesota was no different. After the Twins got swept from the ALCS, owner Calvin Griffith fired the manager, saying he was incorrigible. It wasn't a popular move, even as the Twins repeated as champions of the AL West in 1970, and it grew less popular when they hit tough times as the decade continued. Martin surfaced as Detroit's manager in 1971, solidifying his reputation as the Lindell AC's most recognized customer.

Boswell wasn't long for the Twins after Martin got fired. He went 3–7 with a 6.42 ERA in 1970 and was released in April 1971. The pitcher was picked up by, of all teams, the Tigers, and worked three games for Martin before getting cut loose again. After 15 outings with Baltimore, mostly in relief, he was done. Some have suggested that heavy use in 1969 by Martin—the manager was also accused of burning out pitchers later in his career—might have contributed to Boswell's swoon.

Gladden vs. Lombardozzi

As teammates, they helped the Twins win the World Series in 1987 and bring Minnesota its first major professional sports championship since the NBA Lakers won five titles in six seasons from 1949 to 1954.

As adversaries, however, Dan Gladden and Steve Lombardozzi took part in a brief and regrettable altercation on the front lawn of Gladden's suburban Minneapolis home the following summer.

Both had been valuable contributors to the Twins' AL pennant and subsequent Series victory over St. Louis: Gladden, new to the team that season, gave Minnesota an aggressive leadoff man and hit .350 in the ALCS defeat of Detroit; Lombardozzi, a good-field, light-hit second baseman, muscled up for a home run and a .412 average against the Cardinals that October.

But they had little in common in terms of personality or, it seemed, outlook on their major league endeavors. When the Twins acquired second baseman Tom Herr early in the 1988 season, Lombardozzi's playing time all but vanished, and the 28-year-old got frustrated. A natural reaction perhaps, but some teammates took it as a sign of selfishness.

The friction worsened in Minnesota's 9–7 loss to the Red Sox in Boston on July 20. Manager Tom Kelly used a pinch-hitter for Lombardozzi—playing in his home state of Massachusetts that night—and the second baseman reportedly got upset and went to the clubhouse, rather than stay in the dugout. Words apparently were exchanged, either after the game or on the team's late-night charter flight back to the Twin Cities.

Whatever the inspiration, Lombardozzi drove to Gladden's house on Thursday and confronted the outfielder. A scuffle ensued. When the two showed up at the Metrodome for Friday's game against Baltimore, the residue of their disagreement was evident. Lombardozzi, who denied any knowledge of a fight, had a black eye and scratches on the left side of his face. Gladden had bruises and scratches on his forehead, as well as a cracked bone in his right ring finger.

As some wise guys said that week: "Lombardozzi broke the other Twin's finger when he hit Gladden's fist with his face."

Both men played against the Orioles, with Gladden forced to shorten his swing and choke up almost two inches on the bat to ease the discomfort in his finger. Any discomfort in the clubhouse was left to Kelly and general manager Andy MacPhail to address.

"Two men had a disagreement and they settled it like men," Kelly told the *Minneapolis Star Tribune* when the incident was first reported. "It's done, it's over with. My understanding is that everything's hunky-dory. It's probably better it happened."

Said MacPhail: "I don't think it's all that big a deal.... It was a matter between individuals, and they're both grown boys. I think if you think you can head stuff like this off, that's the wrong assumption."

Actually, at least one report claimed that Kelly had tried to intervene a week before the scuffle. "You could see it coming for a long time, since the trade," the manager said. "It's something that just happened. You don't want to see it but that's the end of it. They're back to getting along. They had a problem and they resolved it. They patted each other on the back the other night and things seem to be fine. When the game's over, they're probably not going to go out and eat together, but on the field is what I'm concerned with."

On the field, the episode had little apparent effect. Gladden, hitting .274, batted .262 the rest of the season. Lombardozzi dipped from .211 to .209. But the Twins went 40–29 in their remaining games to finish 91–71, six more victories than in their Series year. Problem was, Oakland won 104 in 1988.

In spring training the following year, Lombardozzi was traded to Houston. He played just 23 games for the Astros, signed briefly with Detroit, and was out of the majors in 1990 at age 30.

Gladden stayed with the Twins through 1991 and was a catalyst for the team that beat Toronto and Atlanta in October of that year. He signed with Detroit as a free agent for his final two seasons and then returned in 2000 as a Twins radio analyst.

In August 2007 the two men participated in activities commemorating the 20th anniversary of the '87 World Series without incident. In fact, Gladden said that they put the fight behind them the day after it occurred.

Hunter vs. Morneau

The third bout on this card took place on September 29, 2005, near the end of the season that snapped Minnesota's string of three consecutive AL Central titles. Frustration levels already were high, and they bubbled over after a home loss to Kansas City when teammates Torii Hunter and Justin Morneau got into an altercation that was swiftly broken up by other Twins.

Hunter wasn't even on the active roster at the time; his season had ended on July 29 when he fractured his left ankle attempting to make a difficult catch in Boston. He played only 98 games in 2005, hitting a disappointing .269 with 14 home runs, and the Twins apparently missed him. They were 54–48 before Hunter got hurt, good enough to stay close in the AL wild-card race, but just 29–31 after their center fielder's injury. They wound up in third place, 16 games back and 12 out of wild-card contention.

Morneau, at 24, was five years younger than Hunter and had plugged along in 2005 with a .239 average, nearly 100 strikeouts, and still not scratching his vast potential. In early June Hunter,

Torii Hunter and Justin Morneau weren't seeing eye-to-eye as they bickered in the media during the 2005 season.

without naming names, had challenged some of the team's young players not to give in to minor bumps and bruises, pushing harder to play through pain. Morneau didn't necessarily agree—"If I feel like I can't help the team, I'm not going to play," he said—and he definitely didn't appreciate the criticism coming through the media.

So, as with most teammate-versus-teammate scraps, this one had some history. There were other signs of the Twins' wheels coming off, too, cranky that they weren't going to be playing beyond game No. 162: the *Star Tribune* reported that Kyle Lohse had damaged some doors in the clubhouse in a moment of anger, Carlos Silva questioned the effort of some teammates, and J.C. Romero exchanged heated words with manager Ron Gardenhire.

Hunter, who had been rehabbing his injured ankle back home in Texas, didn't like what he saw and heard from afar. "Everybody's got to be tightly knit, and I think that if I was here it wouldn't happen," he said upon his September return. "We'd have to fight, it's as simple as that."

The "we" ended up being him and Morneau. A day later, the Twins slugger said: "When that stuff all happens at the same time, it is hard to win ballgames. When you're not winning, it's a lot of the little stuff that guys get irritated about. It doesn't matter when you win."

It usually doesn't matter as much, either, once the season is over and the tension dissipates. By the time the two players saw each other over the winter, at a Twinsfest appearance, Hunter had apologized, and they had patched things up. "I know this guy is going to hit 30 homers, 40 homers," the outfielder said. "We have to get him right mentally, and thinking positive all the time. He's going to hit, believe me."

Hunter ended up being right, mentally or otherwise. Morneau tore through 2006, particularly the last four months, and won the AL Most Valuable Player Award with 34 home runs, 130 RBIs, and a .321 average. Hunter had 31 homers, 98 RBIs, and his sixth Gold Glove in center. And the Twins won another division title.

Hey, what do you expect from Twins, if not a little sibling rivalry?

RON DAVIS

The most terrifying two words in Minnesota Twins baseball history?

One is Ron. The other is Davis. Put them together, and you've got the stuff Twins nightmares are made of.

Wait a minute, that's not strong enough. Murders have been committed with less motive than Davis, in his role as the team's supposed bullpen closer from 1982 into 1986, had given some of his teammates and coaches with failures on the mound. Keep doing what he did several times too often in blowing save situations, losing games entirely, and damaging a young Twins squad's collective psyche, and it's quite possible that the rangy right-hander might have ended up on the back of a milk carton.

Consider the day in August 1986 when Davis, out of chances for redemption in a Minnesota uniform, was traded to the Chicago Cubs, the organization that drafted and signed him 10 years earlier.

The night before, the Twins had scrapped back from a 4–1 hole against the Angels in Anaheim, tying at 4–4 on a pair of ninth-inning errors by California first baseman Wally Joyner. After reliever Keith Atherton cruised through three innings, manager Ray Miller called on Davis, whose mojo already was long gone. As he stepped to the mound to face the Angels' 2-3-4 hitters, Davis lugged an 8.84 earned run average with him. He had a 2–5 record, had not saved a game since April, and had been relegated by Miller to doing mostly mop-up work.

Some background is necessary here. Like a lot of closers, Davis didn't have a typical ballplayer's personality. Some said he was a little odd. Tales out of the Twins' clubhouse claimed that he would absentmindedly sing while he showered, even after tough defeats or his own poor performances. Patrick Reusse, a sportswriter at the *St. Paul Pioneer Press* at the time, recalled Davis as sometimes favoring the tune "Jimmy Crack Corn."

So Wally Joyner greeted Davis with a single to right, and Brian Downing's single to left moved Joyner to third. Miller called for Reggie Jackson to be intentionally walked and, at that point, yanked Davis in favor of right-hander Roy Lee Jackson.

Doug DeCinces then came through with a base hit to center to win it.

And that was it, Davis's final appearance for Minnesota as vintage R.D. The next day he was shipped off to Chicago. The rest of the Twins wrapped up their series in Anaheim with a complete-game victory by Frank Viola (one of Davis's most outspoken critics near the end) and then headed to the airport for their flight to Seattle. On the ride, Reusse related years later, Kirby Puckett did an impersonation of Davis's Texas drawl and then led a sing-along of—wait for it—"Jimmy Crack Corn."

It wasn't supposed to work out that way for Davis and the Twins. When he arrived in 1982 from the Yankees, he was considered one of the hardest-throwing and most promising young relievers in the game. As the set-up man for Goose Gossage, Davis went 14–2 as a rookie in 1979, never had an ERA above 2.95 in three seasons with New York, and pitched in the 1980 and 1981 postseasons (with an ominous 23.14 ERA in four appearances against the Dodgers in the '81 Series).

When the Twins acquired Davis, they did so with the intention of making him their own Gossage. He was, unfortunately, something of a hood ornament on a clunker in Minnesota. The 1982 Twins club was going nowhere fast with 15 lowly paid rookies on the roster in owner Calvin Griffith's strategy to cut costs. Few teams have ever had less need for an accomplished closer; that club finished 60–102. Davis earned 22 saves but finished 53 games, lost nine times, and pitched 106 innings to get them.

The next year, the Twins (70–92) were a little better and so was Davis. His 30 saves ranked third in the league and he brought his ERA down by more than a full run, to 3.34. Minnesota's record in games in which Davis pitched: 37–29.

By 1984 the kids were maturing and jelling, and expectations were rising. Minnesota was on its way to a .500 season for the first time in five years and would spend 52 days in first place in the AL West. On August 22, the Twins swept a doubleheader in Milwaukee and sat 5½ games ahead of both California and Kansas City.

But their inexperience with meaningful September baseball began to show, and Davis did not save them. A 3–11 skid erased their lead in the standings with three weeks to play and, for a couple of days, they slipped to third. Still, by sweeping Cleveland in the final home series, followed by Viola's 8–4 victory at Chicago on September 24, the Twins were only a half-game back of the Royals, six games to play.

Six too many. Minnesota lost them all, and Davis was right in the middle of the ones that stung most. On September 27 at Cleveland, Davis entered with a 3–1 lead in the eighth, one man on, and no outs. A walk, a sacrifice, a run-scoring ground ball, a single, and an error by Tim Teufel allowed the Indians to tie it. In the ninth, after striking out George Vukovich and Pat Tabler, Davis gave up a home run to Jamie Quirk, a third-string catcher acquired by Cleveland for the final week of the season.

Bleak as that was, the next game was worse. Two games back with three left, the Twins grabbed a 10–0 lead before the Indians batted in the third. But Viola unraveled in the sixth, Cleveland sent 12 batters to the plate, Gary Gaetti chipped in an error to keep the ugliness alive, and the Twins' lead was down to 10–9. Again, Davis got the call in the eighth. He promptly gave up a game-tying homer to Joe Carter and in the ninth walked both Pat Tabler and Jerry Willard, taking the loss when Brett Butler drove in Tabler with a single off Ed Hodge.

Those two misadventures cost Davis serious standing with his teammates.

"There were enough games that got away from him that, if one thing went wrong when he came in, everybody on the club had the feeling, 'Here we go again,'" bullpen catcher Rick Stelmaszek said.

In 1985 the Twins slipped to 77–85 and never seriously contended in the division. Davis's worst performances continued to overshadow his more conventional outings. Like the game in Seattle on April 13, when he turned a 7–4 lead in the bottom of the ninth into an 8–7 defeat by yielding two walks, then a grand slam to Phil Bradley. Or like the May 13 game at Yankee Stadium, when Davis had two outs in the ninth, one man on, and an 8–6 lead. He walked Ken Griffey and then got tagged by Don Mattingly for a three-run homer.

By that point, Davis had a target on his back with Twins fans and media, and he knew it. His nerves frayed, his mood was affected. "Ron Davis was a very hyper guy on the mound," venerable broadcaster Herb Carneal recalled. "Once, in Boston, he was so nervous that he didn't wait for a sign from catcher Mark Salas but threw a pitch before Salas had put his mask on."

A managerial change, with Billy Gardner being replaced by Miller, suited Davis for a while. The Twins went 50–50 over their final 100 games with Miller, highly regarded from his days as Baltimore's pitching coach, at the helm. Davis found a groove in which he was good on 20 of his final 21 save opportunities, his ERA dropped from 4.55 in 1984 to 3.48, and the Twin Cities's chapter of the BBWAA voted him the team's Pitcher of the Year.

Which was nice, while it lasted. The following season, Davis, in consecutive appearances against California six days apart, turned a 4–3 lead into an 8–5 loss, and a 6–3 lead into a 7–6 defeat. And it wasn't just the "what" but the "how" of Davis's implosions. On April 20 he gave up four hits, two walks, a hit batsman, a wild pitch, and a home run in one full inning of work. On April 26, it went single, homer, foul out, walk, strikeout, homer. Roller-coaster rides, too many ending badly, including what for Miller was the last straw, a disaster at Fenway Park on May 19. With two outs, no one on, and a 7–6 lead, Davis loaded the bases on a walk, a Wade Boggs double, and an intentional walk. Next, he walked Jim Rice to force in the tying run. Finally, Davis plunked Marc Sullivan, pushing across the game-winner.

After that, it was only a matter of time before Davis would be gone, in some way, shape, or form. And when the trade to Chicago came, the dark cloud over the Twins vanished. "The tension disappeared," Stelmaszek said. "I've never seen a team react like that to a trade."

Clearly, Davis needed a change. "It's a nice feeling to have it over with," he said the day his stay-turned-ordeal in Minnesota ended. "And I haven't given up a home run in the National League yet."

"Yet" being the operative word. In 17 appearances with the Cubs over the final seven weeks of the season, Davis gave up three homers and went 0–2 with a 7.65 ERA. He split 1987 between Chicago and Los Angeles, getting the call in 25 games of middle relief or mop-up duty. Davis's major league career ended in 1988 with San Francisco, a 1–1 mark in nine appearances.

Davis still ranks fourth on the Twins' all-time list in saves (108), behind Rick Aguilera, Joe Nathan, and Eddie Guardado but four ahead of Jeff Reardon and 32 up on Ron Perranoski. But after going 40–24 in games in which Davis pitched in 1984, the Twins slipped to 32–25 whenever he went to the mound in 1985, and finally 7–29 when he pitched in '86. He became the butt of jokes in Minnesota, the object of scorn, and, by the end, the bearer of good tidings to the opposition whenever he crossed the white lines. Somehow, though, it didn't sour Davis—happily retired to the Scottsdale area of Arizona—on his time with the franchise.

"People ask me, if I had my choice, what team would I want to play for today," he said years later, "and I say, 'Minnesota, without a doubt.' I don't care if they hated me—that's their business—but the people who got to know me and our neighbors in Plymouth and Edina...they were all great."

Davis's final appearance in the major leagues wasn't nearly as upsetting as his final Twins effort. Facing the Dodgers in Candlestick Park, he pitched a perfect ninth inning, striking out John Shelby for the final out. The Giants, of course, lost 7–3 that day.

THE METRODOME

Abraham Lincoln eventually lived in the White House, his final mailing address and about as good as it gets for a residence in terms of prestige, fame, and creature comforts. And yet, historians, schoolboys, and even old Abe himself, if pressed hard in one of his incessantly honest moments, still manage to get misty-eyed over the thought of the 16th president's early days in a log cabin.

Maybe, one day, folks will look back at the Metrodome that way.

A little nostalgia and the passage of a lot of time might eventually do for that sad excuse for a baseball park what 26 seasons of American League activity (and two more to go), two World Series, and all sorts of cosmetic nipping, tucking, tweaking, and camouflaging have not: make it lovable.

At its best, for baseball purists, the Hubert H. Humphrey Metrodome has been barely tolerable. It is to the ideal of our national pastime what the Arena League is to the grand game of football, what Taco Bell is to haute cuisine, what *The Biggest Loser* is to *Masterpiece Theatre*. The Metrodome is a bastardization, a prefabrication, and a borderline sports felony.

The most revered ballparks across the land offer sunshine, blue skies, green grass, fresh air, and all the rewards, psychically and physiologically, that come from a spring day or a summer night spent healthfully outdoors. The Metrodome, by contrast, is air-conditioning, Teflon, gray vistas, navy backgrounds, lots of vinyl, and a synthetically colored carpet that, no matter how true its bounces, couldn't fool the hungriest cow.

The Metrodome has long been a source of national disdain; mercifully, the Twins will move into a new ballpark in 2010. Photo courtesy of AP/Wide World Photos.

It is one part stadium, three parts mausoleum, industrial in color scheme and as warmly beckoning as an IRS audit. In terms of how the game itself is played there, think marbles in a bathtub. Acoustically, the Metrodome ranks somewhere between an alley dumpster and the noise made by talking through one end of a cardboard tube.

And if there's one thing Minnesotans just love to do after fighting cabin fever for six months due to snow drifts and late-afternoon darkness, it is...walk inside to see a baseball game while the sun is still up in the summer.

Its many nicknames expose it as something less than pastoral. In a sport known for its Friendly Confines and green cathedrals, the Minnesota Twins—through the 2009 season, anyway—play their home games in: the Homerdome. The Thunderdome. The Humpdome. At the height of the Chicago Bears–Minnesota Vikings rivalry in the late 1980s, Bears coach Mike Ditka referred to the place as the Rollerdome and even wheeled through the hallways of Halas Hall on roller skates for the videographers before one clash.

Then again, there is this: to the Twins, the dump is home. It is the imperfect joint where they hold a perfect 8–0 record across those two Series appearances, in 1987 and 1991. It is the Massive Doughy Kaiser Roll sitting on the fringe of downtown Minneapolis where, with the stands full and the spectators stoked, the decibels can hit 118 at peak moments and rockers like Mick and Keith have nothing on the normally mild-mannered folks waving Homer Hankies.

What opposing players, coaches, and managers complain about, the Twins embrace or, at least, have learned to embrace as home-field advantage. They get used to the lighting, the bounces, the visual background, the angles, the air quality, and the clamor, and then lean on those things as assets, chips to be used when really needed.

"I think the main thing about this place is, when one team plays here the majority of the time, most of the 'breaks' are going to go in its favor," Twins shortstop Roy Smalley once said. "This place just has enough quirks that you have more funny things happen here, and the home team gets used to them. That builds confidence."

So do good results. The Twins have posted winning records at their Dome for seven consecutive seasons through 2007 and in 16 of the past 24. On the road, they have topped .500 only seven times in those same 24 seasons.

One team's advantage is another team's misery, of course. And we're not just talking about crosswinds, the one-and-only Green Monster at Fenway, the vines of Wrigley, or the intimidating level of tradition (and boisterousness) at Yankee Stadium. We're talking about batted balls that carom off of a *ceiling*, something Abner Doubleday or Alexander Cartwright never anticipated.

As for longtime P.A. announcer Bob Casey's amusing and notorious pregame admonishment, "No smooooooooking at the Metrodome!" well, that's something R.J. Reynolds never anticipated at a ballpark, either, at least before this millennium.

That sense of being indoors for what naturally is an outdoor sport contributed for years, some suspected, to Twins crowds that were more subdued, less raucous, than you typically would find around the big leagues. That, however, changed with the club's 1987 drive to the American League playoffs and World Series. Then, again in 1991 and for every Twins postseason appearance since, the Metrodome was transformed into a college basketball snakepit, a super-sized Final Four atmosphere in which the noise stayed close, rumbled around, and had fans' ears ringing a day later at the office, at school, or on the loading dock. Sound, on those special occasions, became tangible, palpable, in play every bit as much as the bats, ball, or gloves.

Then, of course, there are the speakers, suspended high above the artificial turf and very much in play. According to Metrodome ground rules, a ball hitting a speaker or the roof in fair territory, if caught by the fielder, means the batter is out and runners advance at their own risk. A ball that strikes those obstructions in foul territory is dead.

Early in the 1984 season Oakland's Dave Kingman hit a tremendous pop-up that found its way into a drainage hole in the fabric roof and stayed there. After a few moments of confusion, during which Isaac Newton's theory seemed seriously in doubt, the umpires sent Kingman to second base with a ground-rule double.

Twins DH Chili Davis wasn't as fortunate in a 1992 game. He drove the ball long and far to right field, only to have it bang off a speaker and rebound to Baltimore second baseman Mark McLemore, turning a home run into a loud and misdirected out. Earlier that same season, Milwaukee's Rob Deer popped out to shortstop Greg Gagne on consecutive at-bats with both balls hitting the roof before heading down.

In 1982, its debut year, visiting outfielders complained about the material used on the warning track, a slippery hazard for anyone in cleats. The fences in left and right were just seven feet high, allowing a ridiculous number of ground-rule doubles from balls that bounced out off an especially springy turf. Plexiglas was installed in left for about a decade after that, while a massive vinyl tarp—Boston's trademark left-field wall, reimagined by the folks from Hefty—was added in right.

Baseball? This was getting more like pinball.

"The best home-field advantage ever, with the ceiling and the lights and the baggie," Twins third baseman Gary Gaetti said. "We pretty much adopted it as our favorite place to play. It wasn't a great baseball stadium compared to some that have been built, but it was ours, and we took advantage of playing there."

To an opposing manager, the best thing about the Dome was the fact that it was a road nuisance; he couldn't go home and kick the dog or argue with his wife. Tony La Russa, who dealt with it during his stops in Chicago and Oakland, didn't appreciate a ball hit to short right field in June 1984 that apparently hit a seam and bounced past Harold Baines all the way to the wall for an inside-the-park home run in a 3–2 White Sox loss.

Said LaRussa after the game: "The play was a disgrace to baseball."

Let's face it, the whole place pretty much has been a disgrace to baseball. All utility, no charm. A venue built on time and well within its $55 million budget, but with all the aesthetic appeal of a double-wide.

Sure, there are some terrific baseball memories: Kent Hrbek's grand slam in Game 6 of the '87 Series, Kirby Puckett's leaping catch in Game 6 four Octobers later and Jack Morris's tenacity 24 hours after that, the dogpiles of jubilant Twins players after each championship, the spontaneous love-in that packed the place in the wee hours after the ALCS victory over Detroit in '87.

There are other moments, too, such as the Super Bowl in 1992 and the Final Four barely two months later. In 1988 the Twins became the first American League team to draw more than 3 million fans in a season. Debuting a year later, the Timberwolves played their inaugural NBA 1989–1990 season in the Metrodome and set a league attendance record that still stands (1,072,572).

The Metrodome also has housed University of Minnesota football, rodeos, monster truck shows, Billy Graham services, and Bruce Springsteen concerts, as well as the Vikings, who will continue to play there after the Twins move about 10 blocks west to their new outdoor ballpark in 2010. Few will shed any tears, as long as they lug the retired jersey numbers and those two shiny trophies—symbolizing Minnesota's only major pro sports titles since the Lakers left in 1960—across downtown Minneapolis with them.

TWINS PITCHERS WHO BATTED

Rick Aguilera got to experience, in real life, a dream that nearly every young baseball fan has had at one time or another. You know the one: tie game, World Series, extra innings, bases loaded, two outs, and, hey, guess who's due up at the plate?

One small problem: Aguilera was a pitcher by trade. In the American League. Where the designated hitter rule has taken the bats out of hurlers' hands since 1973.

So when Aguilera was sent to pinch-hit for the Twins in the twelfth inning of Game 3 of the 1991 World Series, his team tied 4–4 with Atlanta, it was less like a dream and more like a nightmare for folks across the nation rooting for Minnesota. Manager Tom Kelly had used up his last position player, infielder Al Newman, in the eleventh inning, putting his batting order in a bind in which a pitcher was going to have to hit.

Might as well be Aguilera at that point, who had broken into the major leagues with the New York Mets. An all-around good athlete, Aguilera had managed 28 hits and a .203 average in parts of five seasons before being traded to the Twins in 1989. He had hit three doubles and three home runs, with 11 RBIs. That made him a better option with a bat in his hands than Aguilera's teammate, reliever Mark Guthrie.

But this was two rusty years beyond Aguilera's last at-bat. In front of 50,878 people at Atlanta–Fulton County Stadium and millions more watching on television. With a World Series game at stake.

"I'm playing for right now, not three innings ahead," Kelly said, shrugging off second-guessers the next day.

Said Aguilera: "It's not something where you can just get in the batter's box and hit the ball again."

Remarkably, though, that's what Aguilera did. Against Braves reliever Jim Clancy, the Twins' closer smacked a line drive to center field. Unfortunately, outfielder Ron Gant was right there.

Aguilera stayed in the game and got tagged for Mark Lemke's two-out single that scored David Justice for the Braves' 5–4 victory. That run snapped a postseason shutout streak for Twins relievers of 32⅔ innings, dating back to 1987.

It marked the first time a pitcher had been used to pinch-hit in a Series game since Don Drysdale did it in 1965 against Minnesota. But then, this game was ripe for it, lasting 4 hours and 4 minutes and using up a record 42 of the 50 players on the two rosters. Aguilera was the eighth pinch-hitter used by the Twins that night.

Little did Aguilera know at the time, but his unexpected thrills in that game nearly continued. Had Game 3 gone beyond 13 innings, Kelly planned to use left fielder Dan Gladden as a reliever, shifting Aguilera to the outfield, where he had never played in the big leagues. "I wasn't going to pitch Aggie more than two innings," Kelly said. "I'm not going to kill him." And the only available bodies on his bench at that point were starting pitchers Jack Morris and Kevin Tapani, who were booked for Games 4 and 5.

Gladden? He didn't mind the idea, since he had pitched single innings against California in 1988 and Cleveland in 1989. Besides, he figured he might have an edge. "They [the Braves] don't have a book on me," he said.

If it makes Aguilera feel any better, lining out to center field wasn't a bad at-bat, all things considered. In the years between the AL adoption of the designated hitter rule in 1973 and the start of interleague regular-season play in 1997, Twins pitchers batted a total of 13 times. And went 0-for-13.

Nine of those at-bats came in the six games of the 1987 and 1991 Series played in the NL ballparks. Considering how out of their element they were at the plate, six of those nine were easy strikeout victims.

Four other Twins pitchers went to the plate and waggled bats in regular-season games in those 24 years. Two of them did it in one game: Vic Albury and Bill Campbell both batted in a 16-inning affair on July 12, 1975. Both of them struck out against New York's Pat Dobson in a game at Shea Stadium that the Twins lost, 8–7, in 5 hours, 11 minutes.

On August 24, 1986, Ray Fontenot batted and struck out against Toronto's Tom Henke in a 7–5 loss in 10 innings to the Blue Jays at the Metrodome. And on June 13, 1989, Allan Anderson became the only other Twins pitcher to pinch-hit in the

20/20 HINDSIGHT

It's not exactly like Barry Bonds's exclusive membership in baseball's 500 home runs–500 stolen bases club. Or even as impressive as Jose Canseco when he became the game's first 40/40 man.

Still, the five Twins who managed to slug 20 homers and steal 20 bases in the same season have nothing to apologize for. They are Larry Hisle (28 HR, 21 SB, 1977); Kirby Puckett (31–20, 1986); Marty Cordova (24–20, 1995); Corey Koskie (26–27, 2001), and Torii Hunter (23–21, 2002).

DH era when he faced Jerry Reed in Minnesota's 4–3 victory over Seattle in 11 innings. Anderson, too, struck out.

Oh, wait, there was one more, a Twins pitcher who batted in the 1992 All-Star Game in San Diego. The manager who sent him to the plate that year? Tom Kelly.

The pitcher who stepped to the plate and struck out against Cincinnati's Norm Charlton was—wait for it—Aguilera.

IN THE CLUTCH

HITS KEEP ON COMING

If someone offered you a friendly wager to name the Minnesota Twins player who put together the longest streak of consecutive games with at least one base hit, to bet your old jalopy up against his spectacularly shiny Bentley Continental GT and was willing to give you not one but two guesses, you would go for it, right?

You probably would name Rod Carew first. You might go with Tony Oliva or Kirby Puckett as your backup guess.

And you would be handing over your car keys.

Carew, the most accomplished hitter in Twins history (.334 career average with Minnesota), twice strung together 18 games in which he hit safely, once in 1973 and once in 1974. Oliva, a .304 lifetime hitter, had two streaks of 17 games, first as a rookie in 1964 and again as a veteran All-Star in 1970.

But they never got close to the franchise record, either as it stood when they played or where it stands now.

The target at the time was a 24-game streak owned by outfielder Lenny Green, set from May 1 through May 28 in the team's 1961 inaugural season. The left-handed-hitting Green had 34 hits in 94 at-bats during his streak, scoring 14 runs and hitting .362. It would be 19 more years before a Twins batter compiled a hitting streak longer than Green's, and both Carew and Oliva were gone by then.

The correct answer, then, is Ken Landreaux, an outfielder who spent two of his 11 big-league seasons in Minnesota. He came to

TOUCHING THEM ALL

Seven different players in Twins history have hit for the cycle, each doing it once. The first was Rod Carew, getting his single, double, triple, and home run in five at-bats in a 10–5 victory over the Royals in Kansas City on May 20, 1970. The most recent was Kirby Puckett, who did it in a 10–1 pasting of the Oakland Athletics on August 1, 1986. In between, Cesar Tovar, Larry Hisle, Lyman Bostock, Mike Cubbage, and Gary Ward pulled off the feat.

Four rival batters have hit for the cycle against the Twins: Fred Patek, Fred Lynn, Paul Molitor, and Travis Hafner.

the club in February 1979, one of the four players packaged by California for Carew, coincidentally enough. That season, Landreaux hit .305 with 15 home runs and 83 runs batted in, and in a July game against Seattle, he rapped two doubles in the same inning.

In 1980 Landreaux was chosen as a reserve for the AL All-Star team, largely on the strength of his early-season hitting streak. From April 23 through May 30, the wiry outfielder hit safely in 31 consecutive games. It was baseball's longest streak since Pete Rose put together 44 games, admittedly just two years before. And it remained the longest until Milwaukee's Paul Molitor hit in 39 straight from July 16 through August 25, 1987.

Landreaux, 25 at the time, started his streak in rather memorable fashion. In a Wednesday afternoon getaway game for California at Met Stadium, Angels pitcher Bruce Kison cruised into the ninth inning with a no-hitter. It was the only reason to stick around that day, too; the Twins were losing 10–0 through seven innings and 17–0 after California roughed up Roger Erickson for seven unearned runs in the ninth. With one out in the ninth inning, Landreaux doubled to left field to spoil Kison's bid before an announced crowd of 4,772.

That got Landreaux going, and he didn't stop for five more weeks. He had 13 multihit games during the streak, with five doubles, one triple, two home runs, and 19 RBIs. He scored 13 runs and went 49-for-125 (.392), boosting his overall average to .356. In 13 of the 30 games, Landreaux rapped two or more hits and came up dry only when he faced Baltimore left-hander Scott McGregor on May 31 in Bloomington, flying out to lead off the eighth in his final chance.

Landreaux did have a highlight in early July, hitting three triples off three Texas pitchers in a 10–3 Twins victory. But the rest of his season was ordinary; after batting .178 in June, Landreaux slumped again in August (.192) and was a .259 hitter over the season's second half. Landreaux also got a little overlooked because Kansas City's George Brett flirted with .400 that summer and had his own 30-game hitting streak before finishing at .390.

Near the end of spring training in 1981, the Twins traded Landreaux to the Dodgers. He earned a World Series ring with L.A. that year and turned himself into a base-stealing threat over his seven NL seasons, but he came up empty in free agency after the 1987 season and wound up playing in the Pacific Coast League.

Ten years after Landreaux's achievement, catcher Brian Harper had a 25-game streak that ran from July 6 through August 4, during which he batted .384 (38-for-99). Harper, a .295 lifetime hitter and a member of the 1991 Twins championship team, added a 19-game streak in 1993. That one lasted from July 20 through August 12 and was immediately followed by a stretch in which Harper got hits in 12 of his next 14 games. If not for an 0-for-4 at Oakland on August 13 and another 0-for-4 against the White Sox seven days later, Harper might have had a 33-gamer. As it was, he batted .352 in those 33 contests.

Four Twins have had hitting streaks of 23 games: Kent Hrbek, Puckett, Marty Cordova, and Cristian Guzman. Shane Mack hit in 22 straight in 1992, and Ted Uhlaender and Chuck Knoblauch each got hits in 20 consecutive games.

ALLISON'S CATCH IN 1965

What made the illness that eventually took Bob Allison's life in April 1995 so startling and so scary was that it robbed the former Twins strongman of his movement, his power, and his athleticism.

All of those were such obvious physical attributes in Allison, the strapping fellow with the Central Casting good looks who came to Minnesota for the team's inaugural season.

The Allison who died at the relatively young age of 60 from a rare nerve disorder most often referred to as ataxia had little in common with the slugger who hit 211 home runs and drove home 642 in 10 seasons after the franchise shifted to the Twin Cities. "My coordination is gone," Allison said in a 1991 interview. "I can't walk. I can't talk. I can't write. I can't do anything."

See, that guy bore little resemblance to the broad-shouldered, competitive outfielder with the big personality and a knack for frightening middle infielders with his locomotive slides into second base. Allison played baseball with a football player's intensity.

"This guy had the ideal body," former Twins pitcher Jim Kaat said. "Very durable. He was a hard-nosed player and he played every day. He was always so fit. Everyone marveled at his condition."

Never more so than in Game 2 of the 1965 World Series, the first in franchise history. It was a chilly, drizzly afternoon at Met Stadium, with soggy grass in the outfield and Sandy Koufax on the mound for the visiting Los Angeles Dodgers. Rough conditions for the home team.

Allison confided years later that, prior to the game, he had noticed how slick the footing was in the outfield, so he donned a pair of football cleats to improve his traction. Little did he know how much that would matter.

The game was scoreless in the top of the fifth when Ron Fairly singled to right off Kaat. The next man, Jim Lefebvre, drove a curving shot down the left-field line that Allison came clomping across for. A few yards shy of the wall, with fans in overcoats peering through and over the chain-link fencing in that outfield corner, Allison lunged with his left arm, made a backhanded catch about a foot off the turf, and then slid through the wetness right into foul territory. He popped up in time to throw to the infield, forcing Fairly back to first base.

Wes Parker followed with a single to the right side, but Kaat got John Roseboro and Koufax on foul pop-ups to end the inning. If not for Allison's catch, the Twins likely would have trailed 2–0 against the great Koufax. Instead, they scored twice in the sixth on an error, a sacrifice, and three straight hits and went on to win 5–1. Their 2–0 Series lead didn't hold, but they did force the Dodgers to a seventh game. That remains the Twins' only home loss in 12 Series games played in Minnesota. But then, it was Koufax again, painting a three-hit masterpiece.

CHANCE'S TWO NO-HITTERS

Baseball hasn't actually used asterisks as much as it has talked about them through the years. It never slapped one on Roger Maris's feat of hitting 61 home runs in 1961—it simply listed Maris's single-season mark for 162 games along with Babe Ruth's 154-game record from 1927. And no one seriously expected commissioner Bud Selig to mandate an asterisk alongside Barry Bonds's career home-run total once he caught and passed, presumably with some unfair chemical advantages along the way, the great Henry Aaron.

But if ever there was an achievement ripe for an asterisk, it was Dean Chance's "perfect game" thrown against the Boston Red Sox on August 6, 1967.

Chance, at age 26 deep into a terrific comeback season in Minnesota after a meteoric rise and fall with the California Angels, faced 15 Boston batters in five innings that day at Met Stadium and retired them all. Unfortunately for all concerned, including a crowd of 26,003 on that Sunday in Bloomington, the rainy weather wasn't cooperating. In fact, after Chance struck out against Jim Lonborg leading off the bottom of the fifth, home-plate umpire Jim Odom and his crew shut the game down. Because the Twins had been up 2–0 and the Red Sox got their at-bats in the fifth, the contest counted. Chance officially joined the ranks of pitchers who had thrown no-hitters, and made an even shorter list of hurlers of perfect games.

A piece of history for 15 measly batters? Hardly seemed right. It's not clear whether anyone scoffed or snickered at Chance's greatness based on a technicality, but there surely had to be doubters.

Dean Chance followed up his five-inning "perfect game" with a more conventional no-hitter 19 days later in 1967.

All of whom Chance shut up 19 days later.

Prevented through no fault of his own from testing his best stuff over a full nine innings against Boston that day, Chance went at the Cleveland Indians on August 25 with something less than his best. In the second game of a doubleheader at Municipal Stadium, the hard-throwing and hard-living right-hander was wild but, again, unhittable.

Not that anything special seemed to be in the offing; in the bottom of the first, Chance walked the Indians' first two batters, struck out the third, and then saw the cleanup man reach safely on an error by third baseman Cesar Tovar. He threw a wild pitch to Max Alvis, bringing home a run, before striking out Alvis and getting Joe Azcue on a fly ball.

Minnesota tied it in the second inning, and then went up 2–1 in the sixth when an otherwise-sharp Sonny Siebert balked in Tovar. And that apparently was enough for Chance. He breezed through the next three innings, allowing just one walk. In the ninth, he got Vic Davalillo, Chuck Hinton, and Tony Horton on routine ground balls and, just like that, he had a full-sized, nine-inning, grown-up's no-hitter to go along with his pocket version from earlier in the month.

Chance became one of the few no-hit pitchers to allow a run, and he walked five with that wild pitch while striking out eight. Still, it was a thing of beauty, especially after Major League Baseball "clarified" its definition of a no-hitter to be "a game in which a pitcher, or pitchers, gives up no hits while pitching at least nine innings."

Not to worry: the Twins still recognize Chance's shorties as two of their five no-hitters. The others were:

- Jack Kralick, August 26, 1962, a 1–0 victory over Kansas City
- Scott Erickson, April 27, 1994, a 6–0 victory over Milwaukee
- Eric Milton, September 11, 1999, a 7–0 victory over Anaheim

The Twins have been the victims of four no-hitters through the years, including perfect games by Catfish Hunter on May 8, 1968, in Oakland and David Wells on May 17, 1998, in New York. The other two hurlers who held Minnesota hitless weren't shabby, either: Vida Blue on September 21, 1970, and Nolan Ryan on September 28, 1974, at California.

YOU CAN GO HOME

The instant that it happened, it seemed wrong. A panic move. Something a beer-league player might try.

And yet, Al Newman's unexpected and unorthodox decision to throw home provided an early spark in a pivotal game late in the Twins' 1987 championship season.

In the team's final home game of the season, with the Twins in first place and the visiting Kansas City Royals in second, manager Tom Kelly went for something of a knockout punch when he started right-hander Bert Blyleven on three days' rest. Everyone in baseball knew that Minnesota was sneaking through its schedule with three legitimate starting pitchers in Blyleven, Frank Viola, and Les Straker (okay, maybe 2½), but Kelly's move pretty much confirmed it. It also looked a little desperate when Blyleven immediately walked leadoff man Willie Wilson and gave up a long single to Kevin Seitzer, with Wilson taking third. That brought up hitting maestro George Brett.

"I felt awful," Kelly recalled years later. "I thought, 'I messed up.'"

Brett hit a short-hop ground ball to Gary Gaetti at third, who threw across to Newman to force out Seitzer at second. But rather than relaying to first for the double play and conceding a run, Newman noticed that Wilson had held up at the crack of the bat, in case Gaetti caught Brett's drive on the fly. Then the Kansas City speedster took off toward the plate.

So the Twins utility infielder, subbing that day for Steve Lombardozzi, uncorked a throw to the plate. It nearly beaned one umpire and Blyleven himself before reaching catcher Tim Laudner an instant ahead of Wilson for the tag. Blyleven got out of the inning without further damage, and the Twins scored five times, with three home runs, in the bottom of the first en route to an 8–1 victory. The next night in Texas, they clinched their first division title in 17 years.

At least in part because of Newman's a) reckless, b) unusual, c) heads-up, or d) all-of-the-above play.

Even Newman admitted later: "I can't believe I threw home."

NABBING DARRELL NAPPING

Tim Laudner had to wait in line for his share of accolades after the Twins' 1987 World Series victory. He had a half-full, half-empty sort of regular season, batting .191 but hitting 16 home runs while handling most of the heavy lifting at catcher. In the ALCS against Detroit, Laudner went to the plate 14 times and got just one hit.

But it was Laudner's reflexes and arm that made the difference in Game 4 at Tiger Stadium that October; since it was Game 4 that more or less put down, and kept down, manager Sparky Anderson's squad, you could say that Laudner had plenty to do with the Twins reaching their first World Series in 22 years.

The Twins led 4–2 when Detroit opened the sixth inning with three straight singles by Chet Lemon, Darrell Evans, and Dave Bergman. With a run in, Mike Heath bunted Evans and Bergman into scoring position. During a pitching change, third baseman Gary Gaetti said a few words to Laudner. And as Gaetti went back to his position, he told the third-base umpire, Joe Brinkman, to be ready.

Sure enough, with left-handed Lou Whitaker batting, Laudner caught a pitch from Juan Berenguer and snapped a throw down to third base. Evans, 40, had strayed too far in the chilly fall air and felt Gaetti's glove slap down before he could dive back to the bag. Two outs. When Berenguer followed up with a wild pitch to Whitaker, Bergman moved to third, but the Tigers missed out on the tying run. A Jim Morrison fly ball to center ended the threat.

"Gary and I have a predetermined signal," Laudner said later. "If he feels we can make it and he puts it on, I'll throw it down there."

Said Evans: "I just got too far off. I was trying to be aggressive. I don't know if it was a set play or a pitchout."

Evans's lousy night wasn't quite over. In the eighth, playing third base—a return to his roots, though Evans mostly was a first baseman or DH at that point—the veteran booted a ground ball by Laudner with one out. The Twins' catcher moved up on a wild pitch and a ground-out. Then Steve Lombardozzi grounded a single that stayed underneath Evans's glove for an insurance run.

Anderson was second-guessed after Minnesota's 5–3 victory for failing to use another fielder at third base and for not using pinch-hitters earlier in the game. But even the Tigers' white-haired skipper had felt the momentum of the game shift with Laudner's strong throw. "I think the pickoff was the turning point of the game," Anderson said.

"T. REX" WRECKS GANT

Kent Hrbek, for much of his professional life as the Twins' first baseman from 1981 through 1994, had an alter ego that many Minnesota fans heard about but rarely saw in action. T. Rex, a professional wrestling character, always was the roughhousing ham and clown in Hrbek trying to get out of the guy wearing pinstripes in a team sport.

"When I was a kid, six, seven, eight years old, my grandpa used to watch it [professional wrestling]," Hrbek told reporters one day. "He'd sit in his chair in front of the TV and watch it. If you'd get in front of the TV while he was watching it, he'd give you the back of his hand."

Largely a figment of the beefy slugger's imagination, T. Rex occasionally would make an appearance on the field during pregame warm-ups or in the Twins' clubhouse before or after a game, clamping a bear hug on an unsuspecting visitor or pantomiming some ominous move.

But in Game 2 of the 1991 World Series, the fans who packed the Metrodome got to see T. Rex in all his glory; contrary to real wrestling, this glimpse was completely unscripted.

The Twins led 2–1 when Atlanta's Lonnie Smith, with one out in the top of the third inning, reached first on an error by third baseman Scott Leius. After Terry Pendleton flied out, Ron Gant drove a single through the left side, with Smith scampering around to third. Dan Gladden's throw squirted past third base to Twins starter Kevin Tapani, who had seen Gant round the bag aggressively at first. So Tapani fired the ball to Hrbek.

In live action and some full-speed replays, it appeared that Gant's momentum—as he lunged back to the bag, reached out with his right leg, and banged into Hrbek—carried him too far, pulling his foot off the bag while Hrbek applied a tag. But in slow motion, especially, it looks as if Hrbek levered Gant off the bag with his right thigh and gloved left hand, an improvised rasslin' move to steal an out, an inning, and who-knows-how-many runs from the Braves.

Umpire Drew Coble, working first base, favored the Twins' interpretation. "In my judgment, his momentum carried him over the top of Hrbek," Coble said.

Local product Kent Hrbek was a key member of both the 1987 and 1991 championship teams.

Reactions of the participants, meanwhile, broke down along party lines.

"He [Gant] knocked me over and pushed me off balance," said Hrbek, who ran off to the Twins' dugout as soon as Coble made his call.

Gant and first-base coach Pat Corrales argued, with the Braves outfielder throwing his helmet to the artificial turf. "I didn't know you could pull people off the bag," Gant said after the game.

Atlanta manager Bobby Cox felt it was obviously a bad call ("Brutal," he called it). And Twins manager Tom Kelly just played coy. "Gant gets a single to put guys at the corners and we start throwing the ball all over the place," Kelly said. "I was starting to throw my hat. Then Tapani heaves it to first base. I started cursing. 'What on earth are we doing?' Next thing I knew, the umpire was saying the inning was over. I had to ask what the hell happened.

"I get nervous when the boys start throwing the ball around the field."

The controversial play got at least as much attention in the gap between Games 2 and 3 as Reggie Jackson's infamous hip play in 1978, when the Yankees slugger appeared to move his hindquarters into the path of a Dodgers' throw. By the time the teams arrived in Atlanta, Hrbek was public enemy number one and actually received some death-threat phone calls to the Twins' hotel. He said that his mother back in Minnesota also had received a telephone threat concerning her son.

That news got teammate Kirby Puckett's attention. "We were down in Atlanta, and me and Herbie were getting introduced next to each other before the game," Puckett said. "I'm standing next to him, asking him if anybody would really take a shot at him on the field, and thinking, 'What if they have bad aim?'"

Prior to that game, when asked about the threats, Hrbek had said: "I'm not that scared. I'm more puzzled. I'll say this: at least they're talking baseball."

The big first baseman admitted later, though, that the calls did concern him. After all, Hrbek never imagined T. Rex as a villain.

"I'd want to be a good guy [in wrestling]," he said. "I think I am a good guy. I like to have fun. I'm just like you guys.... When I go home, I kiss my dogs."

LONNIE SMITH JOINS CLUB

For all of Jack Morris's steely-eyed, gunslinging toughness in demanding the ball for however long it took to decide Game 7 of the 1991 World Series, one fact remains: in all probability, Morris and the Twins would have lost the deciding game and baseball's ultimate championship if not for some misdirection by a pair of crafty infielders and a base-running gaffe by Atlanta's Lonnie Smith.

Smith's name, rightly or wrongly, was added to the long list of World Series "goats"—a list that includes such fellows as Fred Snodgrass, Mickey Owen, Johnny Pesky, Ernie Lombardi, and, of course, Bill Buckner—due to an adventure on the base paths in the eighth inning.

Smith, appearing in his fourth Series with his fourth team, led off the top of the eighth with a single to right. The next man, Terry Pendleton, hit a shot to left-center that bounced off the wall as Dan Gladden and Kirby Puckett gave chase.

It's safe to say that everyone in the packed Metrodome assumed that Smith would motor around with the game's first run, leaving Minnesota in a real jam: down 1–0, runner in scoring position, no outs, only six outs of their own left to catch up, and Atlanta starter John Smoltz in his rhythm on the mound.

Everyone, that is, except Smith. For reasons that aren't entirely clear to this day, the Braves' designated hitter in this game had lingered at second base, looking timid, almost lost. By the time he motored toward third, the Twins' fielders had recovered, and that's as far as Smith could go. So instead of a real jam, it was only a regular jam: men at second and third, still no outs, but no runs in, and the game still tied at 0–0.

Shoot, that hardly felt like a jam at all, relatively speaking.

"We still should have scored," Pendleton said a year later. "That was the crime of it all. People forget what happened afterward."

What happened afterward was that Ron Gant grounded out to first base too cleanly for the runners to budge. The Twins intentionally walked David Justice to give themselves a force-out at any base and to face Sid Bream, the Braves' slow-footed first baseman. And just like room service, only to a room packed with 55,118 crazies, Bream delivered another ground ball to Hrbek at first. He threw home to catcher Brian Harper to force Smith at the plate and then took Harper's thrown a stride before Bream got down to first. End of inning? More like an escape.

"I knew right there what everyone would be talking about," Smith recalled.

No kidding. What showed up more clearly on replays was that, at the crack of Pendleton's bat, Twins shortstop Greg Gagne and Chuck Knoblauch acted as if they were turning a routine ground ball into a double play. That's when Smith hesitated, confused by the fake. And that cost him the precious seconds he would have needed to get all the way home.

Smith, however, contended that he did not react to the trickery of Minnesota's middle infielders. He said he knew the ball had been hit into the outfield but paused because he hadn't seen where.

"I never saw that damn ball," Smith said long afterward. "I just knew it was hit in the outfield. But with the way Kirby was catching everything during the series, I figured he might be catching this one, too."

The plot thickened when Smith revealed that, after he got to first base, Atlanta manager Bobby Cox gave him the steal sign. He said he was not comfortable with it and opted, in his head, for a delayed steal. That might explain what Braves general manager John Schuerholz said about Smith's presence of mind on the ensuing play.

"Smith wasn't looking at Knoblauch. He wasn't looking at his coach. He wasn't looking at anything except second base, just looking at that damned base," Schuerholz said.

PINCH US, WE'RE DREAMING!

Almost 10 percent of Randy Bush's 763 base hits over 12 seasons with Minnesota came in pinch-hit appearances. Rich Reese, who spent all or parts of 10 seasons with the Twins, hit more pinch-hit grand-slam home runs (three) than anyone else in American League history.

Chip Hale holds the club record for most pinch-hits in a season (19). And, in 1991, Scott Leius hit .440 as a pinch-hitter but a mediocre .264 the rest of the time.

Jose Morales is tied for 10th on baseball's all-time list with 12 pinch-hit home runs, but he hit only one of those during his three seasons with the Twins (1978–1980).

As helpful as each of those fellows was, though, the most impressive pinch-hitter in Twins history might have been Rod Carew. With a .323 pinch-hitting average from 1967 to 1985, Carew tops all Hall of Fame players with a minimum of 100 pinch-hit appearances.

One of his most memorable for Twins fans came on July 25, 1976, with the Twins trailing 5–4 in the sixth inning, the bases loaded, and one out in Chicago. White Sox manager Paul Richards brought Francisco Barrios in to replace left-hander Terry Forster, assuming he would have a righty-righty matchup with shortstop Luis Gomez. One problem: it was the first game of a doubleheader, and Twins manager Gene Mauch had given Carew a rest.

"We couldn't believe it," teammate Roy Smalley recalled. "We were in the dugout, saying, 'Did he forget that Gene has Rod Carew, the best hitter in baseball, sitting over here?'"

The lefty-swinging Carew drove a pitch from Barrios to deep center field for a triple, clearing the bases for a 7–5 lead in a game the Twins eventually won 13–8.

(And *that* might explain why, years later, Smith admitted he once concocted a scheme to shoot Schuerholz, blaming him for the unhappy end of his playing career.)

It is worth remembering, too, that Smith had been involved in a base-running gaffe earlier in the Series, with Game 4 tied 1–1 in the fifth inning. He was on second when Pendleton sent a line drive at, then past, Puckett. Holding up initially, Smith was late getting to third, but coach Jimy Williams waved him home. Knoblauch's relay throw beat him there, Harper held onto the ball when Smith slammed into him, and Atlanta cost itself another run (it won anyway, 3–2).

After Game 7, in a visitors' clubhouse that emptied quickly, Smith retreated to a back room while most of the media and his teammates took care of business and then cleared out. Finally, he emerged but walked past the reporters who remained.

"I knew when we didn't score in that game, people would blame me for losing the World Series," Smith said in October 1992, still feeling the sting a year later. "I just knew it. That's why when the game ended, I wasn't talking. I knew no one would believe me."

Smith, nicknamed "Skates" early in his career after some foot-work problems in the outfield, claimed he watched a replay of the pivotal play only once, to hear what the announcers had to say. "Because [Tim] McCarver blamed me and said that Knoblauch faked me out, and Jack Buck said it was terrible base running, why would anyone believe nobody else?"

Smith has lugged around the onus of that play for years. It is etched into his baseball legacy and likely will be mentioned in the second or third paragraph of his obituary. Fortunately, it never got the best of him.

"I think people really thought I was going to commit suicide," he once said. "I was down, real down, but I wasn't going to kill myself. I had to get on with my life, and I wasn't going to let it ruin my family's."

THE HITLESS WONDERS

Fifty-three times, across the first four months of the 1967 season, Twins pitcher Dean Chance lugged a piece of lumber into the batter's box with the idea of doing some damage on the Twins' behalf. Offering some payback to the other guys' hurler. Posting some crooked numbers or, heck, even just a straight vertical one, on the scoreboard.

Fifty-three times Chance dug in. And 53 times Chance did nothing more than produce an out.

In one of the greatest individual arguments for the American League's wisdom in taking bats out of pitchers' hands, Chance's 0-for-53 hitless streak stands, more than 40 years later, as the club's longest drought ever. Which is fitting, because Chance was a horrible hitter over his entire career, batting .066 in 662 at-bats. He struck out 420 times while playing for five teams across 11 seasons.

"I wish I was still in baseball," Chance said a couple of years after retiring following the 1971 season. "The designated hitter rule was made for me."

Chance, of course, wasn't hired for his bat. Among Twins players who were, catcher Butch Wynegar suffered through the long string of at-bats without a hit. Wynegar nearly went 0-for-38 in 1978, going 21 days (September 4 through September 24) without safely reaching base.

Shortstop Greg Gagne is the only Twins player to endure two hitless streaks of 30 at-bats or more; he went 0-for-32 in the middle of the 1991 season, surpassing his 0-for-30 stretch deep in the 1987 season. Funny how neither of Gagne's dry spells seriously cost the Twins—they won their championships in '87 and '91.

NUMBERS DON'T LIE
(OR DO THEY?)

FLIRTING WITH .400

With each baseball season that passes, Ted Williams's magical .406 season in 1941 gets more amazing.

With each baseball season that passes, so does Rod Carew's .388 mark for the Twins in 1977.

Sixty-seven years have come and gone since Williams became the last major leaguer to bat .400 or better over a full season. And more than 30 have ticked off everyone's life calendar since Carew's run at .400, no matter how fresh and vivid it still seems to many Twins followers.

Thirty years? Doesn't seem possible. The image of Rodney Cline Carew crouched over, leaning back, his bat poised and cradled like Itzhak Perlman working magic with his violin, the skin of his right cheek stretched taut with a nasty, baseball-sized chaw of tobacco (the better to see a pitcher from that left side of the plate), it seems so fresh. It's like the old line about Ty Cobb: if Carew played today, what would he hit? Probably no more than .310 because, after all, he'd be a 62-year-old man.

Carew was half that age when he had the most magnificent individual season of his 19-year Hall of Fame career. That this master batsman would lead the American League in hitting again, winning the sixth of his seven batting titles, was almost to be expected. But Carew put up numbers across the board—239 hits, 128 runs scored, 38 doubles, 16 triples, career highs of 14 homers and 100 RBIs—that were breathtaking. Not the least of which was that .388 batting average, the highest since Williams had hit .388 in 1957.

Since 1977, only a handful of professional hit men have come close to either Carew or Williams. Kansas City's George Brett finished with a .390 average in 1980, and San Diego's Tony Gwynn hit .394 in 1994, but those two eventual Hall of Famers had brevity on their side. Brett, for instance, played in only 117 games that season, which kept his at-bats down to 449 and thus required only 175 base hits. Had he turned just five outs into hits, his total of 180 would have gotten the Royals third baseman to .400.

Gwynn appeared in even fewer games in 1994 (110) due to the labor strike that ended his and everyone else's season by the middle of August. All the Padres outfielder needed, then, based on his 419 at-bats, was three more bleeders or fortunate hops to reach the big fat .400.

Carew? Nothing abbreviated about his challenge to that milestone. He played in 155 games and logged 616 at-bats and 694 plate appearances, both career highs. Adding opportunities to fail, tempting the odds over a far greater sample size, the Twins first baseman would have needed eight more hits along the way to have finished at .400974. Williams's legendary .406 was built off a modest 456 at-bats, thanks to 147 walks, so 185 hits got it done for him.

Even Carew, reflecting years later, knew that his chance of reaching and staying safely above .400 declined every time he stepped to the plate. "You wear down when you swing the bat that many times, during a game or during a season, and they're always bringing in fresh pitchers to face you," he said back in 1997. "You would have to be tremendously disciplined at the plate. You would have to take a lot of walks. You would have to hit what you want to hit and not chase pitchers' pitches.

"That sounds easy, but it's not. It requires tremendous discipline every day of a long season."

Carew admitted that he had mental lapses, from at-bat to at-bat or from one day to the next, as the grind of the schedule and the heat of the summer wore on. And he made good points about the changes in baseball from Williams's heyday to his own.

Sure, 1977 was an expansion year—Toronto and Seattle joined the American League, which allowed Carew and every other AL hitter to fatten up on 20 pitchers who wouldn't have been in the league one year earlier. But just about every other trend in the game had gotten stacked against batters in the 36 years between Williams's .406 season and Carew's chase: travel, the number of games (162 versus 154), more and more night baseball, and the size of fielders' gloves. And, of course, that tactic of using "fresh pitchers." That, especially.

Check out the numbers, as presented by the baseball stats website, baseball-reference.com: Carew batted .397 against starting pitchers in 1977, and the more he saw of them, the more he feasted (.426 when facing them for the third time or more in a game). But in his 193 at-bats against relievers, he batted "only" .368.

Comparable data for 1941 isn't readily available, but it is for 1957, when Williams also hit .388. That year, Teddy Ballgame knocked around starting pitchers at a .411 clip and actually fared better (.434) when facing them for the first or second time in a game. But he hit .315 against relievers and faced them only 92 times.

So in this apples-to-apples comparison, Carew faced fresh pitchers an additional 100 times while hitting .388. Given the way baseball was played in 1941, compared even to 1957, Williams's advantage in stalking .400 probably was even greater.

Which isn't to suggest, of course, that Carew was Williams's equal as a hitter. That he could, for one remarkable season, inspire conversations about and be mentioned in the same breath as Williams and .400 was special enough.

One of the highlights of that '77 season, not just for Carew but for Minnesota fans, came in mid-July, when the Twins' line-drive machine was the cover guy of two national magazines. *Time* featured him solo, with the words: "Baseball's Best Hitter." *Sports Illustrated* went one better, putting Carew on its front with Williams for an article titled, "Ted Williams Analyzes Rod Carew: The last .400 hitter and maybe the next."

The only problem with Williams's analysis of the Twins' spray hitter was that the Red Sox great was a consummate pull hitter

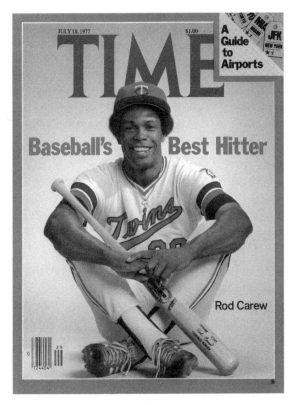

Baseball's   Best Hitter

Rod Carew

Rod Carew's pursuit
of a .400 batting
average landed him
on the cover of *Time*
magazine in 1977.

who expected a man Carew's size to hit with more power. Carew
was fine with his style the way it was, thank you, and was not
about to change.

No one was complaining on June 26, easily the highest of
highlights in a season filled with them. With Gene Mauch in his
first season as manager and an offensive attack that would lead
the AL in hits, runs, and average (.282) while finishing second in
doubles and triples, there was a buzz about the Twins again. Fans
were coming back to Met Stadium, and 46,963—a ballpark record,
boosted by a "Jersey Day" promotion—came out for the rubber
game of a three-game series against the White Sox, who were in a
virtual first-place tie with the Twins.

Forget the giveaway; the game was incredible, with 23 runs
scored in the first four innings and two hours off the clock just to

record those 24 outs. Twins outfielder Glenn Adams had a career day with a grand slam and eight RBIs, yet he was overshadowed by Carew. And by the fans' reaction to Carew.

After a double and a single in the first two innings, Carew finally, officially, was batting .400 (he began the day at .396). The scoreboard flashed that info for the crowd, sparking a standing ovation. They kept it up the rest of the afternoon as Carew singled, walked, and finally slammed a two-run homer in the eighth. He was hitting .403 by the time the Twins' 19–12 slugfest ended.

Carew later called it the best day of his career. Mauch, in his 27th season at that point as a major league player or manager, said, "I've never had a game like this. Not even close."

By the end of June, Carew was hitting .411; he hit .486 that month with eight triples, 30 RBIs, and a .775 slugging percentage. But a July that would have been solid for most players (.304) was a problem for Carew's quest. He had eight games in which he went hitless, dragging his average down to .383 as August began. Then it dropped further when he hit a "mere" .363. The Twins couldn't get much traction, either, going 31–28 to hit September with a 75–59 mark, third best in the AL West.

From that point, the club and its star headed in opposite directions. A pitching staff that wound up 12th in hits and ERA contributed to a 9–18 limp to the finish. But Carew got busy again, punching 43 hits in his final 98 at-bats (.439) and hiking his overall average by .010 points in that final month. As far as the fans at Met Stadium were concerned, Carew *was* a .400 hitter; he hit .401, to be exact, in the Twins' home games.

And yet, with an autumn chill in the air, school back in session, the Vikings off to a 4–1 start, and that September skid, a crowd of only 3,291 came out to see Carew one final time in the year's last ballgame at Met Stadium. Those who did weren't disappointed: he went 2-for-3.

Carew was named the AL's Most Valuable Player after the season, getting 12 of the 28 first-place votes cast. He picked up his sixth batting title and, unexpectedly, a $100,000 bonus from Twins owner Calvin Griffith. "He thanked me for having a great year and said I was one of the big reasons why we drew big crowds and made money," Carew once said.

There were conflicting reports about the relationship between the two men after that. Griffith reportedly referred to Carew as a "damn fool" for signing a multiyear contract that paid him $170,000 annually during his peak years. The owner also was said to have made offensive remarks that offended the player, whose wife was Jewish. With the freedom of free agency approaching, Carew nailed down his final batting title (.333), and then looked to cash in. He and the Twins butted heads in a trade-versus-contract tug-of-war, to the point that commissioner Bowie Kuhn finally intervened to help broker a deal. Griffith, who ultimately didn't want to lose Carew for nothing in return, sent him to the Angels for five players.

Carew still had seven seasons, seven All-Star appearances, two trips to the postseason, and 968 hits left in him from 1979 to 1985. But for all his impressive numbers, the best and most memorable remains .388.

LET'S PLAY NINE!

Cesar Tovar, who spent eight of his 12 seasons in the big leagues with the Twins, put up some of the most interesting and quirky numbers in the team's history. They include:

- 164: That's the number of games Tovar played in during the 1967 season, two more than the regulation 162 and still the record for American League players. The Twins played two games that season that ended in ties due to rain—5–5 at Detroit on June 21 and 1–1 at New York on July 25—and Tovar played in all of them. The only man to appear in more regular-season games in one season was the Dodgers' Maury Wills in 1962, and he did that only because Los Angeles and San Francisco competed in a three-game playoff that was tacked onto the season's end to determine the pennant. (An interesting note: Tovar went 0-for-9 at the plate in those two tie games, so if the stats had been thrown out rather than recorded, he would have batted .270 that season, not .267.)

- 5: Tovar also holds the AL record for the most times having his team's only hit in a game. That's right, he is credited with breaking up five no-hitters, including two in the ninth inning in 1969 against Baltimore's Mike Cuellar and Dave McNally.

- 4: The 5'9", 155-pound native of Venezuela was the first Twins batter to rap four extra-base hits in one game. Tovar went 4-for-6 with two doubles and two home runs, scoring three times in a 12–3 victory at California on May 21, 1967. Three other Twins have since gotten four extra-base hits in a game, including Kirby Puckett twice.

- 11: Tovar went to the plate 11 times in a 22-inning game that the Twins lost 4–3 on May 12, 1972. He had four hits and one walk. Shortstop Danny Thompson also had 11 plate appearances that day, going 0-for-10 with a sacrifice bunt.

Of course, the most intriguing number of Tovar's career as a utility player and leadoff man—who got votes for the AL MVP award for five consecutive years, from 1967 to 1971—was nine. Nine, as in the number of positions on a baseball diamond. Nine, as in the number of innings in a typical game. And nine, as in the number of positions Tovar played—one per inning—on September 22, 1968, at Metropolitan Stadium.

It was a flaky idea at the end of a flop season, a summer-long disappointment that had the Twins stuck in seventh place, 74–81, and 27 games behind the Detroit Tigers, when they took the field on that Sunday afternoon for their home finale. As fan-appreciation gimmicks go, it wasn't an overwhelming success—only 11,340 tickets were sold to witness Tovar's passage into baseball's trivia books. But then, that was better than the 7,997 who turned out for the previous day's game against Oakland or the lonely 1,710 who attended the series opener on Friday.

As a novelty, this scheme to which owner Calvin Griffith gave his blessing wasn't on a Bill Veeckian, send-a-midget-up-to-pinch-hit scale. It wasn't even original. Three years earlier, on September

8, 1965, Kansas City used shortstop Bert Campaneris in the same manner, one position per inning.

But it was pretty cool that, after Tovar strode to the mound as the Twins' starting pitcher that day and threw his warm-up pitches to catcher Jerry Zimmerman, the first batter he faced was Campaneris (the Athletics had moved to Oakland before the season).

"He's probably the best utility player we've ever had," former Twins equipment manager Jim Wiesner said at the time of Tovar's death in 1994. "When we needed a guy to play second base, he played second. When we needed a guy to play the outfield, he played the outfield for you."

Born on July 3, 1940, in Caracas, Tovar faced some intense scrutiny when the Twins acquired the minor leaguer from Cincinnati in a trade of pitcher Gerry Arrigo. Arrigo was a young left-hander who had gone 7–4 as a spot starter for the Twins in 1964, striking out 96 in 105⅓ innings and throwing a one-hitter. In Tovar's major league debut on April 12, 1965, his error at third base with two outs in the ninth inning enabled the Yankees to score the tying run, but he redeemed himself with a two-out RBI single in the eleventh to win it 5–4.

After appearing in only 18 games that season, Tovar established himself with 134 games in 1966 and averaged 609 at-bats

THE HIGHS AND THE LOWS

The highest number ever worn by a Twins player was third baseman Tony Batista's No. 77 in 2006. Coach Bobby Cuellar wore No. 78 when he was with the club in 2003 and 2004.

The lowest number for a Twins player? That would be catcher Junior Ortiz, who wore No. 0 as a nod to his nickname "O."

The most frequently worn number in team history is No. 21, which was worn by 29 different men, from Ray Moore (1961–1963) to Matt Garza (2006–2007).

for Minnesota from 1967 through 1972. He stole 45 bases in 1969, had 13 triples in 1970, and led the league with 204 hits in 1971, batting a career-best .311. And while he played primarily center field during his best seasons, Tovar continued to help defensively in the infield throughout his career. (Arrigo? He went 27–33 after the trade and was out of the big leagues by June 1970.)

Traded to Philadelphia for three players before the 1973 season, Tovar also played with Texas, Oakland, and the Yankees. He finished with a .278 average in 1,488 games in the majors, playing 77 at shortstop and more than 200 each at third and second base.

But he never pitched, caught, or played first base again after that September day in 1968.

Just looking at Tovar's line in the box score from that game is amusing, with the string of position symbols after his name: P-C-1B-2B-SS-3B-LF-CF-RF. For fans who like to keep score, that meant Tovar manned the various defensive spots in not-quite-perfect numerical order: 1-2-3-4-6-5-7-8-9. But he moved around the diamond in a nice orderly fashion.

Other Twins did their fair share of shifting to accommodate him, too. Bob Allison bounced from left field to center, back to left, back to center. Graig Nettles had a 1B-CF-3B afternoon.

Facing Campaneris to start the game, Tovar got the A's short-stop on a foul pop-up to third base. Then he struck out Reggie Jackson. After a walk to Danny Cater and a balk, the novice hurler got Sal Bando to foul out to first base. No hits, and an 0.00 earned run average for eternity.

A composite photo that ran the next day in the *St. Paul Dispatch*, taking up nearly half the page, showed Tovar at all nine positions at once, and even threw him in as the batter and the on-deck hitter. Only cloning would have made that possible. As it was, Tovar's tour around the diamond went pretty smoothly. Pitcher Tom Hall walked two in the inning Tovar caught but pitched out of the jam. The versatile Venezuelan, at first base, gloved a grounder from Jackson and flipped to Hall covering, then singled, stole second, and scored the game's first run in the bottom of the third. Tovar handled a pop-up at second in the fourth, had no chances at shortstop or third, and caught a pair of fly balls in left in the seventh. In the eighth he caught Cater's sacrifice fly to center that scored Allan Lewis to cut Minnesota's lead to 2–1, and that's how it ended.

A stunt that belonged only to Tovar and Campaneris for the next 32 years finally got matched on September 6, 2000, when Texas's Scott Sheldon also played all nine defensive positions. Sheldon jumped all around the diamond, with manager Johnny Oates's blessing, in just five innings; he didn't enter the game until the fourth inning, with the Rangers already trailing 10–1 at Chicago.

A month later, Detroit utility player Shane Halter made it four big leaguers in history. Coincidentally, he did it against the Twins on October 1, 2000, walked the only hitter he faced (Matt LeCroy), and scored the winning run in the ninth inning of a 12–11 Tigers victory.

Still, only Tovar among them served as starting pitcher, went a full inning, and, to Jackson's eternal aggravation, struck out a future Hall of Famer.

WHAT'S YOUR NUMBER?

The Twins have retired five numbers to honor the most talented, the most revered, and the most popular players in their history. Even casual baseball fans in the Upper Midwest can tell you which stars wore No. 3, No. 6, No. 14, No. 29, and No. 34 on their backs.

But the five men whose numbers adorn the outfield wall in Minneapolis's domed stadium weren't necessarily the only ones who wore them. They simply were the most accomplished and the last to do so.

Well, not No. 3. Harmon Killebrew, who came from Washington with the franchise itself, was wearing that number in the Twins' debut game back in 1961, and he was wearing it when he wrapped up his Hall of Fame career in Minnesota in 1974. (He wore it in his final season with Kansas City in 1975, too, but we'd rather ignore that unfortunate farewell lap.) No Twin has worn it since.

BIG, ROUND NUMBERS

The pitcher credited with the 1,000[th] victory in franchise history is the same guy credited with the team's 2,000[th] win. Bert Blyleven beat Milwaukee 7–1 on July 12, 1972, at Met Stadium. Thirteen years later, on September 25, 1985, Blyleven picked up a 5–1 victory at Texas.

Other pitchers who got credit for Twins milestone victories: Pedro Ramos (No. 1, on April 11, 1961, at New York, 6–0), Jim Kaat (No. 500, on August 23, 1966, at Washington, 7–0), Roger Erickson (No. 1,500, on August 17, 1978, against Kansas City, 6–5), Jack Morris (No. 2,500, on September 28, 1991, at Toronto, 5–0), Mike Lincoln (No. 3,000, on May 4, 1999, against New York, 8–5), and Kyle Lohse (No. 3,500, on May 7, 2005, at Tampa Bay, 8–1).

Even before Killebrew was done, Tony Oliva made No. 6 famous at Met Stadium. But he was, in fact, the fifth Twins player to don it. Infielders Billy Consolo and Ted Lepcio both wore No. 6 in 1961, followed by Jim Snyder in 1962. In fact, Oliva played a total of 16 games for the Twins in 1962 and 1963, wearing No. 37. He didn't switch to his more familiar single-digit jersey until '64, and when Snyder rejoined the big-league club for 26 games that season, the second baseman found himself wearing No. 21. In between, first baseman Vic Wertz wore No. 6 when he wrapped up his 17-year career with three months in Minnesota.

Kent Hrbek was the last Twins player to wear No. 14, but the number was in heavy rotation prior to his arrival in 1982. Pitcher Pedro Ramos was the first Minnesota player to wear it, followed by manager Sam Mele until he got fired in 1967. Danny Monzon (1972–1973), Glenn Borgmann (1974–1979), and Pete Mackanin (1980–1981) all kept the number warm for Hrbek.

Six players briefly wore Rod Carew's familiar No. 29 before the artful hitter and second baseman from Panama made it his own. They were Julio Becquer (1961), Fred Lasher (1963), Wally Post (1963), Chuck Nieson (1964), Mel Nelson (1965), and George Mitterwald (1966). By the time Mitterwald came back to the Twins in 1968, Carew was entrenched as the reigning AL Rookie of the Year, so the husky catcher briefly wore No. 34 before finding a home in No. 15 for five final Twins seasons.

As for No. 34, everyone knows it now as Kirby Puckett's uniform number. Before it was Puck's, though, it was Jim Roland's (1963), Dwight Siebler's (1964), Ron Clark's (1966), Ted Uhlaender's (1966), Pete Hamm's (1970), Jim Nettles's (1970), Ron Schueler's (1977), Jose Morales's (1978–1980), and Don Cooper's (1981–1982).

One other number needs to be accounted for here: every major league team has retired No. 42 to honor Jackie Robinson, the Brooklyn Dodgers' Hall of Fame second baseman who broke the major league's color barrier in 1947. While that number was available (before April 1997), however, a number of Twins players and coaches wore it: Gerry Arrigo (1961), Jim Manning (1962), Buzz Stephen (1968), coach Ralph Rowe (1972–1975), coach Don McMahon (1976–1977), coach Camilo Pascual (1978–1980), manager Billy Gardner (1981–1985), and coach Dick Such (1985–1997).

Pascual had worn No. 17 as one of the Twins' early pitching stars from 1961 to 1966, but when he returned to coach, Pete Redfern had settled into that number.

Also, a "grandfather" clause in baseball's Robinson tribute allowed major leaguers active at the time to continue wearing No. 42 if they desired, which explains how outfielder/DH Butch Huskey (2000) and pitcher Mike Jackson (2002) wore it in their brief stays with the Twins.

TWINS PREFER THREES

One of baseball's rarest plays and a guaranteed crowd-pleaser (if the home team is in the field, anyway) is the triple play. In spite of or maybe because of their nickname, the Twins have been pretty adept at turning those triplets.

Over the years, the Twins have turned far more triple plays (11) than they have hit into (seven). And they are the only team in the history of the major leagues to pull off the feat twice in the same game, getting an amazing six outs on two pitches.

It happened on July 17, 1990, a Tuesday night game at Fenway Park in Boston. The first one was typical bang-bang-bang. With the bases loaded, former Twin Tom Brunansky grounded sharply to third, where Gary Gaetti stepped on the bag and fired across to Al Newman covering second. Newman relayed quickly to Kent Hrbek at first base, and Minnesota was out of the inning.

It sounds almost like something out of Little League, but as Brunansky walked to the plate, Gaetti told Wade Boggs, the Red Sox runner at third, that a triple play might be in order. "[He] just looked at me and spit," Gaetti said. "I think he rolled his eyes a little bit."

Said Boggs: "I wasn't taking him seriously."

In the eighth inning, it went the same way. With runners on first and second, Jody Reed was the Boston batter who grounded hard to Gaetti. Step on the bag, throw to Newman, relay to Hrbek. Inning over.

As if Reed's one-hopper wasn't trouble enough, the second baseman said he stumbled getting out of the batter's box. "I said, 'Here we go,'" Reed said. Later, the Red Sox infielder gushed, "It's never happened in 120 years or whatever. We were the first. It's like landing on the moon."

The defensive gems kept the Twins in the game but did not win it for them. They got Dan Gladden as far as second base with one out, but old pal Jeff Reardon retired Junior Ortiz and John Moses to save the 1–0 Red Sox victory.

How's this for irony? The game's only run was scored by Mike Greenwell, who had reached safely in the fifth inning when his ground ball went through the legs of shortstop Greg Gagne, one of the sweetest-fielding Twins players ever. On a night when defense was the story, an E6 lost it for Minnesota.

"That's unbelievable," Newman said in the visitors' clubhouse afterward. "I'm still nervous about it. I just figured we were going to win the ballgame after the second one happened."

But veteran pitcher Dennis Lamp, with Boston at that point, recalled some recent wisdom from manager Joe Morgan. "As Joe always says, 'We've got to stay out of the double plays,'" Lamp said. "And we did."

Here are some details of other Twins triple plays:

The first one in franchise history came on August 18, 1966, when Rich Rollins, Cesar Tovar, and Harmon Killebrew got the putouts from Frank Malzone's grounder to third in a 6–2 victory over California at Met Stadium.

Catcher Glenn Borgmann and shortstop Luis Gomez pulled off the only Twins triple play involving just two fielders. On July 25, 1976, at Comiskey Park, Chicago had runners on first and second when Bill Stein's foul bunt pop-up was caught by Borgmann. He threw to Gomez and, since the runners had gone with the pitch, forcing the lead man and tagging the other snuffed the inning.

Gaetti and Hrbek, both exceptional glove men, took part in six triple-plays in their time together. They worked with four second basemen on those rarities (John Castino, Tim Teufel, Steve Lombardozzi, and Al Newman).

Left fielder Dan Gladden was the only outfielder to start a triple play for the Twins. He caught Joe Carter's fly ball in the fourth inning of a scoreless game at the Metrodome on August 8, 1988, and threw to second to double-up Cleveland's Ron Washington. Willie Upshaw, the Indians' runner at first, had strayed from the bag, too, and Lombardozzi's throw to Gene Larkin got the third out.

Add the Twins' 11 triple plays to the 20 that were made by the Washington Senators during the franchise's first 60 years in the nation's capital and the total of 31 ranks them among the top six in post-1901 baseball history.

Of the seven triple plays turned against Minnesota, three of them were by the California Angels. They came on June 27, 1972; July 23, 1977; and September 8, 1996. Two more have come against Cleveland.

On May 27, 2006, just 13 days after Chicago pulled a triple play against the Twins at the Metrodome, Minnesota reliever Juan Rincon was the epitome of efficiency when he replaced Jesse Crain in the top of the eighth inning, with no one out and three Seattle Mariners on base. Catcher Kenji Johjima hit Rincon's first pitch on the ground to second baseman Luis Castillo, who tagged the runner headed to second and threw to Justin Morneau at first for the second out. Richie Sexson had scored from third, but Carl Everett rounded that bag too aggressively, so Morneau threw across to third baseman Tony Batista for the tag on Everett.

"Rincon didn't follow orders," Twins manager Ron Gardenhire said after the 9–5 home victory. "I told him to get a ground-ball double play, and he got a triple play."

IT AIN'T OVER 'TIL IT'S OVER

ROLLIN' RYAN

Thriving in a job, both personally and by most measurable results, is no guarantee that, sooner or later, the job might not fit. That's the situation Twins general manager Terry Ryan found himself in late in the 2007 season.

"This has been creeping in and creeping in," Ryan said, announcing his unexpected resignation on September 13, deep into another challenging season. "It got to the point where I knew I had to step aside. I didn't like seeing the way I had become, the way I treated people.... I don't have it in me anymore."

Ryan, who finished out the season and then moved into a senior advisory role with the Twins, excelled at his GM job for 13 seasons. After several lean years at the start, the club reached the postseason four times in a span of five years, from 2002 to 2006. His first and maybe second blueprints didn't work out quite right, but Ryan made several shrewd trades (the A.J. Pierzynski and Chuck Knoblauch deals) and, early in the new millennium, had the roster stocked with stars and future stars such as Johan Santana, Joe Mauer, Justin Morneau, Torii Hunter, Joe Nathan, and Francisco Liriano.

Ryan's record at signing free agents wasn't as strong, and he had to pursue that strategy carefully, faced with the payroll limits imposed by owner Carl Pohlad. Releasing future Red Sox hero David Ortiz without tendering a contract after the 2002 season came back to bite Ryan and the Twins, too.

Ryan got out on his own terms and planned to beef up his scouting activities, always his first love in the game. But he left his replacement, Bill Smith, with a full plate of work, including the free agency of Hunter (who signed with Anaheim) and Carlos Silva (who signed with Seattle), contract negotiations with Santana and Nathan before the end of 2008, and navigation of the team's move to an expensive new outdoor ballpark in 2010, while satisfying fans eager to win and the tightfisted ownership of the Pohlad family.

Because longtime Twins owner Calvin Griffith handled contract negotiations and most personnel transactions himself, running the baseball operation like a mom-and-pop grocery store long after his rivals went corporate, the team has had only five official general managers in its history. After Griffith relinquished the role in 1984, Howard Fox took over. In 1985 he yielded to Andy MacPhail, the boy wonder who got the team to the World Series in two of his first six seasons. Ryan's tenure lasted precisely 13 years (1994 to 2007) before he flipped the keys to assistant Smith.

HARDWARE HANKS

When the Twins won a Triple Crown of sorts in 2006—Justin Morneau as American League MVP, Johan Santana earning the Cy Young Award, and Joe Mauer capturing the AL batting title (.347)—they became the first team since the 1962 Los Angeles Dodgers to have three players hog those honors.

When the Dodgers did it, shortstop Maury Wills was the National League's MVP, Don Drysdale won the Cy Young Award (one for both leagues at that time), and outfielder Tommy Davis led all NL batters with a .346 average.

Sticking with the major annual awards for individuals, Minnesota has been most successful at finding prized newcomers, earning the AL Rookie of the Year Award five times. The winners: Tony Oliva (1964), Rod Carew (1967), John Castino (1979, tied with Toronto's Alfredo Griffin), Chuck Knoblauch (1991), and Marty Cordova (1995).

Santana is the only repeat winner of a major award, taking the Cy Young in 2004 (20–6, 2.61 ERA, 265 strikeouts, 54 walks, 156

Justin Morneau (left) and Joe Mauer had sensational seasons in 2006 and form the nucleus of the modern-day Twins.

hits in 228 innings) and again in 2006 (19–6, 2.77, 245 strikeouts). A unanimous winner both times, the native of Tovar, Venezuela, also was seventh in 2003 balloting and third in 2005.

The other two Twins pitchers to earn the AL Cy Young Award were Jim Perry in 1970, when he started 40 times and went 24–12 as Minnesota won a second straight AL West crown, and Frank Viola in 1988. That season, pitching home games with the familiar "Sweet Music Viola" bedsheet down the right-field line, Viola went 24–7 with a 2.64 ERA.

Four Twins—Zoilo Versalles (1965), Harmon Killebrew (1969), Carew (1977), and Morneau—have been their league's MVP. And Tom Kelly was Manager of the Year in 1991 when he took Minnesota from last place in the AL West the season before to a World Series championship.

COMEBACKS AND BLOWN LEADS

On an otherwise ordinary Friday night early in September 2007, the Twins' game at U.S. Cellular Field in Chicago played out like the two teams' mediocre seasons: over eight innings, the Twins and the White Sox scored four runs apiece. Not a lot of excellence, certainly not much urgency.

And then, *whammo!*, the ninth inning broke out. Minnesota racked up six runs in their half of the inning for what seemed like a certain victory. Except that the White Sox countered with six of their own in the bottom of the ninth. In the thirteenth inning, former Twins catcher A.J. Pierzynski—*that* guy!—rapped a run-scoring single off Juan Rincon with the bases loaded for an 11–10 Chicago victory.

It was the first time in major league history that two teams entered the ninth inning tied, only to have each side score at least six runs to knot things up again. And it was the first time in White Sox history that they had come to bat in the ninth inning trailing by so many runs, yet managed to tie.

How did it happen? In a sense, the Twins scored too many runs in the ninth. That fat lead encouraged manager Ron Gardenhire to use rookie pitcher Julio DePaula for what figured to be the game's final three outs, rather than closer Joe Nathan, who had been warming up. By the time the Twins skipper got Nathan up again, it was 10–6 with Jim Thome stepping to the plate, runners on second and third. The White Sox slugger drove a DePaula pitch over the center-field wall.

Still, Nathan came on at 10–9, having converted 29 of 32 save opportunities at that point. A walk to Paul Konerko, a steal by pinch-runner Scott Podsednik, a strikeout of Pierzynski, a wild pitch with two strikes on Darin Erstad, and Erstad's ground-rule double tied it.

If it makes them feel any better, it was the ninth time in Minnesota history that the club blew a lead of six runs and lost. Six times the Twins have let seven-run leads turn into defeats. They have lost after leading by eight runs on two occasions. And then there is the infamous 10–0 lead in Cleveland on September 28, 1984, that turned into a crushing 11–10 loss.

Prefer happier endings? On May 10, 2000, the Twins trailed 8–1 against the Indians, but scored six runs in the bottom of the seventh, got Matt Lawton home with one out in the ninth, and then won 10–9 on Midre Cummings's two-run walk-off homer off Steve Karsay. Through the first 47 seasons, that was their biggest comeback.

THE LEATHER EXPERTS

It was always tough on Tom Kelly and Ron Gardenhire, the Twins managers who had Torii Hunter as their ball-hawking center fielder. Hard as it was to watch Hunter slam into outfield walls or sprawl at full-speed on grass or turf in pursuit of a rocketing base-ball, it would have been just as hard to watch those balls become extra-base hits, frequently even home runs.

Defense has been a major ingredient in the Twins' most successful seasons, a cornerstone of Kelly's and Gardenhire's philosophy of not beating oneself. But Hunter took that a step further by often beating himself *up.*

"I'm suicidal," Hunter said one day, joking. "I've always been that way. When I was younger, everyone said I was nuts." Hunter allegedly knocked himself out running into a pole playing high school ball and, in a minor league game, crashed through a

Center fielder Torii Hunter's flair for the dramatic has helped him win more Gold Glove awards than any Twin in team history. Photo courtesy of AP/Wide World Photos.

plywood outfield fence. He has broken toes just jamming them into walls on some catches.

At least through his first dozen major league seasons, any attempts to persuade Hunter to patrol the outfield more, uh, conservatively have failed. "I have to do it for my pitchers," he said. "I'd rather save a home run than hit one. Defense is what I pride myself on."

Defense is what earned Hunter seven consecutive Gold Gloves, from 2001 to 2007, honoring him as the league's top center fielder. Hunter has a shot at the AL record for outfielders of 10, held by Al Kaline, and maybe even the all-time mark of 12 held by Roberto Clemente and Willie Mays. If he reaches it, he'll do it as an Angel after signing a five-year, $90 million contract with Anaheim in 2007. Hunter's predecessor in center for Minnesota, Kirby Puckett, also won the fielding award six times.

The only Twin to win more? Pitcher Jim Kaat, who shares the record regardless of position with 16, same as pitcher Greg Maddux and third baseman Brooks Robinson.

Gary Gaetti earned four Gold Gloves at third, from 1986 to 1989. Catcher Earl Battey, first baseman Vic Power, and shortstop Zoilo Versalles won two each while with the Twins, and Tony Oliva, Chuck Knoblauch, and Doug Mientkiewicz were recognized once each through 2006.

Most overlooked Twins defensive player? Easily, it was Kent Hrbek, who played first base like a hockey goaltender, "saving" his infielders on countless errant throws and his pitchers with all sorts of fielding gems. Hrbek, a large man, was also surprisingly nimble, giving chase to foul pop-ups and flies to short right field.

SPECIAL Ks

Johan Santana tipped his cap to the crowd at the Metrodome on August 19, 2007, as he walked off the mound after eight innings against the Texas Rangers. That meant two things: first, Santana did not plan on returning for the ninth. And second, he already had done enough.

The Twins' two-time Cy Young Award winner struck out 17 Texas batters that afternoon, allowing only two hits in a 1–0 blanking. Santana didn't take a shot at tying the major league record of 20 strikeouts by sticking around for the Rangers' final three outs. But he did set a Twins record for strikeouts in a game.

Can't blame the fans, though, for booing as closer Joe Nathan walked in to pitch the ninth. Nathan struck out two more, pushing the team's single-game record to 19.

"I felt good, but at the same time, we knew in that situation Nathan would be the right guy to go back out there and shut everything out," Santana said. "I trust all my teammates, especially the bullpen."

Santana's teammates feel the same way about him, which made trade rumors involving Santana, the Yankees, and the Red Sox in 2007 even more disheartening. The pitcher's previous high for strikeouts was 14, and he struck out 13 Rangers earlier in the season on May 22 at Texas. "He's the best pitcher in the game for a reason," said Rangers shortstop Michael Young, who whiffed four times in the August game. "In the past, I've had good at-bats against him, but once he gets a full head of steam, it's tough to break his rhythm."

Twins ace Johan Santana struck out 17 batters in eight shutout innings against the Texas Rangers in 2007.

Santana threw 83 strikes and 29 balls in this one, relying almost exclusively on his fastball and change-up. He had 11 strikeouts in the first five innings, none in the sixth, and then got his final six outs on Ks, too.

The previous mark for a Twins pitcher was 15 strikeouts, accomplished four times: Bert Blyleven versus Oakland on August 1, 1986; Jerry Koosman versus Kansas City, June 23, 1980; Joe Decker at Chicago, June 26, 1973; and Camilo Pascual at the Los Angeles Angels on July 19, 1961.

STARRY, STARRY NIGHTS

Baseball always has mandated that every franchise be represented in its annual All-Star Game, which can rub away some of the luster from a player's selection. A lot of times, it simply meant a guy was his team's best performer through the first half of the season.

So the real honor goes to those teams who place more than one man on the All-Star squad in a given year, and to players who get chosen multiple times. Or participate as starters.

In the Twins' first 47 years of existence, they had a single All-Star 22 times. That included all-time greats such as Rod Carew and Kirby Puckett, and obvious one-hit wonders such as Dave Engle and Ron Coomer.

Twenty Minnesota players have been chosen at least twice, topped by Carew's 12 consecutive selections. Harmon Killebrew was named to 11 All-Star teams, 10 with the Twins. And Puckett went to 10 in a row, from 1986 to 1995.

From 1961 through 2007, Twins players were All-Star starters 35 times. That included Dean Chance (1967), Roy Smalley (1979), Frank Viola (1988), and Jack Morris (1991), who represented Minnesota in the Midsummer Classic once each.

When the Twin Cities hosted the game for the first time in 1965 at Met Stadium, the team was extremely well represented by Killebrew, Earl Battey, Mudcat Grant, Jimmie Hall, Tony Oliva, and Zoilo Versalles. When the event came back 20 years later to the Metrodome, Tom Brunansky was Minnesota's lone All-Star.

THE BAD GUYS

Catcher A.J. Pierzynski, the former Twins catcher turned really annoying rival, might be Minnesota's least-favorite White Sox player in recent seasons. But the Chicago player who did the most damage and broke the most hearts over the years was Frank Thomas.

The Big Hurt did exactly that to the Twins during his 18 seasons, the first 16 as a member of the White Sox. In 180 meetings through 2007, Thomas cranked 52 home runs with 142 RBIs while batting .295 in 647 at-bats. That's his most home runs against any opponent, and it helped him—along with 41 doubles—to a .600 slugging percentage against Minnesota.

The pitching equivalent of Thomas has been Roger Clemens, 24–13 in 44 lifetime starts against the Twins. Clemens has struck out 272 in 312⅓ innings, which isn't shabby—until you notice that Nolan Ryan (20–11 versus Minnesota) rang up 336 Twins in 296 innings. Ryan also—ouch!—plunked eight Twins batters.

HR FEATS

It will help, with the following anecdote, to understand that baseball's Charlie O. Finley was George Steinbrenner a good decade before the Yankees' bombastic owner made his name in the game. He was Mark Cuban with less hair and, despite the neckties, a worse wardrobe.

Finley, who owned the Athletics during their time in Kansas City and Oakland, was both a maverick in regards to baseball tradition and a notoriously hot-tempered boss, and it is the latter that lends credibility to this tale from the Twins' road game against the Athletics on May 2, 1964.

Longtime Twins broadcaster Herb Carneal, as quoted in Alan Ross's book *Twins Pride,* recalled that Finley was out of town but had checked in by telephone with Athletics public relations director Jim Schaaf just as Tony Oliva was heading to the plate to lead off the eleventh inning, the teams tied at 3–3.

"Schaaf reported Oliva's home run as it happened," Carneal said. "Finley's mood worsened as Jimmie Hall's home run was described. Schaaf then told him Bob Allison had hit one out."

Actually, the batting order was Oliva, Allison, and then Hall, but the impact was the same. While Kansas City made a pitching change, bringing in Vern Handrahan to rescue Dan Pfister, Schaaf assured an apoplectic Finley that, uh, yes, sir, the Twins indeed had just hit three home runs in a row. Then Harmon Killebrew stepped into the box.

"Killebrew's home run was too much for Finley," Carneal claimed. "He was so convinced that Schaaf was pulling his leg that he fired him over the phone."

The Twins, from their arrival in Bloomington until well into the 1970s, frequently had the sort of unadulterated power that could pound big crooked numbers onto scoreboards and clobber unsuspecting opponents. The number one reason was the presence of Killebrew, one of the game's consummate sluggers, whose majestic moon shots often were measured not just by runs driven in but by distance traveled. In the so-called game of inches, Killebrew was a tape-measure guy who worked in feet by the hundreds. Sometimes 500.

That's another of the Twins' home-run tales. On June 3, 1967, Killebrew cranked what generally is considered the longest home run in Minnesota history. California's Lew Burdette entered with two outs in the fourth inning, hit Rich Rollins with a pitch, and then served up one that Killebrew drove an estimated 520 feet, the ball landing in the sixth row of the upper deck at Met Stadium. The ball allegedly cracked the seat back, and the club soon painted that seat orange to commemorate the blast.

Killebrew had plenty of home-run help, though. Allison hit 211 home runs in his 10 years with the club in Minnesota, including 67 from 1963 to 1964. The powerfully built outfielder hit the first grand slam in Twins history and had their first three-homer game.

The 225 home runs belted by Minnesota in 1963 ranked second in big-league history only to the Yankees' 240 in 1961. Hall, a left-handed swinger, contributed 33 to that total and hit at least 20 home runs in each of his first four AL seasons. Earl Battey was a catcher with power, hitting 26 in 1963. Role players such as Rollins and Don Mincher had pop in their bats, and even infielders such as Zoilo Versalles and Bernie Allen could reach the seats with some frequency.

If four home runs in a row was impressive, five in one inning surely must have tanned Finley's hide. That's right, the Twins picked on Kansas City again on June 9, 1966, when Rollins, Versalles, Oliva, Mincher, and Killebrew pounded pitchers Catfish Hunter (2), Paul Lindblad (2), and John Wyatt (1). Only a ground-out by Sandy Valdespino, between Versalles's and Oliva's blasts, interrupted the string of long balls. And Hall, with a double to right field after Killebrew's at-bat, nearly added a sixth.

The Twins held a power party on August 29, 1963, in Washington, hitting 12 home runs in a doubleheader against the Senators and sweeping by a combined score of 24–3. Seven different batters went deep against five pitchers, with Killebrew slugging three that day, and Hall, Allen, and Vic Power hitting two each.

It was a big deal when Allison and Killebrew each hit a grand slam—in the same inning—against Cleveland on July 18, 1962. No team before or since has topped that, although several have tied it. But then Fernando Tatis of the St. Louis Cardinals went one better on April 23, 1999, when he hit two grand slams in one inning *by*

TABLE SETTING AND CLEARING

There's not a Rickey Henderson in the bunch—even Rickey Henderson would say that, in his trademark third-person way ("There's not a Rickey in the bunch," Rickey said)—but three Twins hitters did a pretty good job of getting their team on the scoreboard quickly.

Outfielder Jacque Jones, from 1999 to 2005, hit 20 home runs to lead off ballgames. Chuck Knoblauch did it 14 times from 1991 to 1997, and Dan Gladden jacked out 12 in Minnesota's first at-bat from 1987 to 1991. In all, Twins leadoff men started 111 games with homers.

Henderson, of course, did it 81 times over his Hall of Fame–worthy career, more than the number two and number three men in baseball history—Brady Anderson (44) and Bobby Bonds (35)—combined.

himself. Twelve players in major league history have hit two grand slams in the same game—but alas, none of them were Twins.

In the 1980s a fearsome foursome in the heart of the batting order restored some power that had been absent from the lineup. Kent Hrbek (34), Tom Brunansky (32), Gary Gaetti (31), and Kirby Puckett (28) hit 125 of the team's 196 home runs in the World Series season of 1987. Hrbek would wrap up his career with 293 home runs and eight grand slams, second in both categories to Killebrew (475 and 10 in his Minnesota era). Torii Hunter hit three in 2007 to move within one of Hrbek, followed by Puckett (7) and Gaetti (6). Brunansky clubbed three grand slams in six-plus seasons with the team, and he does have the distinction of hitting the only inside-the-park grand slam in Twins history. He got it on July 19, 1982, at the Metrodome against Milwaukee's Jerry Augustine.

After the splurge in '87, however, no Twins batter would reach 30 homers in a season again until Justin Morneau (34) and Hunter (31) in 2006. The shortage of bona fide power hitters in recent years in what was mistakenly thought to be a home-run-happy ballpark, the Metrodome, had a franchise once identified with the long ball running a serious deficit in that statistical category.

In the 1960s the Twins outhomered the opposition in eight of their nine seasons. But they did that only four more times in the next 38 years and only once since 1980. Blame it on the batter, blame it on Minnesota's pitchers, or blame it on the team's general managers and scouts, but through 2007, the Twins had clubbed 6,299 home runs in their first 47 years of existence. To 7,293 by their foes.

PLAYING FAVORITES?

The one year out of seven in which Rod Carew didn't win the American League batting title, when he batted .331 in 1976 and narrowly missed out, wound up as one of baseball's most controversial episodes of the 1970s.

On the final day of the season, the Twins were in Kansas City, wrapping up a three-game series that meant nothing in the standings—the Royals were safely atop the division, the Twins securely in third place—but everything to the batting race. Kansas City's George Brett and Hal McRae began game No. 162 with .331 averages, and there already was a little tension between the teammates and friends. McRae had been sputtering, hitting at a .255 pace in September and October to drop his season average from .350. Brett, meanwhile, was plugging along, hitting .327 during the same span to close the gap between them.

Then there was Carew, hitting .329 down the stretch in pursuit of his fifth consecutive title. It didn't help the two Royals' mood any when, in game No. 161, they sat out while the Twins' first baseman rapped three hits in four at-bats. His teammate, Lyman Bostock, had dropped back to .323 and didn't play at all in the final two games.

So the stage was set for a statistician's adventure and a team-chemistry headache.

"It was so close," Brett recalled years later, "after our second or third at-bats, they had to carry it out five numbers to see who was ahead. It came down to the last at-bat of the season between Hal and me."

Heading into the ninth inning, Minnesota led 5–2—which mattered only because it assured Kansas City of batting one more time. Carew was 1-for-3 and then got a two-out single to finish at .331. As the Twins took the field, Brett was the second man due up, and McRae was third, giving them both one more opportunity—each was 2-for-3 at that point.

"I hit a ball off Jim Hughes to short left field," Brett recalled in Phil Pepe's book, *Talkin' Baseball: An Oral History of Baseball in the 1970s.* "Steve Brye was the left fielder. He came running in and kind of quit on it a little early. The ball bounced over his head [on the artificial turf at Royals Stadium] and I got an inside-the-park home run. After the game, Brye said he lost the ball temporarily in the sun, which happens on occasion. I don't know. I just hit it and ran."

The fluke hit nudged Brett's average to .333 (215-for-645). McRae faced Hughes next and grounded out to short, dipping to .332068. After John Mayberry walked, Jim Wohlford ended the game with a ground-out. That's when things got nasty. McRae became convinced that Brye had let Brett's ball drop because he, Minnesota manager Gene Mauch, or the entire Twins team was racist and didn't want a black player to beat out the white guy (Brett).

"[Hal] pointed to Gene Mauch in the third-base dugout...who flipped him off, gave the old fist up in the air, and the next thing you know, there was an argument," Brett said. "It took a lot of fun out of winning the batting title, and I felt really bad for Hal because he and I were such good friends. He taught me how to play the game of baseball once I got to the major league level, with that all-out style of his. It didn't affect our friendship at all, but I felt really sorry for him."

When Brett went to the plate in the ninth inning, he was batting .332298 to McRae's .332699. Had Brye caught his ball for an out, McRae would have finished ahead of him, regardless of his own at-bat.

"The curious thing is why Brye would want me to win the batting title instead of his own [teammate, Carew]," Brett said.

Could be the Twins had a calculator in their dugout. Carew, with his ninth-inning single, was in the books at .330578. Third place.

Said Brett: "Teed [Carew] off so much, the next year, he went out and hit .388."

CALVIN GRIFFITH

In his later years, he often was referred to as a dinosaur, occasionally with derision but most of the time as affectionately and nostalgically as that sort of label could be applied. *Griffisaurus Calvinychus,* that peculiar species of baseball owner for whom the game was both his passion and his livelihood, doomed to extinction by free agency, network television, corporate ownership of rival teams, and a stubborn determination to keep baseball as his business.

Calvin Griffith, the man who moved the Washington Senators to Minnesota and rechristened them as the Twins, finally reached the tar pits in 1984, when he reluctantly sold the team to billionaire banker Carl Pohlad for an estimated $36 million. Griffith stuck around for another 15 years as one part museum piece, one part mascot in his regular visits to the Metrodome. But he really was of a different way, a different time.

In relative terms, he was strictly Mesozoic.

"You talk about somebody standing up for his principles—about how the game should be run or the ownership of a team—Calvin certainly was one of the dinosaurs," Twins manager Tom Kelly said upon Griffith's death in October 1999.

Said Roy Smalley, a former Twins shortstop: "This really is the completion of old-school baseball. It was sad to me to watch him pass out of the game, and now it's just more poignant with his passing."

From his traditional, some might say antiquated, ways of running the Twins organization, to his physical appearance—a hefty man for much of his life, with heavy jowls and a sometimes quizzical look—to a frugality that frequently verged into penuriousness, Griffith was an easy target for those who competed with him or negotiated against him. Fans who rooted for his team time and again wound up frustrated by the results on the diamond and the blown deals in the boardroom, and the more money became a driving force in the major leagues, the more Twins stars left to suit up elsewhere.

The old-fashioned owner wound up taking the blame within the borders of Minnesota, while hearing laughter from many of the game's other markets. As a businessman, well, Griffith had a good eye for baseball talent, and respect for him broke down pretty much along those lines.

For instance, pitcher Mike Marshall, a former Twins reliever who had his best years with the Los Angeles Dodgers and Montreal Expos, generally considered himself the smartest guy in any room. But when he sat across a bargaining table from Griffith, unable to convince the owner to incorporate deferred payments into his next contract, Marshall's view of the boss was hardened.

"I said, 'Calvin, I agree with you,'" Marshall recalled years later. "'I think deferred payments are ruining baseball, but I'll tell

Five years after moving from Washington, D.C., to Minnesota, Calvin Griffith's Twins reached the World Series. Photo courtesy of AP/Wide World Photos.

you what I'll do. You want to pay me X dollars for that first year, that's great, but I don't need all that money, Calvin. Let me loan half of it back to you, and you pay me prime interest on it. And he said, 'Good, I'll do that.'

"So I not only got deferred payments, I got prime interest on it, the buffoon."

Buffoon? Kind of harsh for a fellow who kept baseball alive in Washington, D.C., for much of the 1950s, saw a golden opportunity to pounce on a new market in the Upper Midwest, brought the major leagues to a Twin Cities area that only the year before had lost the NBA's Minneapolis Lakers, and then, in the franchise's fifth season after the move, steered them to the World Series.

Even if Griffith never was *not* about the money, he always was about the baseball.

It was the family business, after all. Clark Griffith, one of the game's top pitchers before and after the start of the 20th century, had moved into a managing role with the Chicago White Sox, the

New York Highlanders, and the Cincinnati Reds even as he continued to play. In 1912 he joined Washington as its manager and eventually assumed ownership of the club.

Clark Griffith and his wife Addie were childless in 1922 when Addie's brother Jimmy Robertson fell ill, leaving him and wife Jane too impoverished to support their seven children. Calvin, the oldest of five sons, and his sister Thelma were sent from Montreal to Washington to live with their aunt and uncle. A year later, Jimmy Robertson died at age 42, and Clark Griffith unofficially adopted his nephew and niece; Jane and the other children moved to Washington and received financial help from the Senators' owner.

Calvin Griffith, for a spell, was a batboy for the Washington team—most notably in 1924, when the Nationals (as the club also was known) won their only World Series championship. He pursued a baseball career, first as a catcher and later as a manager, the latter while helping his uncle operate minor league teams in Charlotte and Chattanooga.

First as a boy, then as a young man, Griffith picked up the game and the business from his uncle, who was inducted into the Hall of Fame in 1946.

"After every [game], we would go home and talk about what happened at dinner," Griffith said. "I learned the strengths and weaknesses of players. The little things it took to hit a baseball, to pitch a certain way to a batter, or to throw a runner out."

He learned, too, the value of a nickel. "My uncle could break even on an attendance of 325,000 a year, which would hardly pay the salary of some players today," Griffith said a few years before his death. "Of course, we owned Griffith Stadium in Washington. We made money off concessions.... We also rented out the stadium to football teams and the Homestead Grays black baseball club. My uncle only charged the Grays 10 percent of the gate, unheard of today. He felt the black leagues of those days were important to baseball."

Beginning in 1942, Calvin Griffith took an active role in the team's management and even butted heads with his uncle over the St. Louis Browns' move to Baltimore; it was Calvin, not Clark, who fretted about the Senators' loss of turf and fan base. But when the elder Griffith died at age 85 in 1955, he left the controlling interest in the ballclub (52 percent) to Calvin and Thelma.

By then, business headaches were trumping baseball issues for the family. The Senators, from 1955 through 1959, finished last in the American League in attendance, drawing anywhere from 425,000 to 615,000 fans each year. Having already told District of Columbia politicians that he wanted a new stadium, Griffith began to listen seriously to overtures from baseball-hungry sites such as Louisville, Houston, Los Angeles, San Francisco, and the Twin Cities. With recently constructed Met Stadium ready and waiting in suburban Bloomington, Minnesota, Griffith made his move in 1961; the other AL owners, nervous about vacating Washington and alienating Congress, offered an expansion Senators club to fill the void.

Hapless as they were, then, the new Twins were more ready-made than their replacements back in Washington. Players such as Harmon Killebrew, Bob Allison, and Camilo Pascual blossomed in Bloomington, and the farm system of the Griffith franchise continued to produce players. The club won 91 games in its second and third seasons in Minnesota, then 102 in reaching the World Series in its fifth—with the game's fattest payroll, no less.

Griffith still held tightly onto his wallet. Pascual often told a story about tearing up one contract proposal, mailing it back to the club, then getting the same one—"all Scotch-taped back together"—returned in the mail. The owner played hardball, too, with his managers, running through six different skippers in the Twins' first 12 seasons.

And as the 1960s turned into the '70s, and the players union got stronger and the owners lost leverage, the Twins' negotiations became a battleground. A pitcher named Dick Woodson got the best of the team in binding arbitration. Jim Kaat and Jim Perry exercised their five-and-10 trading rights. Free agency opened a floodgate, with players such as Bill Campbell, Larry Hisle, Lyman Bostock, and eventually even Rod Carew leaving outright or being traded to salvage something from their losses. Baseball still appealed to Griffith as much as ever, but the business side had overrun it.

"Those first few years at the Met were paradise. We got big crowds all the time. Everybody was so gol-darn happy," Griffith said years later. "I got a license plate that said 'Twins,' and people would drive by me, honking their horns and smiling and waving.

"Not like later on, when they'd give me the finger."

Admittedly, saying a sports team owner was adept before free agency is like complimenting someone for being good-looking before electricity. Modern times shed a whole new light on things. Baseball changed before its fans did, and Griffith, well, he never really changed at all. That made life, professionally at least, trickier than ever.

After their second consecutive American League West division crown in 1970, the Twins topped .500 only four times in their final 11 seasons at Met Stadium. Their farm system essentially was stocking other teams with established players, once the Twins took the time and spent the money to develop them. Then Griffith, a lightning rod of fan complaints but also an avuncular sort, good for occasionally amusing malapropisms, caused some bumps in the road that made business and baseball even harder.

At a Lions Club speech in Waseca, Minnesota, in September 1978, a possibly inebriated Griffith made a number of coarse and racist comments that got reported back in the Twin Cities. For instance, the owner suggested that catcher Butch Wynegar's disappointing performance stemmed somehow from chasing his wife around the bedroom. Worse, he said he preferred Minnesota to Washington for its smaller number of black residents. "Black people don't go to ballgames, but they'll fill up a rassling ring and put up such a chant it'll scare you to death," Griffth said.

Despite his claims that the words were taken out of context and that he was not a bigot, Griffith paid a stiff price. Carew announced he would no longer work on the "plantation." The public began wearing "Trade Calvin" buttons or, worse, staying away from Met Stadium entirely.

By 1982 unhappy fans had a new ballpark to kick around. Griffith accepted the dreary, plastic, enclosed excuse for a baseball park as a concession to Minnesota's harsh spring and fall weather. But in the Twins' first season indoors, in the quirky Hubert H. Humphrey Metrodome, they finished 60–102 and drew only 921,000 fans. Griffith stocked the roster with a bunch of relative kids, not because they were ready for the big leagues but because they kept his payroll in check—the team's average salary that season was $67,000, compared to $242,000 for the typical major league player.

"The interesting thing is that the organization has always seemed to come up with good young players," Carew once said, "but then they mature into veterans, and it's not economically feasible for them to stay."

That pattern likely would have continued into the mid-1980s, with players such as Kent Hrbek, Gary Gaetti, Frank Viola, and Kirby Puckett, who formed the nucleus of the first World Series champions, except that Griffith—after flirting with selling or moving the team out of state—cut a deal with Pohlad. Witnesses said that, when the final papers were signed in September 1984, Griffith wept.

In his post-ownership years, Griffith's image softened again, and he was a frequent visitor to the Dome, in the stands and in the media dining room where he took one or two meals daily. He was like a walking, talking natural history exhibit, bleached bones with plenty of flesh still in place.

"I think I'm a person who looked out for the fan," Griffith said one day. "I think I was always honest with them. I don't lie.... We made mistakes. But my mind has always been open for the betterment of baseball."

HOME INVADERS

Eleven times in 47 seasons, a Twins player has had a "pure" steal of home plate (as opposed to being part of a double-steal). Five of those came courtesy of Rod Carew—and three of those came in a span of less than six weeks.

On April 9, 1969, Carew raced home to break a 2–2 tie at Kansas City in the fifth inning, a game the Twins would lose (they are 9–2 through the years when one of their base runners steals home). Ten days later he took advantage of Hoyt Wilhelm's knuckleball floater to steal home again. Then, on May 18, Carew took off again when Detroit left-hander Mickey Lolich's back was turned.

Years later Carew credited former Twins manager Billy Martin, who had worked with him as a young player and ran the club in 1969, for showing him what a weapon it could be. "After I got into it, I really enjoyed doing it because I wasn't just stealing home for the sake of stealing home," Carew said. "I only did it at opportune times, when I felt it was important for the team."

Not to mention exciting for the fans, home or away. "It was high-emotion time," said Carew, who studied and timed opposing pitchers. "They knew I was going to do it, but they couldn't stop me.... Everyone in the ballpark knew that I could do this. Everyone was anticipating. At times people would yell, 'Steal, steal, steal!' They knew it was going to happen, but they didn't know when."

Carew added two more "pure" steals of home later in his Twins career, pulling the stunt in the first inning in games against Cleveland on May 14, 1975, and Oakland on May 17, 1976. He stole home seven times overall in 1969, coming within one of Ty Cobb's single-season record. Carew ended his career with 17 steals of home plate (Cobb holds the lifetime record of 54).

One thing working against Carew after 1969 was the fact that Martin managed in Detroit, Texas, Oakland, and New York and knew what his old protégé was up to. "He'd jump up on the top step and yell to the guys to hold me on," Carew said. "Because he knew in the back of his mind that I'd timed a couple of his pitchers and I was going to do it. The master caught the student."

Outfielder Dan Gladden is the only other Twins player to steal home more than once, doing it twice during the 1988 season.

KIDS IN THE HALL (OR NOT)

"THE KILLER," HARMON KILLEBREW

By the end of the year in which he turned 31 years old, George Herman "Babe" Ruth had hit 356 of his 714 career home runs. Not quite half.

Harmon Killebrew, at the same point, had hit 380.

No wonder Killebrew became the first "franchise" player for the Minnesota Twins and the most feared slugger in the American League throughout the 1960s. It is more of a tribute to Ruth, frankly, that he outhomered Killebrew the rest of the way, 358–193, and rather surprising, too, given the differences in their lifestyles and nocturnal activities. The Babe was one of the game's legendary carousers, whose appetites clashed even with the most basic training regimens of his time. Killebrew was a family man not known for any of the off-field pursuits made famous by Mickey Mantle, courtesy of pitcher-and-author Jim Bouton in his groundbreaking baseball book, *Ball Four*.

About the worst thing Bouton had to say about Killebrew in that memoir framed by the 1969 AL season was referring to the Twins star as the "Fat Kid." As in: "How the hell can I be nervous about starting a baseball game? Even if it is against the Fat Kid and his wrecking crew." So even with that misguided shot—at 5'11" and a listed 213 pounds, Killebrew was stocky but hardly fat—the wise-guy former Yankee was paying homage to a Twins team that had boosted its power production from 105 home runs in 1968 to

Harmon Killebrew was the first face of the franchise and remains one of the most feared sluggers in baseball history.

163 the following season, thanks in large part to Killebrew's career-best 49.

It should be noted, too, in acknowledging Killebrew's inability to keep pace with Ruth or Henry Aaron (398 at age 31) that the Babe, heading into 1927, was on the brink of his 60-homer season and baseball's reputed lively ball era. Killebrew, at the end of 1967, was facing what quickly became known as the "Year of the Pitcher" in 1968. He also suffered serious injuries in two of his remaining seasons (a torn hamstring in 1968 and left knee surgery in 1973) and, admittedly, a rather abrupt loss of his skills near the end of his 22 pro seasons.

Still, the Fat Kid—or as he was more commonly nicknamed, "Killer"—did all right for himself, his proud native state of Idaho, and legions of Twins and, before that, Washington Senators fans.

"He kept us in business," Twins owner Calvin Griffith once said. "He was the backbone of the franchise."

Killebrew also was something of a baseball rarity: a streak *power* hitter. His home runs often came in bunches, with long arid stretches in between. When he hit 42 in 1959 in his first season as an everyday player for Washington, 15 of them came in May, compared to his total of 12 in July and August. Late in August 1962 Killebrew and Detroit's Norm Cash were tied for the AL home-run lead with 34 each—before the Twins star mashed 11 in the season's last 12 games to take the HR title easily, 48–39.

Even in 1969, when he slammed 49, Killebrew found a way to go 23 straight games without clearing a fence. And in 1971 as he approached membership in the 500-home-run club, he took seven weeks to go from number 498 to number 500 (and just five more innings to get number 501).

Much of it had to do with Killebrew's all-or-nothing philosophy at the plate. He always had been encouraged to hit the ball as hard and as far as he could, and, long after he retired, Killebrew spoke of some advice he got from Pirates home-run champ Ralph Kiner. "He told me that I should be hitting for power, and that I needed to move up on the plate and pull the ball," Killebrew said. "That lowered my average and caused me to strike out a lot more, but he was right—I hit for power."

Killebrew never batted higher than .288 over a full season, and he struck out 100 times or more in seven seasons, with three more years topping 90. But he was selected for 11 All-Star teams. He led the AL in home runs six times, hit at least 40 in eight seasons, ranked fifth on the all-time list when he retired, and (until Alex Rodriguez catches and passes him) still ranks second among American Leaguers. Also by the time he retired, Killebrew was third in home-run frequency, averaging one for every 14.22 at-bats, trailing only Kiner (14.11) and Ruth (11.76).

Certainly Killebrew's backstory would rank him among those old black-and-white newsreel heroes. Raised in Payette, Idaho, he came by his sports achievements naturally; his father was considered an outstanding athlete, and Killebrew once said that one of his great-grandfathers was known as the strongest man in the Union Army during the Civil War. Growing up on the plains in the 1940s and '50s, the first major league game Killebrew ever saw, he played in.

It's part of the legend that the future Washington Senator actually was discovered by an Idaho senator. Herman Welker, who had grown friendly with Washington baseball owner Clark Griffith during his years in the Senate, told the Old Fox about this Killebrew kid in 1954. The last time Welker had volunteered such information, Griffith reportedly ignored it—and the player turned out to be Vernon Law of Meridian, Idaho, who went on to win 162 games in 16 seasons for Pittsburgh and led the Pirates to the 1960 World Series with a Cy Young–winning record of 20–9.

So either to satisfy Welker or cover the organization's hind end, Griffith sent scout Ossie Bluege to Payette in search of Killebrew. On a soggy day, the folks running Killebrew's semipro team learned that a big-league scout was on site, so they hurried to prepare the field when the rain stopped. On one pitch, the 17-year-old, fresh out of high school, really muscled up. "He hit one a mile over the left-field fence," Bluege said later. "I stepped it off the next morning and measured it at 435 feet. That convinced me."

The Senators signed Killebrew as a "bonus baby," paying him a $30,000 package that included $6,000 per year and an annual bonus of $4,000. By the rules in effect at the time, he had to stay on the major league roster, which explains his meager 113 game appearances from 1954 through 1958. His home-run frequency was a more modest 23.09 in those five seasons of part-time usage. Finally, in December 1958, the Senators opened up a position for him by trading third baseman Ed Yost to Detroit.

Calvin Griffith, running the Senators' baseball operation even before his uncle's death in 1955, was a staunch believer in Killebrew. So, still, was Bluege: "He hit line drives that put the opposition in jeopardy. And I don't mean infielders, I mean outfielders."

Killebrew rewarded them almost immediately, with 18 homers, 39 RBIs, 40 runs, and a .609 slugging average in the first two months. After hitting 42 that season and 31 in 1960, Killebrew smacked 46, with 122 RBIs and 107 bases on balls in 1961 in the franchise's first season in Minnesota. He hit 48, 45, and 49 the next three seasons, putting a pleasant face on a young team loaded with strong hitters. In fact, if you didn't know better, you might have thought that Killebrew actually had modeled for one of the two brawny guys in the caricature for the team's logo, shaking hands across the river as a teaming of Minneapolis and St. Paul.

The term "Killebrew fly" referred to the towering moon shots that the Twins slugger typically hit, and while the methods of measuring home-run distance were crude at the time, his prodigious clouts frequently did have a Paul Bunyan or John Daly quality to them. As former Baltimore manager Paul Richards said one time: "The homers he hit against us would be homers in any park—including Yellowstone."

Fans of a certain vintage will remember the 1971 All-Star Game in Detroit, the night six legends—Roberto Clemente, Aaron, Johnny Bench, Frank Robinson, Reggie Jackson, and Killebrew—hit home runs, and Jackson's banged into a transformer on the right-field roof at Tiger Stadium. Well, in 1960 Killebrew became the first player in 25 years to hit a ball onto the left-field roof. Two seasons later he hit a ball that *cleared* that roof. He recalled hitting another homer in 1960, off Herb Score in Chicago, that hit one of the posts in the upper deck beyond left field and bounced all the way back to the shortstop.

The home run that Killebrew hit off New York's Pete Mikkelsen on July 11, 1965—what they called a "walk off" nowadays, turning around a 3–2 pitch with two outs in the ninth to transform a 5–4 loss into a 6–5 victory—arguably was the most dramatic and important of his career. It sent Minnesota into the All-Star break with a first-place record of 53–29 and served notice to the Yankees that their domination of the league (14 pennants in 16 seasons) was ending.

But the one he hit off California's Lew Burdette at Met Stadium on June 3, 1967, was Killebrew's longest, no argument necessary. The ball slammed into a seat back in the upper deck

SOMEHOW, THEY MANAGE

Tom Kelly is the winningest manager in Twins history and guided the team to two World Series championships.

Over the years, the Twins have had two owners, six general managers, four players who won batting titles, four who won AL MVP Awards, and three who won Cy Young Awards.

They have had 12 different managers, which suggests it is a lot harder to find extreme talent and willing billionaires than it is skippers to steer from the dugout.

The most successful Twins manager, obviously, was Tom Kelly, who ran the ballclub from late in 1986 through the end of 2001. He deflected credit with both World Series champions, kept preaching defense, pitching, and smallish ball through some lean years that eroded his own winning percentage, and then got Minnesota up to second place in his final season. That put Ron Gardenhire in position to go first, first, first, third, first, and third from 2002 through 2007.

Here are the Twins field managers, with their records:

- 1961 Cookie Lavagetto (23–36, .390)
- 1961–1967 Sam Mele (524–436, .546)
- 1967–1968 Cal Ermer (145–129, .529)
- 1969 Billy Martin (97–65, .599)
- 1970–1972 Bill Rigney (208–184, .531)
- 1972–1975 Frank Quilici (280–287, .494)
- 1976–1980 Gene Mauch (378–394, .490)
- 1980–1981 John Goryl (34–38, .472)
- 1981–1985 Billy Gardner (268–353, .432)
- 1985–1986 Ray Miller (109–130, .456)
- 1986–2001 Tom Kelly (1,140–1,244, .478)
- 2002–2007 Ron Gardenhire (534–437, .550)

in left field, a blast estimated to have traveled 530 feet. The location was painted orange and allegedly never sold again, and it was later commemorated by a chair fastened high to a wall at the Mall of America, the shopping center built where the old ballpark once sat.

One day later, on June 4, Killebrew hit another ball to almost the same spot, this hit pounding off the upper-deck facing. "I got the book on how to pitch to Harmon Killebrew from my room-mate," joked Jack Sanford, the Angeles pitcher who bunked on the road with Burdette.

Too bad Killebrew couldn't have saved all the extra distance beyond what he actually needed to clear those fences and walls around the American League. He might have had Ruth's record easy.

Then again, he might not have. Injuries were unforgiving, in terms of games lost and home-run opportunities foregone. Killebrew missed 48 games in 1965 after Baltimore's Russ Snyder ran into his glove arm near first base and dislocated the slugger's left elbow. In 1968 Killebrew ruptured a hamstring in the third inning of the 1968 All-Star Game in Houston, stretching for a throw from shortstop Jim Fregosi. He didn't play again until September 1, totaling only 100 games and 17 home runs. The knee surgery in 1973 limited him, at age 37, to just five home runs, and his production spiraled down from there.

Rare among Hall of Fame–caliber players, Killebrew was known for playing no particular defensive position, which hurts him a little bit when people start batting around the all-time this and all-time that teams. He isn't going to knock Mike Schmidt, Brooks Robinson, George Brett, Edgar Martinez, or Pie Traynor off a lot of people's lists of top third basemen, since he didn't have a strong reputation there as a fielder. But he sometimes gets lost in the shuffle at first—behind Lou Gehrig, Jimmie Foxx, Willie McCovey, Jeff Bagwell, and others—because he wasn't seen as a full-timer there, either. Baseball insiders say Killebrew was effective enough wherever he was used, but in being moved around without grumble, it looked from afar as if his managers were trying to hide him a little defensively.

Almost universally, Twins fans feel that Killebrew never should have had to wrap up his playing days in a uniform other than Minnesota's. Seeing their franchise slugger in the powder blue double-knits of the Kansas City Royals in 1975 was sort of like watching Johnny Unitas finish with the San Diego Chargers or Michael Jordan on the court for the Washington Wizards.

Neither should Killebrew, in a perfect world, have been made to wait an extra three years for his invitation into Cooperstown's famous shrine and museum. The voting members of the Baseball Writers' Association of America left him 62 votes short of the 75 percent needed in 1981, 66 votes short in 1982, and 12 shy in '83. When he finally made it, Killebrew was still six votes behind Luis Aparicio—who had been 191 votes behind the Twins star in 1981. Go figure. Some folks apparently dismissed Killebrew as a one-dimensional player, fixating on his .256 batting average or lack of foot speed or Gold Gloves.

"It's so hard for the average fan to understand what Harmon meant," longtime teammate Jim Kaat once said, "because when you look at his batting average you say, 'Well, he didn't hit for a high average and he wasn't a great fielder.' I remember one writer saying, 'I'm not going to vote for him on the first ballot because all he did was hit home runs.'

"Yeah. But he hit 573 of them."

Kaat saw Killebrew from the inside-out, leaving no doubt as to his Hall-worthiness. "Unfortunately, for a lot of you who didn't see him, you don't know how many he hit in the clutch," Kaat said. "Besides that, he was a model citizen, he was a great teammate, and he's still, I think, the most revered Twin up there."

Little doubt why. Killebrew helped introduce Minnesota to the major leagues, provided more long-ball thrills than anyone else in the league during the Twins' first decade, helped the team reach the World Series, and provided clubhouse leadership in that by-example way, rather than a Reggie Jackson, straw-that-stirs-the-drink style. That suited the straightforward, rarely boisterous Upper Midwest sensibilities of the folks who went to Met Stadium.

"Killebrew gives us class," catcher Earl Battey said. "He makes us feel like we're all riding in a Cadillac."

Killebrew made a vast audience feel that way with his Hall of Fame induction speech, a humble and gracious talk in which he spent nearly half the time thanking those who helped him and the other half praising the game's other great players. At one point, though, he related a story that cut to the chase of what baseball and his sense of family meant to him. It's a tale he has told often but bears repeating:

"Dad used to work with my brother and me on different things that were important in all sports—football, basketball, baseball. One evening we were out in the front yard, and my mother came out on the porch and said to my father, 'Clay, the boys are digging holes in the yard, tearing up the grass.'

"And my father went over to my mother and very sternly said: 'Kate, we're not raising grass here. We're raising boys.'"

They raised themselves a Killer, didn't they?

HALL OF FAMERS

Three of the six players who have worn Twins uniforms *and* been elected to baseball's Hall of Fame are featured elsewhere in this book or this chapter. That only makes sense: Kirby Puckett, Harmon Killebrew, and Rod Carew spent all or most of their illustrious careers with the organization and would be three of the names most frequently spoken in a word-association game that began: "Minnesota Twins."

That leaves three others, at least until enough voting writers or old-timers see things differently on candidates such as Tony Oliva, Bert Blyleven, Jack Morris, and Jim Kaat. Or until guys such as Torii Hunter, Johan Santana, Joe Mauer, and Justin Morneau string together a few more seasons of brilliance before they're done and then wait the requisite five years for their eligibility clocks to begin ticking.

As for Paul Molitor, Dave Winfield, and Steve Carlton, they spent anywhere from three seasons (Molitor) down to the proverbial "cup of coffee," Venti-sized (Carlton), with the ballclub. One contributed big (Molitor's .341 average, 225 hits, and 113 RBIs in 1996). One contributed small (Winfield averaged 15.5 homers,

59.5 RBIs, and .264 in two seasons). One contributed hardly at all (Carlton's 1–6 record and 8.54 ERA).

Still, all three lent something to the franchise's pedigree and history, doubling the number of plaques at Cooperstown that list "Minnesota" somewhere on them.

Paul Molitor

Probably the most amazing thing about Molitor and his three seasons with the Twins is that he was still active and playing in 1996, when he arrived at age 39. The overriding trait of Molitor's early career in Milwaukee was the problems he had with injuries and the likelihood that various ailments, mishaps, and one well-chronicled struggle with drug abuse would undermine his longevity and potential.

Molitor missed 50 games in his third season, played in only 64 in the strike year of 1981, and then was sidelined for all but 13 games in 1984. By age 28, the folks at baseball-reference.com claim Molitor's career had the most in common with Rafael Furcal, hardly a first-ballot Hall of Famer. Then the St. Paul native and former University of Minnesota star missed another 100 games at age 29 and 30.

Hometown hero Paul Molitor collected his 3,000th career hit in 1996.

"The injuries were frustrating, and I couldn't really pinpoint what it was," Molitor once said. "I thought that I worked out and took care of myself. Some were more flukish, and some were recurring things."

Gorman Thomas, a teammate of Molitor with the Brewers, told the *Milwaukee Journal-Sentinel* in 2002: "In my mind, if Paulie hadn't gotten hurt so much, I think he would have been able to catch Pete Rose for total hits.... It's just an absolute shame he got hurt."

Rose played 24 seasons to Molitor's 21, saw action in an extra 846 games, and had 699 hits after age 40 to Molitor's 530. But Rose was 38 when he had his final 200-hit season, two years younger than Molitor. And the Hall-ineligible Charlie Hustle, in setting baseball's record for base hits (4,256), averaged 1.1948 hits for each game played. Molitor averaged 1.2370. (For comparison, Ty Cobb averaged 1.3802.)

Rather unexpectedly, and with little change in his workout habits or diet, Molitor's durability improved midway through his career. After playing 150 games or more in a season only twice in his first 10 years, he reached 150 six times in nine seasons—from 1988 to 1996—and played a maximum 115 in 1994's strike year. The opportunity to fill his teams' designated hitter spot 1,174 times definitely helped, restricting his exposure to injuries to only the offensive side of the game. Could be, too, that his luck merely changed.

With it, though, his prospects for Cooperstown improved dramatically. Through Molitor's first 10 seasons in Milwaukee, he averaged 9.5 home runs, 46.5 RBIs, and a .297 average. Over his next 10 with the Brewers, the Blue Jays, and the Twins, those averages spiked to 13.5, 77.3, and .315. By the time he retired, he was one of only four players in big-league history to have more than 3,000 hits, more than 500 stolen bases, and a .300 lifetime batting average. None of the others—Cobb, Honus Wagner, or Eddie Collins—came close to Molitor's 234 career home runs.

Among the highlights of Molitor's 15 seasons in Milwaukee was the 1982 World Series, in which he batted .355 and had a record five hits in the Brewers' 10–0 victory over St. Louis in

Game 1. Another was his 39-game hitting streak in 1987, the majors' longest since Rose hit safely in 44 straight in 1978.

Molitor went to Toronto as a free agent after the 1992 season and was remarkable in 1993, hitting .332 with 22 home runs, 111 RBIs, 121 runs scored, and 22 stolen bases. He made the sixth of his seven All-Star appearances, finished second in AL MVP voting that year, and, in the World Series, batted .500 to earn the championship round's MVP award.

After a significant dip in production in 1995 (15 homers, 60 RBIs, .270 average), Molitor came home, signing with the Twins for what many thought was a sentimental ending. Then he had a monster year, helping the club when it needed help most—Kirby Puckett had been forced to retire suddenly that spring, so the two never played together—and in September, rapping out the 3,000th hit of his career. Fittingly, he smacked a triple, a baseball first for that milestone, and belly-flopped into the bag.

"I remember the Minnesota media saying it was a nice story that I was coming home to play, but 'why would they invest in an older player when they were trying to find a way to get back to winning?'" Molitor said, reflecting on his hometown return. "It wasn't my motivation to prove those people wrong, but it was nice to say that it was a good decision they brought me back."

Dave Winfield

Like Molitor, Winfield was a local boy who came home—after winning his World Series ring up in Canada. Winfield spent one season with the Blue Jays, his fourth major league team, and helped them beat Atlanta in the 1992 World Series. Then he signed with the Twins, with Molitor taking over as Toronto's designated hitter and helping that squad beat Philadelphia in 1993.

By the time Molitor got to the Twins in 1996, Winfield had moved on again; he played the last of his 22 big-league seasons with Cleveland and, five years older than Molitor, retired at the end of 1995. Still, the two shared a lot, from each getting his 3,000th hit wearing a Twins uniform to starting out on those St. Paul playgrounds. Factor in Jack Morris, who nailed down the

1991 World Series for Minnesota with a pitching performance for the ages in Game 7 and grew up in the Highland Park area of St. Paul, and the confluence of baseball talent, drama, and achievement is staggering.

"It's pretty incredible to imagine the possibility of three guys from a town known for hockey going on to accomplish all that we have," Molitor said the night in Kansas City when he got his 3,000[th] hit. "And to all come back and play for the Twins...it's pretty amazing."

Winfield knows amazing, as in being drafted in three professional sports and four leagues (MLB, NFL, NBA, and ABA). As in never playing a game in the minor leagues for the San Diego Padres, going directly from the University of Minnesota and the College World Series in 1973 to the Padres and batting .277 in 56 games. As in producing some of the biggest all-around numbers in the game's history—3,110 hits, 465 home runs, 1,833 runs driven in, and seven Gold Gloves—yet being even more impressive in his sprints from first to third, with those long elegant strides, on someone else's base hit.

Behind that grace, behind the veneer that Winfield developed across two decades in the big leagues (and a stay in New York that felt nearly that long), Winfield broke sweats plenty of times. He was just good at not letting anyone see it.

"I didn't have an easy, smooth career," he said in 2001, soon after hearing the news of his Hall of Fame election. "I worked very hard, and [making the Hall] is a testament to the hard work that I put into it. It doesn't matter that I was big, tall, strong. You're not good in baseball because of those things."

The 6'6", 220-pound Winfield learned the game at St. Paul's Central High, played American Legion ball, and also played for the Gophers. Like most local kids, he got caught up in the arrival of the major leagues to the Twin Cities—Winfield was 10 when the Twins moved from Washington and 14 when they reached the World Series. "Killebrew, Zoilo Versalles—my first glove had his name on it," Winfield said. "Carew, Oliva. Then going through the University of Minnesota, I can still see the people I had on my wall—people like Willie McCovey, because of his strength and dominance yet gentlemanly demeanor. Juan Marichal, then people like Aaron and Mays because they were so great."

Winfield made as many headlines in his career for business reasons as for baseball. There was his unprecedented 10-year multimillion dollar contract with New York in 1981, which led to a feud with Yankees owner George Steinbrenner over delinquent contributions to the outfielder's charitable foundation. He battled with the club when it sought to trade him in 1990, and he declined to be depicted in a Yankees cap on his Cooperstown plaque. Instead, he went in as a Padre, in part because of a $1 million deal from that team.

Despite his overall numbers, Winfield only once led his league in any of the major hitting categories (118 RBIs, 1979), and his .283 lifetime average is near the bottom in the 3,000-hit club. But his 108 RBIs with Toronto in '92 were the most by a player his age (almost 41 by season's end), and it was his two-out, two-run double in the eleventh inning of Game 6 that won the Series for the Blue Jays that fall.

Winfield and Puckett enjoyed being inducted into the Hall in the same year (2001) after developing a friendship that began soon after Puckett's promotion to the big leagues and flourished in two seasons as teammates. Winfield never felt what it was like to be beloved by a team's fans the way Puckett was—he played for too many franchises and sort of glided through the game, keeping the public at arm's length—but always, he was admired. And ultimately honored.

"I left Minnesota and went out on my own," Winfield once said. "I improved as a player and grew in stature as a person. But when people ask, 'Where you from, Dave?' I say, 'Minnesota.' This is where I got the foundation for everything."

Steve Carlton

It isn't as if the Twins or their fans really claim Steve Carlton as one of the franchise's Hall of Fame players. It is simply a fact that the great left-hander, famous for his slider and infamous for his refusal to do interviews with sportswriters, spent chunks of two seasons with Minnesota at the end of his career.

All of Carlton's greatness came before he joined the Twins for the final two months of 1987. Rather than a late-season boost from a savvy veteran pitcher, the move by general manager Andy MacPhail showed how desperate that club was for starters in a threadbare rotation. Carlton had gone 1–8 in his final full season in Philadelphia (1985), then flushed through three teams with a 9–14 mark in 1986, and struggled to 5–9 earlier in '87. He had one glimmer from the past with Minnesota, a 9–2 victory over Oakland on August 8 in which he gave up seven hits in 8⅔ innings, but wound up 1–5, with the Twins also losing Carlton's three no-decisions. In April 1988 the reticent 43-year-old appeared in four games, all Twins defeats, and got rocked for 20 hits and 18 earned runs in 9⅔ innings.

Still, it's not as if Carlton achieved nothing during his stay in Minnesota. If not for his stint with the Twins, he would have retired with 4,111 strikeouts instead of 4,136, a career ERA of 3.16 rather than 3.22, and only 328 lifetime victories, not 329. Oh, and even though he wasn't included on the postseason roster, there probably was a ring and a chunk of winners' share cash in it for Lefty, too.

HALL OF THE VERY GOOD

Six men who wore the Twins uniform as players have made it all the way from Bloomington or Minneapolis to Cooperstown, New York.

Three of them—Harmon Killebrew, Rod Carew, and Kirby Puckett—spent most or all of their playing careers with the Minnesota franchise. Two more—Paul Molitor and Dave Winfield—were St. Paul native sons whose best years were spent elsewhere but who still had productive stints with the Twins of varying lengths.

One other—Steve Carlton—probably would prefer to white-out the 234 days that he spent as Twins property in parts of the 1987 and 1988 seasons at the end of his otherwise illustrious career. The man known as Lefty, with the gaudy lifetime stats (329–244, 3.22 ERA, 4,136 strikeouts), was an unsightly 1–6 with an ERA of 8.54, giving up 74 hits and 12 home runs in 52-plus innings pitched, striking out 25 while walking 28. But then, it's not like he planned on posing in a Twins cap for his bronze HOF plaque.

However, the Twins have employed, and benefited from, several popular franchise stars who would happily wear an "M" or "TC" logo to Cooperstown immortality, if only they could get in without a ticket. When the Baseball Writers' Association of America sends out its Hall ballots each December, or whenever the Veterans Committee considers its next crop of candidates, the names of four former Twins always seem to merit discussion.

Alas, just not inclusion, at least to this point.

Tony Oliva

Tony Oliva burst on the scene like few rookies in major league history in 1964, becoming the first American League newcomer to win a batting championship (.323), the first to get 200 hits, and tying Hal Trosky's first-year mark of 374 total bases. A native of Pinar del Rio, Cuba, the lithe left-handed batter slammed 32 home runs and 43 doubles, both career highs, and was named AL Rookie of the Year.

The next season, Oliva won the AL batting crown again—no one had ever led a major league in hitting in each of his first two seasons—drove in 98 runs, scored 107, and helped Minnesota to its first World Series appearance. He also was one of the Twins' big sticks when they reached the AL Championship Series in 1969 and 1970. By the end of Oliva's eighth full major league season, he had hit safely 1,462 times, had hit 177 home runs, and had driven in 723 runs. His career average was .313, he had worked hard enough as an outfielder to win a Gold Glove (1966) and, at age 32 with a slender build, he realistically could have had another six, seven, or eight strong seasons left. That would have made enshrinement in Cooperstown almost automatic.

But during his eighth season, in which he won his third batting title, Oliva badly wrenched his right knee chasing a fly ball in a late June game in Oakland. He missed the All-Star Game—Reggie Jackson took his spot for the AL and clubbed his famous rooftop homer in Detroit—and limped his way through the rest of the '71 season.

That fall, Oliva had his first knee surgery. In time, he would have seven more. He played only 10 games in 1972 and hit .291 with 16 home runs and 92 RBIs essentially on one leg as the Twins' inaugural designated hitter in 1973. But he never hit more than 13 home runs, drove in more than 58, or batted higher than .285 after that, and after taking only 123 at-bats in 1976, Oliva retired.

DESIGNATED HISTORY

Lots of baseball fans know the answer to the following trivia question. Who was the first designated hitter in the American League? Answer: Yankees slugger Ron Blomberg.

Far fewer, however, know the answer to this one: who hit the first home run by a designated hitter?

On April 6, 1973, Twins legend Tony Oliva—his outfield career curtailed by knee injuries—hit a home run from the DH slot, contributing three RBIs, a run scored, and a walk on a 2-for-4 day at Oakland.

For some teams, the much-debated DH rule has extended the careers of great players who lost mobility or agility to advancing age. Others plugged in regulars, like Seattle with Edgar Martinez, and left them there to thrive. But the Twins generally have used the spot in their batting order on a situational basis, using a variety of position players.

For instance, in 2006, the Twins used 17 different players as their DH and got a total of nine home runs, 63 RBIs, and a .258 batting average. The nine homers ranked last in the league among all teams' designated hitters; Baltimore, with 16, was next-to-last.

Only two players in franchise history got more than 502 at-bats in a season as DH. In 1991 Chili Davis hit 29 home runs with 93 RBIs, while batting .277, as the everyday DH. Five years later, in his first season with the club, Hall of Famer Paul Molitor batted .340 and had eight homers and 100 RBIs. Davis and Molitor each was named the AL's Outstanding Designated Hitter in those seasons.

Later, Oliva worked as a hitting coach with the Twins and was a great ambassador of the game, both in the United States and in Cuba. But his injury-thinned career totals and an abundance of superstars from his era caused the former Twins outfielder to slip through the 15-year Hall eligibility period without ever receiving sufficient votes from the baseball writers. He has been kept waiting by the Veterans Committee, too. Consider this: Oliva finished ahead of Bill Mazeroski and Orlando Cepeda 14 times in the writers' balloting, yet he could only watch as the Veterans Committee saw fit to open the door for them.

To many of those who played with or against Oliva, though, there is little question that he belongs among the game's elite.

"Tony Oliva was critical in teaching me the art of hitting," Carew once said. "He deserves to be in the Hall of Fame, and I want to go to Cooperstown for him."

With each year that passes, Oliva wonders if he might miss out on the honor. A posthumous enshrinement? No thanks. "It's better to go into the Hall of Fame when you are living," Oliva said.

Like some others whose excellence might not have been fully appreciated back in baseball's pre-ESPN, pre-Internet days, Oliva can only wait...and try not to get bitter or too disappointed.

"Without baseball," Oliva once shrugged, "I would have stayed in Cuba and been a farmer, maybe played amateur ball and coached. I wouldn't have met my wife [Gordette] or had my family."

Sounds like the makings of a pretty good induction speech, if he ever gets the chance.

Jim Kaat

As a pitcher, Jim Kaat was one heck of a fielder, as certified by the 16 Gold Glove Awards he won over the span of 25 years in the big leagues. That's as many as the great Brooks Robinson, the Baltimore Orioles' Hoover-handed third baseman, won in his Hall of Fame career, and matched in history only by pitcher Greg Maddux.

Lest anyone forget, though, Kaat was one heck of a pitcher, too. On longevity alone, he was amazing. When he retired, his 25 seasons were a record for a hurler (Nolan Ryan and Tommy John eventually passed him). He pitched in a pair of World Series, 17 years apart. With a career mark of 283–237, Kaat ranks eighth all-time among left-handers in total victories. He won at least 20 games three times, and 15 or more in five other seasons.

Oh, and he hit 16 home runs from the supposedly easy-out spot in the batting order, and he even subbed at times as a pinch runner.

At 6'4" and 217 pounds for much of his career, there always was a strapping, James (*Gunsmoke*) Arness quality to the raw-boned product of Zeeland, Michigan. Well, maybe not always.

"I was a little guy as a kid, so Bobby Shantz was my hero," Kaat said of the 5'6" southpaw, a three-time All-Star who went 24–7 for the Athletics in 1952. "I was a Philadelphia Athletics fan because my father liked Lefty Grove. The Tigers always turned me down for a tryout. But finally I grew a little bit and, during my freshman year at Hope College in Michigan, there were a couple of scouts who saw me, and one of them offered me a tryout."

Signed by Washington as a free agent in 1957, Kaat pitched in 16 games for the Senators. When the team moved to Minnesota in 1961, Kaat, 22, moved into the starting rotation. In 1965 he went 18–11 to help the Twins break another Yankees stranglehold on AL pennants, and when he locked up with the fabled Sandy Koufax in Game 2 of the World Series at Met Stadium in Bloomington, Kaat emerged with a 5–1 victory.

"I remember warming up next to him in the bullpen," Kaat recalled of that October afternoon. "It was cold and raw, and he was just throwing so hard…. He was, in my baseball lifetime, the greatest and most dominant pitcher that I'd seen. Just maybe a tip ahead of Bob Gibson, Tom Seaver, Juan Marichal, and Steve Carlton."

But Koufax got the better of Kaat in Games 5 and 7 as the Dodgers won the championship, and the L.A. star beat Kaat out again after the 1966 season. That was the year the Twins' pitcher finished 25–13 with a 2.75 ERA and led the AL with 41 starts, 19 complete games, and 304 innings. Since 1960, only 14 different men have had 25 victories or more in a season.

Still, Koufax topped him in every category—27–9, an incredible 1.73 ERA, 323 innings, and 317 strikeouts—and, in the days when baseball gave out only one Cy Young Award, the Dodgers' left-hander won that trophy, too. By 1967, each league would honor its top pitcher with a Cy Young Award; an AL version in 1966 might have helped Kaat's Hall of Fame bid when he became eligible.

"Jim threw what we call a 'heavy' ball, which is a catcher's nightmare," former Twins backstop Earl Battey once said. "He kept the ball fairly low, and that was back in the days of two-handed catchers. When you catch a low ball, you have to catch it palms up, and it's hard to cushion. Jim's heavy ball with sinking rotation would tear up my hands, but it was hard to hit."

Only slightly better than .500 over the next several seasons, Kaat was 11–12 with a 4.41 ERA in 1973 when the Twins put him on waivers. The Chicago White Sox claimed him, reuniting Kaat with pitching coach Johnny Sain. Together, they developed a quick-release delivery for the 34-year-old, and Kaat used it—to the consternation of opposing batters—to win 21 and 20 games the next two years. Traded to the Phillies in 1976, Kaat spent three more seasons as a starter, and then moved into the bullpen for the Yankees at age 40. He homered at age 41 for St. Louis and helped the Cardinals beat Milwaukee in the 1982 Series, appearing in four games.

Since retiring midway through the 1983 season, Kaat has established himself as one of the game's most savvy TV analysts, working for the networks as well as for several franchises. Not bad for the kid who started out too small to even get a tryout.

"I was kind of happy when I got two or three days in the big leagues," Kaat said. "I took it a day at a time after that and, fortunately, it lasted for about 25 years."

Bert Blyleven

The curveball, as thrown by Bert Blyleven, wasn't just his trademark. It might have been the best of its kind in major league history.

What started out as a "drop" pitch developed by Blyleven as a teenager growing up in Orange County, California, to imitate

Bert Blyleven's devastating curveball and 287 career wins haven't been enough to land him in the Hall of Fame—yet.

Dodgers star Sandy Koufax evolved, soon enough, into one of the most unhittable offerings ever and, with Koufax's, the standard against which breaking pitches get measured to this day. Blyleven at various times has credited his long fingers—and their ability to snap rotation into the ball—or the games of catch he played with his father and the way he avoided throwing fastballs so as not to hurt his pop's hands. In fact, it was natural ability, terrific lower-body and leg strength, and coaching from Twins scout Jesse Flores and a former L.A. pitcher named Ed Roebuck that unleashed Blyleven's big bender in all its glory.

"He was as good as there was for a long time," Kansas City third baseman George Brett said. "Bert is up there with the toughest four or five guys I faced in my career." Legendary hitters such as Reggie Jackson, Johnny Bench, and Rod Carew testified to the elusiveness of Blyleven's curve, which often came in shoulder-high and wound up near the batter's knees. Or, to the pitcher's consternation, could cross the plate as a strike but be called a ball because the catcher gloved it in the dirt.

With the curveball as a weapon, setting up his Grade A fastball, Blyleven—easily the most successful major leaguer born in The Netherlands—compiled a 287–250 lifetime record, with a 3.31 earned run average. He struck out 3,701 batters, threw 60 shutouts, and logged 242 complete games, retiring after 22 seasons in 1992 as one of the last innings–eating workhorses from the game's old school of pitching. Teams on which he pitched twice won the World Series: Pittsburgh in 1979 and Minnesota in 1987.

Thirteen victories shy of the nearly automatic 300 threshold, however, and with a career winning percentage of .534—the equivalent of a 14–12 mark—across 20 years, Blyleven has waited, some years more patiently than others, to be voted into the Hall of Fame. His stats argue strongly for enshrinement, except for those who dwell on his loss total, his lack of Cy Young Awards, or the fact that he won 20 games in a season only once. Then again, some of the voters don't know, or have forgotten, that Blyleven suffered from some unusually hard luck—for instance, in the 24 games he lost in 1970 and 1971, Minnesota's lineup scored a total of 18 runs. As it was, a startling 15 of Blyleven's lifetime victories were by the slimmest margins possible, 1–0.

For the first nine years of his Hall eligibility, Blyleven's vote total rose, reaching a high of 277 in 2006, which gave him 53.3 percent of ballots cast (75 percent is required for election). But in 2007, with Cal Ripken Jr. and Tony Gwynn grabbing the spotlight for the baseball writers who elect Hall members, Blyleven slipped to 47.7 percent.

"If you vote for me one year, how can you not vote for me the next year?" Blyleven said after the 2007 results were announced. "I don't think I lost any more games. I didn't give up any more home runs."

Good thing. Blyleven gave up enough during his playing days: 430, eighth-most in history, including a record 50 in 1986 in his second Minnesota stint, only this time in the Metrodome. Fact is, Robin Roberts, Ferguson Jenkins, Phil Niekro, Don Sutton, and Warren Spahn all gave up more but made it to Cooperstown. You have to be pretty good, the old saying goes, to be around to give up that many home runs. The same goes for losses: every eligible pitcher with 250 defeats or more in the modern era is in the Hall.

Still competitive, but comfortable after a decade in his role as a color analyst on Twins broadcasts, Blyleven wrote a piece for his website after another Hall disappointment in 2005. "I would love to have all those writers that didn't vote for me step up to the plate and let me pitch to them," it said. "I would love to throw a high hard one inside."

Or make them look silly chasing a curveball from their shoulders to their ankles.

Jack Morris

After seeing and hearing the rationale of Hall of Fame voters for not electing Tony Oliva during his 15 years of eligibility ("career didn't last long enough due to injuries") and for passing on both Jim Kaat and Bert Blyleven ("longevity, sure, but neither was dominating"), one might reasonably assume that Jack Morris would be a mortal lock to be enshrined.

After all, there was no more dominant starting pitcher in the American League for the duration of the big right-hander's career, certainly no one better over the full decade of the 1980s. Morris, with Detroit for 14 of his 18 major league seasons, won 162 games in that 10-year span, twice won 20 or more in a season, pitched a nationally televised no-hitter against Chicago in April 1984, and, in October of that year, beat San Diego twice to help the Tigers to their only World Series title since 1968.

Intense to the point of nasty, Morris's temper and sometimes surly demeanor earned him nicknames ("Black Jack," "Mount Morris") but gave him the competitive edge he craved. Worked for him, worked for his team.

"He is, without a doubt, one of the nastiest, meanest, most self-centered, and highest-strung people I've ever met," Sparky Anderson, Morris's manager in Detroit, once said. "He'll waltz

St. Paul native Jack Morris cemented his legacy with a brilliant performance in Game 7 of the 1991 Series.
Photo courtesy of AP/Wide World Photos.

around and prance around as if he truly thinks he's God's gift to the world. But I have to say something else about Jack Morris: he is, without question, the best pitcher I've ever managed."

Minnesota's Tom Kelly felt the same way, and he had Morris for only about eight months. In 1991 the native of St. Paul—whose earlier attempts at free agency had been undermined by baseball's notorious collusion years—signed an incentive-laden contract for one season with his homestate Twins. It wound up being one of Twins GM Andy MacPhail's shrewdest signings and one of the most timely marketing moves by a big leaguer ever.

Morris anchored Minnesota's rotation (and helped a youngish staff learn how to win), went 18–12, beat the Blue Jays two times in the ALCS, and then won twice more in the Series against Atlanta. His Game 7 performance, a complete-game 1–0 victory in

10 innings, lifted the Twins to their second championship in five years and helped Morris, at age 36, cash in with a huge-at-the-time, two-year, $11 million deal from Toronto.

"I've got to do the best I can for my future," Morris said that winter. "I have some mixed emotions. Some good things happened in Minnesota, but good things could happen [in Toronto]."

No fooling. Morris went 21–6 in 1992 for the Blue Jays and won his third World Series ring with his third team. He went 17–18 over his final two seasons with Toronto and Cleveland, settled not far from his hometown, and provided radio analysis on Twins broadcasts.

As for his Hall of Fame credentials, Morris's career totals aren't overwhelming. Over his final six seasons, his ERA got below 4.04 only once. And his off-field personality—for chasing the money late in his career, for his snarly ways—probably alienated some writers with ballots. Morris never has gotten more than 41.2 percent of the vote and, like Blyleven, his support slipped in 2007 after building slightly for years.

"Al Gore ran against George Bush in 2000, and 50 percent of the people voted for one guy and 50 percent for the other," Morris told the *Detroit News* after missing out in 2007. "So why is this different? That's America."

America ought to remember, a little more clearly, what American League hitters faced in Jack Morris through the 1980s. One very nasty decade, plus.

SCREWBALLS, ODDBALLS, AND OTHER FAVORITES

A CAST OF CHARACTERS

Baseball seasons are long, arduous grinds, and even the best teams can count on losing about 60 times in an otherwise rewarding campaign. The game is humbling like that—the best hitters still fail two out of every three times—and the need for comic relief typically goes up as a club's winning percentage goes down.

Winning, after all, is fun all by itself, no other ingredients necessary. Losing is far more challenging. Either it becomes unbearable or short-lived—managers get fired, players get cut or traded—or someone on the team finds a way to relieve the tension, allowing the group to relax and play free and easy, the only way that works in baseball.

The label most often attached to those invaluable human pressure valves has been "flake." It allegedly was first used to describe Jackie Brandt, an outfielder primarily for the Giants and the Orioles in the 1950s and '60s, thanks to a teammate who claimed that thoughts seemed to "flake" off Brandt's brain.

The list of notable flakes in baseball lore is a long one. Some toted nicknames that fit their off-kilter personalities, such as Rube Waddell, Babe Herman, Dizzy Dean, Bill "Spaceman" Lee, or Steve "Psycho" Lyons. Some were less obvious: Bo Belinsky, Chico Ruiz, Andy Van Slyke. Occasionally, a player arrives as a breath of fresh air for the game and then departs almost as suddenly—think Mark "the Bird" Fidrych and "Super" Joe Charboneau. There have even been flaky managers on a time line stretching from Casey Stengel to Ozzie Guillen.

The Twins have had their share of flakes through the years, most fondly remembered from—but not strictly limited to—their leanest years. Fellows such as Mickey Hatcher, "Disco" Danny Ford, and Bombo Rivera made hard times and losing seasons a wee more bearable. Then again, characters such as Joe Niekro and Juan Berenguer emerged during the Twins' first World Series championship drive in 1987. And Bert Blyleven, a class clown with a serious side worthy of Cooperstown, spanned two or three generations of Twins teams, from laudable to laughable and back again.

As far as managers, Billy Gardner qualifies, given his well-publicized lodging at a Super 8 motel in the Twin Cities suburbs while he was Minnesota's field boss from 1981 to 1985.

Here are some of the personalities who put some fun into Twins baseball through the years, even when the scoreboard wasn't cooperating.

Mickey Hatcher

One of the most hallowed names in baseball is Mickey (as in Mantle and Cochrane, both Hall of Famers). One of the most revered names in cartoons is Mickey as well (as in Mouse). Mickey Hatcher somehow managed to combine the two.

If any modern-era player ever seemed like a younger version of famed baseball clown Max Patkin—except with a real big-league contract in his back pocket—it was Hatcher. His upbeat demeanor, goofy facial expressions, and fun-loving ways eased some of the angst from the struggles of the teams for which Hatcher played. And while he occasionally irritated a straight-laced manager or coach, he was popular with teammates and fans, who saw his wackiness as sincere enthusiasm for the game.

A fifth-round pick in 1977 who signed with the Dodgers, Hatcher spent two seasons as a bit player with L.A.'s parent club before being traded to Minnesota in a package deal for outfielder Ken Landreaux. He played in all but 10 games of the strike-shortened 1981 season. Surrounded by rookies the next

Mickey Hatcher kept teammates and fans laughing as a member of the Twins from 1981 to 1986.

season, Hatcher, at 27, assumed an unofficial leadership role, which to him mostly meant keeping the kids loose. In 1983 he hit .317, a boost of nearly 70 points from the year before, and in 1984 Hatcher had his most productive season ever (a .302 average, 174 hits, 35 doubles, 69 RBIs, and eight sacrifice flies). He even was named AL Player of the Week after a hot stretch in August.

In the meantime, Hatcher was having fun. He would sprint to his outfield position while the ballpark organist played "Charge!" and took first base after walks in the same manner. He was known to forget pitch counts or the number of outs in an inning, and after Oakland's Dave Kingman clubbed a pop-up that disappeared through a hole in the Metrodome's Teflon roof in 1982, Hatcher staged an elaborate prank the next day. He enticed a stadium worker to drop a ball from the roof and planned to catch it, appealing to an umpire to call Kingman out about 24 hours after his at-bat.

Hatcher, unfortunately, missed the ball, and it reportedly hit him in the upper thigh—which he then milked by writhing in pain on the artificial turf for several long seconds.

By spring 1987, the Twins' talent had risen beneath Hatcher, and a deal at the end of spring training for Giants outfielder Dan Gladden made him expendable. Minnesota cut him on March 31, so 10 days later, Hatcher signed again with the Dodgers.

After leaving L.A. just in time to see the his old pals go to and win the World Series in 1981, Hatcher left the Twins only to watch them beat the Cardinals in October 1987. The Dodgers finished 73–89 that season, so Hatcher was back to laughably losing. "I said, 'My gosh, I'm rebuilding from scratch again. I'm never gonna be with a winner.' Then, after the first half of [1988], I knew we had a chance to win it all," Hatcher said.

In 1988 the Dodgers improved by 21 wins, due mostly to Orel Hershiser and the rest of a strong pitching staff. They beat the Mets in seven games in the NLCS, and then faced the heavily favored Oakland A's in the Series. Hatcher homered in the first inning of Game 1, scampered around the bases as if the ball had stayed in the park—"He's running like he's afraid they're going to take it off the board," broadcaster Vin Scully said—and made sure the Dodgers never looked back.

L.A. needed only five games in the best-of-seven clash to win the title, and Hatcher, after hitting one home run all season, hit his second of the Series in the finale. As well as Hatcher fit the underdog role for a home-run hero, it almost didn't seem fair, one guy having the most fun and winning a ring all at once.

"What's happened to me the last couple of months has been amazing," Hatcher told a reporter a few months after the Series. "I get stopped in the street. I'm the kind of guy who usually walks around in sweat suits and stuff and could go for months without being recognized. Soon as I got back here after the World Series and the parade and the White House and everything, everybody started coming up to me, slapping my back, saying, 'If it wasn't for Orel, you'd have been MVP of the World Series!' and stuff like that."

The legitimizing of Mickey Hatcher continued after he wrapped up with the Dodgers at age 35 in 1990. He worked a succession of minor league coaching and managing jobs, eventually linking up as a hitting instructor under old teammate Mike

Scioscia at Class AAA Albuquerque in 1999. When Scioscia took over as manager of the Anaheim Angels, Hatcher joined him, the onetime class clown becoming an authority figure of respect.

What?

"Sometimes you've got to dig a little deeper from the surface of some people before you really see the oyster," Scioscia said back in 2002. "You peel those layers off of Mickey—looking at him as a clown or a flake—and underneath is an incredible baseball mind and an incredible teacher."

With Hatcher aboard, whether coincidental or not, the Angels have had some of their best offensive seasons, hitting .282 in 2002 and 2004 and slamming 236 home runs in 2000. Scioscia likes his energy with the hitters and knows that Hatcher has the sort of storybook tale to tell that impressionable players don't forget.

"I told them, 'Any one of you right here can be a hero. I want every one of you to be the hero,'" Hatcher said on a stop back in Minnesota.

And for once, he wasn't joking.

"Disco" Danny Ford

His lawful name is Darnell Glenn Ford, but Twins fans knew him as "Disco Danny," a stylin' outfielder who spent four years in Minnesota before being traded away during owner Calvin Griffith's salary-slashing of the late 1970s.

A right-handed batter with an exaggeratedly closed stance, Ford was a slasher in his own right, seldom showing much patience at the plate. He broke in at age 23, batting .280 with 15 home runs in 1975. He drove in 86 and stole 17 bases the following season, slipped a little in 1977, and then came back with 36 doubles, 10 triples, and 82 RBIs in 1978.

Minnesota fans could see where this was headed: the same place it had gone with Larry Hisle and Lyman Bostock and, soon enough, with Rod Carew, too. Becoming too pricey for Griffith to pay, Ford was traded to California in December 1978 (two months later, Carew would follow). The former Twin helped the Angels win the AL West in 1979, and Ford had his best season (.290, 21 home runs, 101 RBIs, 100 runs).

The outfielder-DH left behind no hardware in Minnesota, but he did leave some vivid memories. Ford earned his nickname for his love of fun and nightlife, and he seemed to heed a motto that it was better to look good than to be good. The game's fundamentals weren't his strength.

For instance, longtime Twins observers recall a 1978 game when Ford, backpedaling the final few yards from third base while waving in base runner Jose Morales behind him, failed to step on home plate and was called out, even though Morales slid in safely behind him. Manager Gene Mauch bolted from the Minnesota dugout after that call.

"I didn't go out to argue with the umpire," Mauch said. "I went out to ask him if I really had seen what I thought I had seen."

Joe Niekro

Cheating in baseball has come to mean something far more sinister these days than a Gaylord Perry greaseball here, a Don Sutton scuffed pitch there, or even bats loaded with cork (Sammy Sosa) or a half dozen Super Balls (Graig Nettles). Or, for that matter, a Joe Niekro fingernail file.

Until a game at California on August 3, 1987, Niekro was best known as the knuckleball-throwing right-hander who, with his eventual Hall of Fame brother Phil, would win more games than any pair of siblings in major league history (539). Working for seven teams across 22 seasons, Niekro—five years younger than Phil—went 221–204 with a 3.59 ERA, won 20 games or more in a season twice, and was named to the 1979 NL All-Star team.

Though he clearly was near the end of the line by June 1987—Niekro had gone 9–10 with a 4.87 ERA for the Yankees the previous season—the Twins were desperate for functional starting pitchers and traded catcher Mark Salas for him. "This is a deal that's definitely not for the future," general manager Andy MacPhail said of Niekro, 42 years old at the time.

But Niekro rewarded MacPhail quickly, winning his first two starts while allowing only four earned runs in 12 innings. He settled into the rotation and was tied at 2–2 against the Angels

Pitcher Joe Niekro was embarrassingly caught scuffing the baseball with an emery board in 1987 against the California Angels. Photo courtesy of AP/Wide World Photos.

that Monday night in August when, with one out in the bottom of the fourth inning, events took a bizarre turn.

Responding either to the complaints of California batters or their own suspicions that he might be doctoring baseballs, the umpires descended on Niekro to "frisk" him. The pitcher acted shocked—shocked!—and as manager Tom Kelly came out to join the discussion, Niekro dramatically turned the pockets of his uniform pants inside-out, raising his hands in a single motion to gesture, "What? What?"

One problem: one of the umps noticed something flutter to the dirt from Niekro's right hand and tracked it. The slow-motion replay was hilarious: Niekro's hands going up and, wait, there it is, something falling from his fingers as the ump's head slowly turned.

It was an emery board. In other words, a disposable fingernail file. Niekro claimed that it was part of his grooming kit that

151

allowed him to properly grip his knuckleball—which, despite its name, actually is held by the pitcher's fingernails rather than his knuckles. But the umpiring crew wasn't buying it—and wondered, too, about a small scrap of sandpaper found on Niekro during the search. Home plate ump Tim Tschida, a St. Paul native, ejected the veteran right-hander. The Twins won that night anyway, 11–3.

Per baseball policy, Niekro remained active while appealing a 10-game suspension and, on August 7, held Oakland to five singles in eight innings for another key victory, 9–4.

But Niekro finally had to do his time. So on August 14, the temporarily idled Twin showed up on *Late Night with David Letterman*, wearing a tool belt with a power sander, a nail file, toenail clippers, tweezers, sandpaper, Vaseline, and shoe polish. He and Letterman had an amusing chat a week after Letterman's staff had produced a Niekro-related "Top Ten" list of excuses, including:

8. I needed [the emery board] to scrape dried wads of chewing tobacco off the bullpen telephone.
4. Rules of fair play are for saps and squares.
1. I like to give pedicures to the ballboys.

Back at work, Niekro went just 1–5 the rest of the season, and the Twins wound up 7–12 in his 19 appearances that year. But one of the seven was special; Niekro started and pitched into the seventh inning on September 28, exiting a half-inning before the Twins scored twice in the eighth to win at Texas, 5–3, and clinch the AL West division crown.

When Minnesota made it all the way to the World Series that autumn, Niekro made it into the baseball record books: he had played the most seasons in the majors (19 years, 138 days) before appearing in the Fall Classic. The record previously was held by Walter Johnson, who waited 18 years before reaching the Series with Washington in 1924.

"The first thing you want is just to be part of something like this, even if you're on the bench," Niekro said before Game 4, when he logged two innings in middle relief. "But then you get here and that's not really enough. It's not a life or death situation, but I think everybody wants to play."

Niekro returned to the Twins in 1988 but was released and called it quits in May after giving up 13 runs in 11⅔ innings, good for a 1–1 record. Over 22 seasons, Niekro faced 15,166 batters to rank 53rd all-time, and pitched 3,584 innings, good for 62nd all-time. He also saw his son Lance reach the major leagues as a first baseman for the San Francisco Giants. On October 27, 2006, the 61-year-old Niekro died from a brain aneurysm suffered at home in Plant City, Florida.

Jim "Mudcat" Grant

"Free spirit" is probably a more apt description of Grant, who spent most of four seasons with Minnesota, than "flake." It was Grant's outlook on life and zest for the people and things around him that he inherited or learned from his mother Viola that made him stand out from the gray-flannel guys around him.

That and, of course, his pitching. Grant was the first black pitcher to win 20 games in the American League when he went 21–7 for the Twins in 1965. He also led the league in winning percentage and shutouts (six), helping that crew to the first World Series in Minnesota history. He pushed the event to the maximum with a three-run homer in Game 6 at Metropolitan Stadium, while throwing a 5–1 victory over the L.A. Dodgers.

As something of a pioneer—only 13 African American major leaguers have won 20 games in a season in the 60 years since the color barrier was broken in 1947—Grant was proud of his accomplishments. And none more so than in 1965.

"There was magic to that season. For me and more for my team," Grant said at the time of the club's 40th reunion.

Grant refined his repertoire of pitches with the Twins, learning a sinker near the end of spring training in 1965 that took him from 14 victories split between the Indians and the Twins the season before to 21 in the best performance of his career. Grant would have earned a Cy Young Award that season, except that baseball honored only one winner for the two leagues in those days, and the 1965 trophy went to Los Angeles's Sandy Koufax.

Not that Grant was without an impressive arsenal, in name alone, when he arrived in Minnesota. As author Jim Thielman wrote in his richly detailed book *Cool of the Evening: The 1965 Minnesota Twins*, Grant always credited veteran hurler Satchel Paige with sharing some of his more unusual pitches, including a "kickapoo" pitch, a "hop and jumper," and a "cloud ball" that would arrive a little wet. As in spitball, Thielman noted.

The fact is, Grant learned to pitch in the first place only because he was about to wash out of baseball as an infielder. He was an outstanding multisport athlete growing up in Lacoochee, Florida, a small town east of Orlando, and had been invited to a low-level minor league camp by Cleveland in 1954. He was close to being sent home when someone whispered to Grant, "Tell them you can pitch."

"Teams always want pitching," Grant said.

A couple of coaches, on the sly, gave the teenager a crash course in pitching fundamentals for an intrasquad game that day and told him to dust off the first batter to impress the managers and to keep the other team uneasy. Grant reportedly did just that and then struck out "12 in seven innings, something like that," he said.

After going 5–6 with a 4.72 ERA in 1967, Grant was traded with 1965 AL MVP Zoilo Versalles to the Dodgers. Over his final four big-league seasons, pitching for five different franchises, he won just 28 more times. He wrapped up with a 145–119 record, 3.63 ERA, and was typically frank about his decline toward the end.

"You lose something every year you throw," Grant said. "If a pitcher says he is just as strong as last year, he is just a liar."

Among other highlights in a life interestingly lived: Grant had a nightclub act as a singer in the off-season ("Mudcat and the Kittens"), a sideline that displeased Twins owner Calvin Griffith. Griffith and most of the baseball establishment wasn't pleased, either, that Grant was married to a white woman, Trudy. And one time, after taking abuse from spectators on the road, Grant told a reporter: "The fans say things about your mother that makes you want to get up in the stands and punch a few of them."

Along the way, Grant penned a poem in which he linked the lessons of baseball to a much bigger picture. The final stanza of "Life" reads: "So stand behind your team, my boy / There'll be many who'll applaud / Just remember that you're the player / And the umpire here is God."

Finally, if Grant achieved nothing else in his baseball odyssey, he left the game with one of its most colorful nicknames. Its origins have changed through the years, with even Grant relating different versions. But one that many believe is that he was dubbed "Mudcat" by a teammate in the minor leagues, Fargo first baseman LeRoy Irby.

However he got it, Grant liked it; after being acquired by the Oakland A's before the 1970 season, he asked that "Mudcat" be sewn onto the back of his uniform shirt rather than his last name.

After all, there have been several players in major league history named James Timothy. But there has been only one Mudcat.

Bombo Rivera

As long as we're going by nicknames, that surely was the most remarkable thing about Jesus Manuel (Torres) Rivera during his brief stay in Minnesota and modest career in the major leagues— the nickname "Bombo" and the way an ordinary platoon outfielder captured the imagination of a market's baseball fans desperate for entertainment.

Rivera was a product of Ponce, Puerto Rico, better known as the home of more accomplished baseball stars such as Orlando Cepeda, Benito Santiago, and Roberto Alomar. He came up through the Montreal Expos' system but got gridlocked in the minors behind a deep Expos outfield cast, with his rights finally sold to Minnesota. The Twins weren't nearly so deep—with the departures of Larry Hisle and Lyman Bostock, they were rolling with an outfield of Dan Ford, Hosken Powell, and Willie Norwood—so Rivera got into 101 games in 1978, batting .271.

The ticket buyers at Met Stadium took a liking to Rivera. Heck, more than that—they downright adopted him the way sports fans often do with underdogs or appealing personalities. And from that, the legend of Bombo Rivera grew. Garrison Keillor, the noted Minnesota author and radio star, wrote a song titled "The Ballad of Bombo Rivera." W.P. Kinsella, author of *Shoeless Joe*, mentioned him in the novel that became the basis for the movie *Field of Dreams*. And in his 1982 *Baseball Abstract*, statistics wonk Bill James wrote this: "A chart of numbers that would put an actuary to sleep can be made to dance if you put it on one side of a card and Bombo Rivera's picture on the other."

The only problem was that, by 1982, Rivera's career in Minnesota was over and was winding down in the majors overall. Rivera had hit .281 in 1979 and, working mostly from left field, showed off his powerful arm with 12 outfield assists. But he broke his left kneecap early in the 1980 season and was limited to 44 appearances and a .221 average. The Twins released him in March 1981, and he played in only five more games with Kansas City in 1982.

Rivera did achieve some success in Japan in 1985 and 1986. In two seasons with Kintetsu, he hit .240 with 37 home runs and 86 RBIs. In 1989 and 1990 Rivera's name recognition earned him roster spots in the short-lived Senior Professional Baseball League, first with the St. Petersburg Pelicans and then with the Florida Tropics, before the operation folded.

Billy Gardner

During his playing days as a scrappy infielder in the 1950s and '60s, Billy Gardner—who was Minnesota's original second baseman, starting and batting eighth in the 6–0 opening victory at New York on April 11, 1961—occasionally was called Whitey or Shotgun. But during his four-plus seasons as Twins manager (1981–1985), he was known to everyone as Slick.

It was one of those ironic nicknames, the way a portly guy gets dubbed "Tiny" or a tight-lipped fellow becomes "Gabby." One thing Gardner wasn't was slick. He was a simple man enjoying a simple life, with a job he loved and a salary he never imagined as compensation for the 353 losses he endured while skipper of some not-yet-ready-for-prime-time clubs in Minnesota.

In contrast to some of the tough guys, drill instructors, and martinets who managed in the big leagues, Gardner was as easy-going as a peanut vendor. He didn't "big league" a soul; in fact, he was known to rent a room at a Super 8 motel in the Minneapolis suburbs during his tenure with the Twins—he never felt he needed a whole apartment.

The New England native was notorious for his malapropisms and appreciated for his candor. Players seemed to enjoy playing for him, even though they seldom won, and generally felt bad when Gardner was fired 62 games into the 1985 season, replaced by Ray Miller.

Gardner got one more chance to manage, moving up from his job as Kansas City's third-base coach when Dick Howser, terminally ill, resigned in 1987 in spring training. But he got fired in August with the Royals two games under .500.

Still, the sportswriter's dream left behind a wealth of anecdotes and quotes. There was, for instance, the time in 1983 he noticed a left-hander named Jack O'Connor warming up in the bullpen a few hours before a game in Baltimore. "Look at my guy out there," Gardner told a writer. "He's pitching, but there ain't nobody there."

O'Connor, in fact, was pantomiming his pitching motion, making imaginary deliveries to an imaginary catcher.

As another Twins pitcher, Brad Havens, ran in from the bullpen and passed Gardner, the manager asked how O'Connor was doing. "He's throwing strikes," the player said.

On the day in 1984 that the Twins promoted Kirby Puckett, Gardner penciled him into the leadoff spot, saying, "When they draft you into the army, they put you at the front lines, right, pal?" But the future Hall of Famer didn't play until a day later, because "Punkett," as Gardner mistakenly called him, was late arriving in Anaheim from Portland, Maine.

Gardner's humor served him especially well in 1982, when owner Calvin Griffith squeezed the payroll and gave him 15 rookies. There was talent there—the core of the 1987 World Series team—but it wasn't ripe yet. And there were a few duds in the mix, too, that lost 102 games.

Such as Al Williams, a pitcher from Nicaragua who allegedly had been a guerrilla fighter. Gardner never saw the sort of killer instinct in Williams that such a background would have suggested. "Guerrilla fighter? I can tell you where Al was when the bullets started flying. He was hiding in the nearest cave," the manager said.

Finally, there is this possibly apocryphal tale: the Twins had returned home from another miserable road trip, and Gardner, who might have quenched his thirst a little too generously on the plane, got pulled over on the freeway later by a patrolman.

Since it makes such a good story now, the officer allegedly asked Gardner *why* he had been drinking.

"I manage the Twins," he replied, avoiding a ticket.

Bert Blyleven

At the moment, Bert Blyleven can't get into even one Hall of Fame, but he has done enough in his baseball career to deserve a spot in three. There is the one in Cooperstown, naturally, where several pitchers with numbers and accomplishments inferior to Blyleven's already are enshrined. There is, as the pitcher himself once said, the Dutch Hall of Fame; no native of The Netherlands has ever come close to Blyleven's big-league success.

And then there is the Unofficial Sports Jokers Hall of Fame, the one with the funhouse mirrors, shaving cream on the telephone handset, and a blast furnace at the entrance simulating the sensation of a hotfoot for every fan who enters.

A strong case could be made that Blyleven either was the most talented of baseball's clowns and practical jokers, or he was one of the funniest great players in history. It's hard to recall any of Ty Cobb's knee-slappers from back in the day and next to impossible to compile a list of Walter Johnson's high jinks. The next time Barry Bonds shows his puckish, devil-may-care side will be his first. But with Blyleven, the trick wasn't chronicling his pranks and humorous moments, it was avoiding or surviving them.

Or as longtime Angels pitcher Chuck Finley once said, after working for a while alongside Blyleven, "I'm glad of the days Bert is pitching. That's the only day my shoes are safe."

An overgrown juvenile with too much time on his hands or a good teammate interested in keeping a club loose and united? Both, probably. But Blyleven's fellow Twins raved about his antics as a big part of the team's chemistry when they won the World Series in 1987. And when Blyleven went to the Angels in 1989, he was quickly credited with boosting the spirits in what had been a dreary clubhouse. After winning 75 games in 1988, California won 91 the next season, and the difference wasn't all Blyleven's pitching (though he was a stellar 17–5).

"Want to know why morale's so much better?" manager Doug Rader said midway through that season. "Bert Blyleven. That's self-explanatory. He's terrific. All his pranks are innocent stuff. But there are now others involved in his ring, less known but just as effective."

Some of Blyleven's tricks were classic baseball gags, from crawling on his belly in the dugout to light the shoelaces of an unsuspecting player or coach, to sneaking up behind a teammate

HR INTRODUCTIONS

Welcome to the Show!

Four players in Twins history slammed home runs in their first at-bats in the major leagues. The most recent? Andre David, who turned around a 1–2 pitch from Jack Morris at Detroit on June 29, 1984.

Prior to that, Gary Gaetti (versus Charlie Hough at Texas, September 20, 1981), Dave McKay (versus Vern Ruhle against Detroit, August 22, 1975), and Rick Renick (versus Mickey Lolich against Detroit, July 11, 1968) homered the first time they stepped to the plate in the big leagues.

Four other Twins went deep in their first games but needed more than one at-bat to do so: Hal Haydel (second AB, versus Al Downing against Milwaukee, September 7, 1970), Eric Soderholm (second AB, versus Diego Segui against Oakland, September 3, 1971), Kent Hrbek (fifth AB, versus George Frazier at New York, August 24, 1981), and Tim Laudner (third AB, versus Dave Rozema against Detroit, August 28, 1981).

during a TV interview and slapping a towel laden with shaving cream on the guy's kisser. Other times, he might don a rubber fright mask as he walked through an airport terminal or take a ride on the baggage carousel.

Once, in the on-field bullpen at Chicago's Wrigley Field during his NL days, Blyleven reportedly mixed some red gum and chewing tobacco, feigned a coughing fit, and produced what appeared to be an internal organ for fans in the nearby grandstand to see. Another time, in spring training with Cleveland, Blyleven led a small group of early-arriving fans in a sing-along of "Take Me Out to the Ballgame."

At the end, he doused his chorus with a cup full of water.

Juan Berenguer

One of the indelible images of the Twins' 1987 postseason run came long after a ballgame ended, with a player who wasn't even in uniform.

Fresh from their ALCS victory over the Detroit Tigers in a surprising five games, the Twins flew back to the Twin Cities and were bused to the Metrodome, standard traveling procedure for them. Little did they know that the roofed ballpark was full of jubilant fans waiting in the dark for the newly crowned AL pennant winners to arrive.

The players, in street clothes, were joined by their families and Twins officials on the Dome's artificial turf. Then, at first unrecognizable in a trench coat and Panama hat, clutching a leather briefcase in his left hand, relief pitcher Juan Berenguer hopped off a bus and joined the others for introductions and accolades.

When Berenguer was introduced, he set down the briefcase, slapped his right fist into his left palm, cranked the right arm down and the left arm up...and the joint went nuts.

Thus was the Berenguer Boogie born.

Berenguer, a hard-throwing, lusty-looking Panamanian right-hander, achieved folk hero status in a matter of weeks during that title run. Already an emotional player, the team's and his own individual success pushed his intensity and his theatrics higher. After tours with five other clubs, Berneguer signed with Minnesota in

January 1987 and, at age 32, hit his stride. He went 8–1 with a 3.94 ERA, striking out 110 in 112 innings while providing perfect setup work for the team's newly acquired closer, Jeff Reardon.

As the crowds at the Dome grew in September, Berenguer got into the spirit after some of his strikeouts, banging his fist into his glove and then yanking them apart, sort of an exaggerated umpire's out call.

It was the sort of thing that could offend opposing teams...if Berenguer had cared.

When the Twins reached the ALCS against Detroit, Berenguer had a secret agenda of his own. He had spent four seasons with the Tigers, starting 27 times and winning 11 games in 1984, the year Detroit beat San Diego in the Series. Unfortunately, Tigers skipper Sparky Anderson hadn't bothered to use Berenguer in any of the five championship games.

"My friends from Panama said, 'What's wrong with you, Juan? You did not pitch in the World Series,'" Berenguer explained years later. "After I won 11 games, Sparky should have let me pitch a couple of innings. That's why I pitched so well in the playoffs against Detroit in '87. My arm was sore, but I wanted to show Sparky that I was a good ballplayer."

In four games against the Tigers, Berenguer gave up one hit and one run in six innings, earned a save, and struck out six. Exuberantly. In the Series against St. Louis, some of the magic was gone. The right-hander gave up 10 hits and five runs in his 4⅓ innings of work, with only one strikeout.

But it didn't matter. The Twins won, and Berenguer—called Senior Smoke by some, El Gasolino by others—was validated as a fan favorite.

Berenguer played three more seasons for the Twins—by April 1990, he was the only pitcher left from the '87 staff—and he wrapped up his big-league career in 1992 with Atlanta and Kansas City. For the next decade, he flirted with comebacks and pitched for independent minor league teams. In time, he settled in the Twin Cities, raised a family, and worked at a car dealership.

But at his hottest, in the winter after the Series, Berenguer was the star of a music video. It had a funky beat, dancing girls, and some very shaky steps from the pitcher and a backup crew of Twins (coach Tony Oliva, Al Newman, and Les Straker). All wore Berenguer's trademark trench coat and hat, with Juan's mustache and shades making him look like a bit player from *Miami Vice*. As for the briefcase...

"A lot of people want to know what was in there," Berenguer's old teammate Bert Blyleven once shared. "And there was absolutely nothing in that briefcase. There was maybe a comic book."

INFINITY AND BEYOND

Archibald "Moonlight" Graham got immortalized in a major Hollywood motion picture, got portrayed by not one but two actors (including the legendary Burt Lancaster), and forever will be associated with one of the great baseball fables of all time, *Field of Dreams*, a film starring Kevin Costner and based on an even more lyrical book, W.P. Kinsella's *Shoeless Joe*.

Frederick John Bruckbauer got, by comparison, the proverbial one-way ticket to Palookaville.

Yet their stories have much in common. Each appeared in precisely one game in his major league career. Each spent significant portions of their lives in Minnesota: Graham, a native of North Carolina, settled in the town of Chisholm, Minnesota, and Bruckbauer was born in New Ulm, in the southwestern part of the state, but was raised in Sleepy Eye, Minnesota. And each wound up beloved for reasons having nothing to do with baseball. Graham served as the school doctor in Chisholm for 44 years before his death in 1965. Bruckbauer raised four children and enjoyed 13 grandchildren, retiring to Naples, Florida, after working 34 years in sales for John Deere.

Then there is this: Graham, a hitter, never got to bat in his lone appearance for the New York Giants. Bruckbauer, a pitcher, never got anyone out in his lone appearance for the Minnesota Twins.

Graham played his one game for the New York Giants on June 29, 1905, across the East River at the Brooklyn Superbas' ballpark.

He subbed in to play the outfield but never got to the plate, and the portions of his baseball career before and after that day were spent in various minor leagues. For Bruckbauer, the big day was April 25, 1961. A rookie just a couple of years removed from his mound heroics at the University of Minnesota, the 6'1" right-hander had spent two weeks on a major league roster for a team just two weeks into its relocation from Washington to the Twin Cities. Everything was new and exciting for all of them, especially the club's unexpected 8–2 start.

The Twins' 11th game, however, wasn't quite as exciting. In Kansas City, wrapping up a two-day series against the Athletics, seven Minnesota pitchers were on their way to a 20–2 pounding. Starter Ted Sadowski allowed six hits and seven runs before being yanked with two outs in the third. Paul Giel, another former University of Minnesota sports star, entered in the sixth, faced nine men, and got just one out, giving up eight runs on five hits and a pair of walks.

So Bruckbauer's brief appearance in between, to start the fourth inning with the Twins down 7–2, didn't seem all that bad in relative terms. K.C. shortstop Dick Howser led off with a double to left and scored on Jay Hankins's single. Jerry Lumpe walked, after which Lou Klimchock doubled to right to score both Hankins and Lumpe. At that point, Minnesota manager Cookie Lavagetto made one of his many strolls to the mound that day and took the ball from Bruckbauer, calling on Chuck Stobbs from the bullpen.

And that...was...that.

Bruckbauer, unbeknownst to almost everyone at the time, had been hiding the fact that his right shoulder was in pain, damaged by what only later became known as a torn rotator cuff. A couple of decades later, he would have been a candidate for reconstructive surgery, with a strong chance of resuming his career. In 1961, though, the 22-year-old was simply diagnosed with "stretched tendons" and stuck with an arm that, compared to his days with the Gophers, felt dead. As Bruckbauer said years later, by the time he reached the big leagues, his fastball looked more like his changeup.

He ended up in Syracuse, New York, back in the minors for the rest of that season, and then retired in the spring of 1962. The abrupt end—really, not even the beginning—of what had been a young man's dream ate at him for years. But real life intruded, distracted, and carried Bruckbauer forward, to a job, a family, and his wife Kathy.

Besides the disappointment that he was never healthy enough for another shot in the majors, there was this: because he did not retire an Athletics batter, the runs he gave up translated into an earned run average of "infinity" on Bruckbauer's permanent record. Officially, it was three hits, a walk, and three runs, but it could have been as few as one run or as many as, well, infinity, because according to baseball math, that's what this pitcher's ERA will be. Now and forever, one of only a handful of pitchers in history to retire that way.

"I don't give a [bleep] about it," Bruckbauer said, shrugging it off more than 46 years later, many of them spent comfortably and happily fishing the waters around Naples, Florida. "That's nothing; that's just a record. Doesn't bother me one bit."

Bruckbauer passed away in October 2007 at the age of 69.

THE VOICE: HERB CARNEAL

Baseball gets a great deal of its lyricism from the fellows who give the sport its voice, most effectively and memorably on the radio. In fact, for most fans and for most games, any sense of nostalgia for the Twins almost necessarily includes voice-over narration by Herb Carneal, fondly recalled.

Carneal served as the Twins' play-by-play broadcaster from their second season in Minnesota (1962) right up to the brink of the 2007 season. He died on the eve of Opening Day, of congestive heart failure, at age 83.

Kent Hrbek, who spent 14 seasons with the Twins, grew up in Bloomington, Minnesota, and remembered Carneal's voice, thanks to his mom, as the soundtrack of most summers. "If she was out in the backyard picking flowers or picking things up around the house, the ballgame was on, and it was Herb's voice on that radio," Hrbek said after Carneal's passing.

Born in Richmond, Virginia, Carneal had radio jobs in his hometown, Syracuse, New York, and Springfield, Massachusetts, before landing as an announcer of Philadelphia Phillies and Athletics games in 1954. He joined Baltimore's broadcast crew in 1957 and spent five seasons there before moving to Minnesota.

Though he never labored to create a "signature" phrase or home-run call, Carneal's gentlemanly descriptions and "Hi, everybody!" affable demeanor made him an easy companion for listeners. He was honored in the Twins' Hall of Fame in 2001, five years after receiving the Ford C. Frick Award in 1996, essentially putting him in the baseball Hall of Fame in Cooperstown, New York, with the game's other revered broadcasters and sportswriters.

"He never had a great 'flair,'" longtime booth partner John Gordon said. "But the secret of a good broadcaster, as far as I'm concerned, is you don't try to imitate someone else. And that's one of the reasons Herb had the success he did. He never wavered or changed his style from when he first started to the end."

THE VOICE: BOB CASEY

Fans in Los Angeles established a tradition across more than five decades: carrying radios with them to the games at Dodgers Stadium so they can listen to Vin Scully's elegant play-by-play announcing.

As good as Twins broadcaster Herb Carneal was, any Minnesota fan who did that risked missing some of the grandest entertainment available at Met Stadium or the Metrodome. Because public address announcer Bob Casey was a show in his own right.

A native of Minneapolis who started with the minor league Minneapolis Millers, Casey served as the Twins' in-ballpark voice for their first 44 seasons and worked about 3,500 games. He was best known for his distinctive introductions—and sometimes hilariously mangled pronunciations—of the players' names, none more famous than "Kirbeeeeeeeee Puckett!" And one of the amusing elements of the otherwise dismal Dome was a Casey reminder before the first pitch, "There is n-o-o-o-o-o-o smoking in the Metrodome!"

Casey, who died in March 2005, at age 79, got noticed by the participants, too. Sometimes it came from butchering their names: calling Nomar Garciaparra simply "Garcia Parra," for instance. Or introducing Otis Nixon as "Amos Otis," or Baltimore's Clay Dalrymple as "Clay Dairy-maple."

When Detroit's Don Pepper had one of his three at-bats in the big leagues at Met Stadium in 1966, Casey still was seeking out Pepper's first name after the youngster had two strikes on him. Legend has it that, as soon as Casey announced him as "Salty Pepper," the rookie heard it and gave a look up to the press box level. At which point Mudcat Grant fired a third strike by Pepper.

"Sometimes I do it on purpose," Casey once said of his tongue-tying adventures. "Sometimes it's by accident."

Cranky on the outside, a gentleman on the inside, Casey was fondly referred to as the "angry" P.A. announcer by ESPN's Jon Miller. And when former Twins second baseman Chuck Knoblauch came to town with the Yankees in 2001, inspiring unusually raucous taunting from the Metrodome stands, Casey scolded the fans: "Please stop throwing things. This is an important game! Now quit this!"

But he was respected and liked by players and managers, too, because of his long association with the club. You thought of a Twins game, you thought of Casey's voice. Period.

"As a kid from Miami, I'd always come [to Fort Myers] to watch the Twins," Yankees star Alex Rodriguez said in 2005. "And I just loved listening to his voice, the way he would say Kirby Puckett and Kent Hrbek."

Casey told the story of his intro for Puckett, playing with the syllables of the outfielder's name after Twins coach Johnny Podres told the P.A. man that this player was going to be special one day. After hearing Casey for the first time, Puckett said, "Man, that's cool. I ain't even done nothing yet. That's how they do it in the big leagues."

At the Metrodome, Casey worked from a booth behind home plate—the Hole, it was called—that kept him at field level before and during games. That helped him become a target for Twins players' practical jokes, such as shaving cream on a towel he used during games or shoe polish on the ear cups of his headset. In between innings of Game 7 of the 1987 World Series, someone from the home team locked Casey in the dugout bathroom, and he wasn't released until he pounded and screamed his way to freedom mere seconds before play resumed.

Still, the funniest incident for which Casey is remembered came on August 25, 1970, during a game at Met Stadium between the Twins and the Red Sox. Several pipe bombs had gone off across the Twin Cities, and a threat had been phoned in to the ballpark. It was Casey's job to get the 17,697 fans to file out to the parking lots while the place was searched.

"Ladies and gentlemen, please do not panic," Casey intoned calmly enough, at least at first. "But we have been informed by the Bloomington Police Department that there will be an *explosion* in 15 minutes."

TRADING PLACES

LET'S MAKE A DEAL!

Some of the greatest players in Twins history have been home-grown, tremendous credits to the organization's scouting staff and farm system through more than five decades. Harmon Killebrew, Tony Oliva, Rod Carew, Kirby Puckett, and Kent Hrbek—the five players whose uniform numbers have been retired by the club—all were scouted and originally signed or drafted by the Twins.

The same goes for Jim Kaat, Bert Blyleven, Lyman Bostock, Gary Gaetti, Chuck Knoblauch, Brad Radke, Doug Mientkiewicz, and A.J. Pierzynski, continuing right up to new-millennium stars such as Torii Hunter, Justin Morneau, and Joe Mauer. Even when owner Calvin Griffith was squeezing nickels with the major-league payroll, he always made it a priority to invest in the team's minor league operation; it made good business sense, beyond the baseball, because young players generally are the cheapest players. When Andy MacPhail, followed by Terry Ryan, subsequently ran the baseball department during Carl Pohlad's ownership of the franchise, they kept the farm system their top priority.

Still, no one builds a championship-caliber team along only one dimension, and the very best ballclubs—the Twins included—always have plugged holes and added depth by seeking help on the open market. Sometimes that has meant a carefully selected free agent, but more frequently, it has meant some good, old-fashioned baseball horse trading.

Trades are the sort of thing that really open up a GM and his advisers to serious second-guessing. But our purpose here is to look at some of the best trades in Twins history, the deals since the team's arrival in the Twin Cities in 1961 that worked out the best for Minnesota. And while it is always nice if a deal doesn't go well for the other team, that's not a prerequisite for ranking a Twins trade high on the franchise's all-time list.

Here, then, are five of the club's proudest player swaps:

1. February 3, 1987—The Twins send pitchers Neal Heaton, Yorkis Perez, and Al Cardwood and catcher Jeff Reed to the Montreal Expos for reliever Jeff Reardon and catcher Tom Nieto.

    Without this deal, the wonderfulness of the 1987 season might have been a déjà vu reckoning with 1984, when an unreliable bullpen—more than any other weakness—undermined a young team's flirtation with a pennant race. Reardon acquired in a vacuum would have been a significant help; Reardon in essence replacing the doom-and-gloom of previous closer Ron Davis allowed the everyday players to *breathe* again. And it's hard to win a World Series if you can't breathe.

    Reardon saved 104 games in his time with Minnesota, with '87 as the statistically shakiest of his three seasons (4.48 ERA, 14 home runs allowed). But it didn't matter—his main contribution was boosting the team's confidence and ending the indoor thunderstorms that accompanied Davis to the mound near the end of his Twins tenure. Perez went 14–15 with six teams over nine years, and Heaton went 41–40 for five clubs following the trade, while Reed caught more than 1,000 games for five National League teams. He even hit 17 home runs for Colorado in 1997, eight years after Reardon left Minnesota and three years after the bearded reliever retired. But that didn't matter, either.

2. November 14, 2004—The Twins send catcher A.J. Pierzynski to San Francisco for pitchers Joe Nathan, Boof Bonser, and Francisco Liriano.

Pierzynski did a nice job for the Twins, batting .300 or better four times, making it to the All-Star Game once, helping the club to two postseason appearances, and lasting all or parts of six seasons before thoroughly wearing out his welcome as an irritating presence in the team's clubhouse. But with wunderkind Joe Mauer rising quickly through the system and ready for a starter's role behind the plate, Pierzynski had to go. At that point, whatever GM Terry Ryan got would have been a bonus—except that he hit a mother lode of pitching talent.

Nathan has been one of baseball's best closers, saving 160 games in his first four years with Minnesota while spinning a 1.94 ERA, making the All-Star team twice, and finishing fifth or higher twice in Cy Young voting. Bonser was a nice addition to the team's rotation in 2006 before skidding badly the next summer, but the former Giants first-round pick will be just 26 in 2008 and presumably in better shape. Liriano looked like the second coming of Johan Santana in 2006, going 12–3 with a 2.16 ERA while striking out 144 in 121 innings. He hurt his elbow in early August and missed all of 2007 after having "Tommy John" reconstructive surgery, but he was expected to be rested, pain-free, and just 24 when he began his comeback in 2008.

3. July 31, 1989—The Twins send pitcher Frank Viola to the New York Mets for pitchers Rick Aguilera, Tim Drummond, Jack Savage, Kevin Tapani, and David West.

Two and a half months before the NFL's Vikings' blockbuster Herschel Walker trade and 18 years before the NBA's Timberwolves sent Kevin Garnett to Boston for seven players or draft picks, the Twins shipped Viola, the reigning AL Cy Young winner, to the Mets for half of a pitching staff. Never mind about Drummond, Savage, or the overhyped West— what Viola did in getting Minnesota to the World Series in 1987 (17–10, 2.90), Tapani and Aguilera did in 1991 for the new-look world champions. Tapani went 16–9 with a 2.99 ERA that season, while Aguilera saved 42 games. Tapani started 180 times in all or parts of seven seasons, winning 75 games, and Aguilera logged 254 saves for a team that had trouble winning, period, near the end of his stay. There was a bonus, too: the Twins traded Aguilera twice and reaped pitcher Kyle Lohse from the Cubs in 1999 when Aguilera was just about done.

Viola went 20–12 for the Mets in 1990, finishing third for the NL Cy Young, and was a two-time All-Star with New York. But he was ready to leave Minnesota in 1989 after a contract squabble, and the left-hander went 39–40 over his final six seasons with the Mets, the Red Sox, and (in cameos) the Reds and the Blue Jays.

4. June 15, 1964—The Twins send pitcher Lee Stange and third baseman George Banks to Cleveland for pitcher Jim "Mudcat" Grant.

Stange went 12–5 for Minnesota in 1963 but started poorly the next season. He never won more than eight games in a season the rest of his career. Banks was a guy from South Carolina whose career just petered out, from 63 appearances with the Twins in 1962 to just four games played in 1965 and 1966.

Then there was Grant, whose zesty personality and 21–7 record helped the Twins to their first World Series in 1965. He also helped them push that Series against the Dodgers to seven games with his home run and pitching (nine innings, one run) in Game 6 at Met Stadium. Grant went 50–35 in his four seasons with Minnesota, but he gets bonus points for the trade that sent him to the Dodgers in 1967. Shipped out with shortstop Zoilo Versalles, Grant helped the Twins acquire pitchers Ron Perranoski and Bob Miller and catcher John Roseboro. Perranoski saved 65 games when the team won the AL West in 1969 and 1970.

5. May 2, 1963—The Twins send pitcher Jack Kralick to Cleveland for pitcher Jim Perry.

Kralick, the season before, had become the first pitcher in Twins history to throw a no-hitter, beating Kansas City 1–0 on August 26, 1962. He went 25–16 in his first two seasons with the Indians, initially making this deal look iffy. But some

Twins insiders pegged Kralick as a guy who wouldn't have a lengthy career, and sure enough, he went just 8–17 after age 29. Perry already had made one All-Star team for Cleveland but brought a reputation as a nibbler and spot starter. The Twins eventually made him a workhorse in their rotation, and Perry responded by going 20–6 in 1969 and 24–12 in 1970, the year he earned the AL Cy Young Award. The Twins won their division both seasons. Perry made two more All-Star squads and went 128–90 for Minnesota before being dealt in 1973 to Detroit.

THREE-PACKS, FOUR-BAGGERS

When you look back across Twins history to identify the sluggers who managed to crank out three home runs in a game on behalf of the good guys, the names make sense. Bob Allison did it at Cleveland on May 17, 1963, Harmon Killebrew muscled up at Boston's Fenway Park on September 21, 1963, and Tony Oliva, in his first season as the team's designated hitter, slammed three homers at Kansas City on July 3, 1973.

Fine. But then you look at some of the names of the opposing batters who did the same thing to the Twins, and it's not exactly a Murderer's Row. Joe Lahoud, who slugged three for Boston in a June 1969 game? Ernie Young and Geronimo Berroa, who did it for Oakland in games three months apart in 1996?

Edgar Martinez was a great hitter for Seattle, but he wasn't known for his multi-home-run games when he jacked three of them in a 10–1 Mariners victory in May 1999. And when the Twins played at Dodger Stadium on June 12, 2005, they gave up three homers to Hee-Seop Choi and lost 4–3.

If it makes anyone feel any better, some of the 21 men who had three-HR games against Minnesota were known for their power or, at least, their hitting prowess. That includes Al Oliver, Eddie Murray, Jeff Burroughs, Harold Baines, Cory Snyder, Joe Carter, Dave Winfield, Dave Henderson, Juan Gonzalez, and Ellis Burks.

DON'T MAKE A DEAL!

One might reasonably assume that any rundown of the worst trades in Minnesota Twins history would focus rather quickly on David Ortiz.

Ortiz, most Twins fans will cringe to be reminded, went from Minnesota to Boston in 2003 and blossomed into one of the most feared sluggers in the American League. More than that, his effervescent personality and flair for the dramatic turned him into one of the leaders of a Red Sox team that made it all the way to a World Series championship in 2004 and 2007.

Ortiz had been a promising and frequently impressive hitter with the Twins, hitting 18 home runs with 48 RBIs in 303 at-bats in 2001, then upping those numbers to 20 and 75 in 412 at-bats the next season. But he had several strikes against him, as far as the Minnesota organization was concerned. He was prone to injuries. His fielding skills were subpar, essentially relegating him to full-time designated-hitter status. The Twins felt that they had several players in their pipeline who would soon fill that role and, even if they lacked Ortiz's power, that never had seemed like a priority in the Tom Kelly/Ron Gardenhire system. Finally, there was the money factor—Ortiz was becoming eligible for arbitration, and the small-market (and sometimes small-minded) Twins didn't want to continue their relationship when the big man's paychecks headed north of $1 million annually.

So lavish power potential or not, it was time for Ortiz to go.

One problem, at least for our purposes: the Twins did not trade him. They simply released him.

Hard to believe, but the Twins let Ortiz go at the end of the 2002 season and got absolutely nothing in return. Which, technically, eliminates him from consideration for this list.

Lucky them, eh?

Granted, someone could make a pretty compelling case that giving up a player as good as Ortiz and getting nothing in return is a de facto horrible trade. Worse than the worst possible trade, which would send back a farmhand, a long shot, or someone at least to fetch doughnuts for the clubhouse in spring training. Even if we accept the claims that Ortiz wasn't nearly as good when he played for the Twins as he quickly became for Boston—hitting more than 200 home runs in his first five seasons after leaving Minnesota and finishing in the top five of AL MVP voting every year from 2003 through 2007—that's a world-class slugger gone from a team short on sluggers since the days of Kent Hrbek and Tom Brunansky or even Harmon Killebrew.

There was one quote from GM Terry Ryan the day after Ortiz was released, noting that the team failed to get any takers in trade talks. Ryan also framed the acquisition that day of shortstop Jose Morban, a fringe player picked up from Texas that day in the Rule V draft, as a swap, since Morban needed a spot on the Twins' major league roster. "We ended up trading Ortiz for Morban," Ryan said then.

When they released him at the end of the 2002 season, the Twins had little reason to believe David Ortiz would blossom into a perennial MVP candidate for the Boston Red Sox.

But in fact, they didn't. And we're going to give the Twins just enough wiggle room on that technicality to spare Ryan that embarrassment on the list of the organization's worst trades ever.

For what it's worth, a review of the Twins' many deals since they began play in 1961 reveals few disastrous trades and none that would qualify among the game's all-time worst. They never shipped out a Lou Brock for an Ernie Broglio. Or dealt Frank Robinson for Milt Pappas. Or sold off Babe Ruth for a potted plant or whatever it was the Red Sox got—okay, $125,000—in January 1920.

Of the bad moves they have made, few were driven by misjudging talent. Rather, they were done out of financial concerns and the fear they might eventually lose a player to free agency or, maybe worse, have to pay him.

Kind of like David Ortiz.

1. April 22, 1988—The Twins send outfielder Tom Brunansky to St. Louis for second baseman Tom Herr.

    No athlete in pro sports history hated coming to a Minnesota team more than Herr, who pouted his way through a miserable season individually (.263 with one home run and 21 RBIs in 86 games for the Twins) and then hurriedly was packaged with two more players for a broken-down Shane Rawley (5–12, 5.21 in 1989). The Twins in 1987 had won the World Series as much on their chemistry, with a core of youngsters from 1982 who matured together, as on talent or strategy; Brunansky had been a key part of that chemistry. "Worst mistake I've ever made," former GM Andy MacPhail said on more than one occasion.

2. December 12, 1969—The Twins send pitchers Dean Chance and Bob Miller, outfielder Ted Uhlaender, and third baseman Graig Nettles to Cleveland for pitchers Luis Tiant and Stan Williams.

    Nettles, after leaving the Twins, played another 19 seasons, hit 378 more home runs, and drove in another 1,280 runs. He made six All-Star teams and won two Gold Gloves, which is the funny part because Billy Martin, who coached and managed Nettles in Minnesota, liked the guy for his bat but didn't think he could handle the job defensively. Well he did. For Martin. On two World Series winners in New York. Tiant won 229 games in his career but only seven in his one season with the Twins.

3. February 3, 1979—The Twins send first baseman Rod Carew to the California Angels for pitchers Paul Hartzell and Brad Havens, catcher Dave Engle, and outfielder Ken Landreaux.

Okay, so we know that the Twins had no real options. Carew was determined to leave, had the trade leverage of a 10-and-5 player, and wanted no part of the National League or George Steinbrenner's Yankees. That severely limited the market for what Minnesota could get in return. Still, for the record, we have to put this on the list, even if a gun was being held to the organization's head.

4. June 1, 1976—The Twins send pitcher Bert Blyleven and shortstop Danny Thompson to the Texas Rangers for shortstop Roy Smalley, pitchers Jim Gideon and Bill Singer, and third baseman Mike Cubbage.

It's true that Blyleven had grown increasingly unhappy with the Twins, generating friction with management in his duties as the team's union rep and eager to be paid more. But it makes no sense that a team would trade a healthy, 25-year-old starting pitcher who already had 99 major league victories under his belt. It's not likely that Blyleven would have picked up the 13 extra victories he needed to reach 300 by staying with the Twins—they were worse than Pittsburgh and Cleveland in the years he was gone—but Minnesota missed out on the prime of the Dutchman's career.

5. December 7, 1983—The Twins send outfielder Gary Ward to Texas for pitchers John Butcher and Mike Smithson and catcher Sam Sorce.

Ward was a solid player and a dangerous bat—he had 28 homers and 91 RBIs in 1982—but beyond that, he was a clubhouse leader for a team carrying 15 rookies that lost 102 times that season. He followed up with an All-Star selection in 1983, along with 19 home runs and 88 RBIs. Butcher and Smithson were a combined 71–76 in their time in Minnesota, and Sorce never reached the big leagues.

MET STADIUM

By the spring of 2010, in time for the Twins' 50th season in Minnesota, the ballclub and its fans are expected to be settling into a brand-new outdoor ballpark in downtown Minneapolis. That means lawn mowers again instead of the Metrodome's vacuum cleaners in a return to real grass and the open air.

Maybe, just maybe, that will take some of the sting out of the nostalgia longtime baseball fans in the region have always felt toward Metropolitan Stadium, the team's home for its first 21 seasons.

Nowadays, when folks think back to their experiences at the Met (as the place commonly was known), they do so with Vaseline smeared on the lens of their memories and soft, tinkling piano music playing somewhere in their heads as a soundtrack. It is an idealized memory, partly about baseball and the Twins' great teams and players back in the 1960s and '70s, but even more so about themselves at a much younger, more innocent time. Maybe they were kids then, experiencing the big leagues in awe and wonder. Maybe they were dads and moms then, rather than grandpas and grandmas, enjoying family time when the pace of baseball and the pace of everyone's lifestyle more closely meshed.

Met Stadium, to a lot of people who attended games there, is a state of mind. It wasn't around long enough to earn the landmark status of a Wrigley Field or a Fenway Park. Neither Babe Ruth nor Alex Rodriguez ever played there, neither Lou Gehrig nor Cal Ripken Jr., and it didn't have character so much as it had quirk. Forget about ivy-covered bricks or a Green Monster outfield wall; this place was a crazy-quilt of triple-decks, double-decks, open grandstands, and bleachers. Because it went up in pieces—dedicated in 1955, opened in 1956 for the Class AAA Minneapolis Millers, and put to use by the Twins and the Vikings in 1961—the football team had more sway than with many older, permanent

LIFETIME TWINS

The Twins haven't been around as long as the New York Yankees or, for that matter, even the Boston Celtics. So they can't rival those two storied franchises when it comes to retired uniform numbers.

Minnesota has honored only five of its very greatest players in that way, hanging the numbers that resonate most with Twins fans on the outfield wall and making them unavailable to any future pretenders. The five: Harmon Killebrew (3), Rod Carew (29), Tony Oliva (6), Kent Hrbek (14), and Kirby Puckett (34).

Heading into the 2008 season, those five and seven more former Twins players had been honored with membership in the team's own Hall of Fame. A relatively new source of recognition, this Hall "opened" in August 2000 with the inaugural class of five—the players already cited—and longtime owner Calvin Griffith.

Since then, Jim Kaat, Bert Blyleven, Bob Allison, Earl Battey, Frank Viola, Zoilo Versalles, and Gary Gaetti have been added to the list of players. Joining Griffith as coaching, front office, or other personnel have been broadcaster Herb Carneal, manager Tom Kelly, P.A. announcer Bob Casey, current owner Carl Pohlad, and director of minor league operations Jim Rantz.

There is one more level of honor within the Minnesota organization's ranks that, while less formal than those cited here, is every bit as exclusive: Lifetime Twins. Only six players in team history played at least 10 seasons in the major leagues and spent their entire careers with the Twins. Here is that short list:

- Tony Oliva (15 seasons)
- Kent Hrbek (14)
- Randy Bush (12)
- Kirby Puckett (12)
- Brad Radke (12)
- Bob Allison (10 as a Minnesota Twin, 3 as a Washington Senator)

stadiums. That explained the outsized section of stands in left field, lousy for a ballgame but prime locations for football.

Based on its vintage, Met Stadium had visual similarities to Milwaukee County Stadium, which had welcomed the Braves from Boston in 1953. Constructed at a cost of $8.5 million, with a capacity that grew from 30,637 to nearly 46,000 as seats were added and reconfigured, the ballpark in semi-rural Bloomington was ready to lure a big-league team several years before it housed one. The New York Giants flirted with the Upper Midwest before heading to San Francisco. Finally the Washington Senators, with owner Calvin Griffith seeing greener financial pastures, made the move.

With a legitimate emphasis on pastures.

"In the early years before they put a double deck in left field, you could actually stand around the batting cage and see cows grazing out beyond the left-field fence," said pitcher Jim Kaat, who relocated with the club at age 22. "It was kind of like a little country town. They made everybody feel so comfortable. It was good for guys and their families."

It was, of course, Minnesota, which made for some grueling conditions in April and October. Some years, May and September weren't so comfortable either.

"We played in some brutally cold weather early in the year," Kaat said. "But as the years went on, it was kind of to our advantage because we became accustomed to playing in that kind of stuff."

Part of Griffith's enticement to choose the Twin Cities over alternative markets such as Houston, Atlanta, or Louisville were the guarantees made by the Minneapolis Chamber of Commerce's baseball committee, including expansion of Met Stadium to at least 40,000 seats, cozy terms with local banks, and attendance of at least 750,000 for each of the first three seasons. There was one additional detail to address: the team's name. The nickname Twins was the easy part (Twin Cities, get it?). But at that time, teams were always named for the cities in which they played. When Griffith agreed to go by the entire state's name, it was a compromise of sorts, just like basing the team in Bloomington was a compromise to avoid alienating fans from either St. Paul or Minneapolis.

The attendance guarantees weren't a problem, by the way. The Twins drew 1,256,723 in their inaugural season, third best in the AL despite a seventh-place finish (70–90). They topped 1.4 million in each of the next two seasons and sold at least 1.1 million tickets annually through their first decade at the Met.

One obvious draw was the vast amount of parking around the ballpark, which fans put to use with tailgating parties before and after games. In fact, one of the first criticisms of the Metrodome—and one that never was satisfactorily answered—was the downtown facility's shortage of parking lots for grills, lawn chairs, and beverages.

The competition and entertainment provided by the ballclub itself was a quick and deep hook into the region's fan base, too. The early Twins teams were packed with sluggers, offering—in relative terms—the sort of long-ball explosiveness that brought fans nationally back to the game during the great (and since tainted) McGwire–Sosa home-run derby of 1998. Minnesota slugged 225 homers in 1963, 112 of them at home, and another 221 (115) the following season.

By 1965, Met Stadium was the site of baseball's All-Star Game, with the Dodgers' Sandy Koufax credited with the NL's 6–5 victory. Maybe that helped him get comfortable—Koufax pitched at the Met twice that fall in the 1965 World Series, including a three-hit shutout in Game 7. The 50,596 in the Met that October day didn't leave happy, but then, going from a minor league market to the major leagues' championship tournament in less than five years, thanks largely to the ballpark on the prairie, still was something to celebrate.

Oh, and so was a one-night stand there by four lads from Liverpool. On August 21, 1965, while the Twins were beating the Angels in Anaheim, the Beatles played at the Met.

Certainly, there was more. Two no-hitters (Jack Kralick and Dean Chance), 15 one-hitters, and five triple-plays. Fans saw 38 grand slams by the Twins and 10 inside-the-park home runs. Cesar Tovar (1972) and Mike Cubbage (1978) hit for the cycle at the Met, and Tovar played all nine positions in one game there at the end of the 1968 season. The ballpark was a host to two more postseason series but, alas, just three games—one in 1969, two in 1970—because the Twins were swept 3–0 by Baltimore each year.

Killebrew hit 244 of his Twins home runs at the Met, clubbed two more there in his final season as a visitor from Kansas City, and personally accounted for 8.6 percent of the 2,866 homers hit there overall in 21 seasons. Two of them came against the Orioles' Mike Cuellar on August 10, 1971, the 500th of his career in the first inning and the 501st five innings later.

Met Stadium appeared to fall into disrepair in its later years—some would say by design to expedite the funding of a new ballpark—and, by 1981, access to the third deck overlooking the left-field bleachers was restricted due to the safety hazard of broken railings. When the Dome opened the following spring, the ballpark in Bloomington became the game's newest facility to be

SLUGGING IN THE SERIES

In the 102 World Series played through the 2006 postseason, a batter had collected a double, a triple, and a home run in one Series a total of 52 times. Forty-eight different players accomplished the feat—Lou Brock, Hank Greenberg, Emil "Irish" Meusel, and Gene Woodling did it twice each—and three of them were Twins.

Zoilo Versalles was the first when he rapped eight hits overall, with one each of the extra-base hits, in 1965 against the Dodgers. When Dan Gladden and Gary Gaetti did it against St. Louis in 1987—each had two doubles, a triple, and a home run—it marked the sixth time in Series history that teammates had managed the feat.

And in something of a Twins asterisk, Paul Molitor did it, but as a member of the Toronto Blue Jays in 1993. In fact, Molitor is the only one in Series history to have at least two doubles, two triples, and two home runs in a Series. That performance, when he batted .500, earned him his Series MVP award.

abandoned. Home plate is marked there these days by a plaque sunk into the floor of an indoor amusement park at a shopping mall.

On the day of the Twins' last home game at the Met— September 30, 1981—an announced crowd of 15,900 came out on a Wednesday afternoon at the end of a strike-scarred season and saw the Royals win 5–2. For the record, Larry Gura allowed only four hits to the Twins and got Roy Smalley on a pop fly out to shortstop for the game's, and the ballpark's, final out.

On that rainy, windy day, Griffith sat in his private box and reminisced for a sportswriter. "I tell you, there's been a lot of feeling of grandeur here," the Twins owner said. "We won more than we lost, that's something to be proud of. We had great parking facilities, a good place to watch a ballgame, and we gave the fans a lot of wins. That's a lot better than a lot of major league ballclubs can say."

PAIN AND SUFFERING

DANNY THOMPSON

Heading into the winter of 1972–1973, Danny Thompson was, from all outward appearances, in high spirits and great shape. Why not? He had recently completed his breakthrough season at shortstop for the Minnesota Twins, easily the most productive of his three so far. He had played in 144 games as the team's every-day shortstop; had batted .276 to lead all AL players at his position; had banged out 22 doubles, six triples, and four home runs; and had driven in 48 runs.

Thompson already was getting pumped for spring training when he went in for a routine physical exam with the team doctor. The date was January 31, 1973, one day before the short-stop's 26th birthday. It seared itself into his mind because of what happened next: there was something off in his white blood cell count. Abnormally high. More tests needed to be run. Then Thompson got the word.

The word, indeed.

"L-e-u-k-e-m-i-a has to be among the most dreaded collection of syllables in the language," sports columnist Jim Murray wrote in the *Los Angeles Times* several years later. "They belong right up there with 'melanoma,' 'carcinoma,' 'cirrhosis,' 'sclerosis,' and the other frightening consonants of the age. Where they don't belong is in the lineup of a major league pennant contender, you would think."

183

In a professional sports culture where physical strength and fitness rule, where youth and athletic skills frequently get confused with immortality, and where weakness is defined as the inability to consistently hit a curveball or something along those lines, the diagnosis dropped in Thompson's lap was a slap of reality, right in the face. Not just for the player and his family, but for everyone around him in the Twins' extended family.

Tom Mee, the team's longtime media relations director, has told the story many times: Thompson was hosting a pool tournament in his basement for some teammates and staff employees one weekend that winter. The day before, he had found out in a telephone call that he had cancer. But at no point during the happy gathering did he ever let on about the bad news. The team found out a day later from the doctors.

"You never would have known it by the way he acted," Mee said. "You had to love him. He was 100 percent competitive, 100 percent team-oriented. One of those people about whom you said, 'God didn't save the mold after the day he was born.'"

On paper and in retrospect, Thompson's career is fairly ordinary, in the relative way that anyone good enough to reach and play in the major leagues can be termed "ordinary." In 694 games, all but 64 late in 1976 with the Twins, Thompson batted .248, with 70 doubles, 11 triples, 15 home runs, and 194 RBIs. He scored 189 runs, walked 120 times, struck out nearly twice as often (235), and got caught stealing (11) more often than he stole (eight).

That was the player. The man? Nothing ordinary about him, according to those who knew him.

"Desire," said Harmon Killebrew, a close friend. "That's the thing that was most typical of him. He loved the game. He loved to play ball."

Thompson had been drafted three times (by the Yankees in 1965, by the Reds in 1967, and by the Senators in early 1968) and declined to sign each time, playing at Oklahoma State instead. Finally, after the Twins drafted him in the first round in June 1968, Thompson turned pro. He got his chance in the big leagues in 1970, when Rod Carew was injured in a play at second base,

HEROES HAVE HEROES

Before they became the heroes of other young fans, baseball's greatest players were kids themselves, and most of them had their favorite ballplayers.

That includes some of the Twins' most beloved players, as shared by Jeff Idelson, vice president of communications for the Baseball Hall of Fame, in a 2004 article for *Baseball Digest*:

- Harmon Killebrew: "Without question, my hero was my father, when I was a boy and always. He taught me more about sports and life than anyone else."

- Paul Molitor: "Growing up in Minnesota, I was an avid Twins fan, and their best player, the one I followed religiously, was Harmon Killebrew. He wasn't overly big or tall but just had certain charisma that was very attractive to a young guy who aspired to get to the major leagues. He turned out to be a great choice because now, having had to get the chance to know him through the years, I know he was not only a prolific slugger, but a true gentleman and a great ambassador for the game. He was certainly a guy I imitated a few times in the backyard."

- Kirby Puckett: "My boyhood heroes in baseball were Ernie Banks, Billy Williams, and Willie Mays. In football, they were Walter Payton and Earl Campbell. In life, it was my mom, Catherine, and my dad, William."

- Dave Winfield: "Other than my mother, who was my best role model, growing up in St. Paul, Minnesota, I liked the Twins baseball players—Zoilo Versalles, Harmon Killebrew, Earl Battey, Mudcat Grant, Lenny Green, etc.—more than other major league All-Stars. Baseball was my game from when I was eight years old and on. The people who played it are the ones I followed and imitated."

bowled over by Mike Hegan, in Milwaukee in June of that season. Thompson filled in at second until Carew returned and then moved in at shortstop when Leo Cardenas got traded after the 1971 season.

After Thompson's illness was diagnosed, he glommed onto any shred of positivity he could find. Doctors at the Mayo Clinic acknowledged that Thompson's case had been detected much earlier than most, which typically show up after patients complain about fatigue or immune-system deficiencies. So that was good, the player felt. Also, the type of leukemia he had ("chronic granulocytic leukemia") was considered to be slow-acting, sometimes rearing up only after many years. Best kind to have then, Thompson figured.

Still, he wasn't ready for any sort of public transformation from Danny Thompson, shortstop, to Danny Thompson, cancer patient. "I didn't want the world knowing," he said. "I didn't want sympathy. I didn't want to make an error and have people say, 'Well, you can't blame him because he has leukemia.'"

There was no keeping this secret, though. Thompson began experimental treatments at the Mayo Clinic in which live leukemia cells were injected into him in hopes of provoking his defense system to fight. "Without the treatment, they told him he might live three years," Mee recalled. "With it, no one knew, but they thought it could help."

The injections opened up welts on Thompson's upper body—about the size of quarters—that never seemed to heal over. They began the program with injections every two weeks, then monthly, then tapering to four times a year.

"It brings you to your knees all right. I don't own an unstained T-shirt," Thompson told the *Times'* Murray. "But the worse thing is, the people who want to clap you on the back or arm. When you go around with big, open sores like that, you fear the backslapper more than the low curveball."

Through it all, Thompson kept playing. His struggle was complicated when minor injuries—a pulled muscle, a turned ankle, or a bruise—would take abnormally long to heal, too. As his batting average dropped to .225 in 1973, Twins owner Calvin Griffith wondered, rather opaquely, about his shortstop's droop at the plate. "I can't understand what's wrong with Thompson," Griffith said. "There must be something on his mind besides baseball."

Thompson laughed about that, freeing everyone else to laugh, too. Of course, Griffith knew about the player's illness. But the Twins owner was known for his, uh, occasional intellectual disconnects.

Thompson batted .250 in 97 games in 1974 and was presented after the season with baseball's Hutch Award, created to honor manager Fred Hutchinson, who was with Cincinnati when he died of cancer in 1964. The honor was given annually to the player who "best exemplifies the fighting spirit, desire, and character" of Hutchinson. The year before Thompson received the award, it went to Detroit reliever John Hiller, who recovered from a heart attack in January 1971 to save 38 games in 1973.

"I've tried to lead a normal life, and I think people in baseball are thinking of me as just another athlete and not something special, and that's the way I want it," Thompson said in news reports of the award. He spent that winter on a farm in Cherokee, Oklahoma, with his wife's family. And he said he never thought of quitting baseball. "This is my life. I love it," Thompson said.

In 1975 Thompson asked Twins outfielder Larry Hisle if he would become his roommate on the road, and while it wasn't the first time a black man and a white man had roomed together, it wasn't all that common, either. Thompson also worked that season on a book—*E6: The Diary of a Major League Shortstop*—with sportswriter Bob Fowler, chronicling his and the team's experiences.

Thompson got his average up to .270 in 1975, played in 112 games, and batted 355 times. Hisle said that he talked openly about his leukemia and believed that he would beat it. But Thompson also grew increasingly religious, like a man who understood he might face a different way out.

On a sunny Saturday in May 1976, Thompson banged out five hits in nine at-bats in a doubleheader against the Angels in Anaheim. The next day, he spoke at length with Murray, the L.A. sportswriter who then wrote: "The World Series has been on for two years now inside Danny Thompson's body.... The Twins will owe him a great deal if they win the pennant. But the long, frail line of future leukemiacs will owe him far more than that."

Two weeks after that, the Twins traded Thompson along with pitcher Bert Blyleven to Texas for Mike Cubbage, Jim Gideon, Bill

Singer, and Roy Smalley. He played in 64 games for the Rangers as a utility infielder, hitting .214. In the last game he started, on September 29, he singled in three at-bats at Met Stadium, facing his old pals in Minnesota.

In November, Thompson began feeling ill and went back to Rochester, Minnesota, to be examined. He underwent surgery to have his spleen removed. While at the Mayo Clinic, on December 10, 1976, just 29 years old, Thompson died.

"I was asleep, and my wife woke me up and she said, 'Larry, Danny died,'" Hisle said later that month. "I remember thinking she had to be wrong, somehow I would wake up and she would be wrong. The total impact of it didn't hit me right away. When it did, I cried."

Killebrew, sickened over Thompson's fate and the thought of his widow and two children left behind, searched for some way to help. He settled on a Danny Thompson Memorial Golf Tournament in Sun Valley, Idaho, an event that has run for more than 30 years and raised in excess of $9 million for cancer research.

Not long before Thompson's death, he and Killebrew spoke. "I talked to him on the phone," said the Twins slugger, already retired for a year. "He had just bought a new hunting dog. We talked about going out hunting together when he got home."

DEVASTATING INJURIES

Catcher Joe Mauer, his manager, and his Minnesota Twins teammates were all a little upset in early September 2007 with what they felt was a storm of hype over his position on the baseball diamond.

Both Twin Cities newspapers had carried sports columns either urging Mauer to move out from behind the plate or challenging the Twins' baseball bosses to force the move on him. The idea would be to spring him from a defensive position with a high risk of injury, stick him somewhere safer in the field (third base, first base), and therefore keep the number one pick from the 2001 draft—and his bat—healthier and more available. Then the sports radio talk shows had whipped the topic into a lather.

Mauer, after all, had been hampered by various leg ailments in 2007, after missing games (including most of 2004) earlier in his young career with similar injuries. Having the first American League catcher to win a batting title—as Mauer did in 2006, batting .347 to place sixth in MVP balloting—doesn't mean all that much if the fellow isn't healthy enough to catch. Or, worse, hit.

But the Twins were more than a little touchy on the topic.

"If it's deemed that he can't play catcher, then obviously we'll find another position for him," manager Ron Gardenhire said. "But you're talking about an All-Star catcher. This guy's pretty good. He can stop a running game. He can do things that you're not going to find anywhere else.

"To sit here and all of a sudden have all this hype about, well, 'He needs to move to fill one gaping hole at third base, and let's just make another gaping hole behind the plate.' Tell me, which one is more important?"

Mauer was bothered more by the suggestion that his injury layoffs hurt his reputation with teammates, who saw him returning to action more slowly than they might expect.

"Guys in here know that I play hard and play hurt and play through all sorts of things," the catcher said. "When you get hurt early in the season, you've got to deal with it the rest of the year, because in baseball, you play every day."

People weren't really picking on Mauer, Gardenhire, or Twins management. But no one could blame them for being particularly cautious, given the catcher's early history with injuries and, frankly, this franchise's familiarity with them. Minnesota has had more than its share of mishaps and debilitations in its first five decades.

Obviously, in 1996, Kirby Puckett's Hall of Fame career ended abruptly when glaucoma robbed him of the sight in his right eye. Less clear was whether the blood flow to that eye, which led to the glaucoma, was itself connected to the beaning Puckett suffered from pitcher Dennis Martinez at the end of the 1995 season. (Medical experts, Twins insiders, and Puckett himself always said it was not.)

Luis Tiant developed a sore arm and was released in March 1971, only to pitch his way back to prominence (15–6 in 1972), followed by consecutive 20-victory seasons, with Boston. Harmon Killebrew suffered serious injuries in 1965, 1968, and 1973 that didn't limit his Hall of Fame eligibility the way Tony Oliva's chronic knee problems did, but they surely kept Killebrew out of the ultra-exclusive 600-home-run club.

Don't forget about dazzling left-hander Francisco Liriano, at 23, sitting out all of 2007 after undergoing elbow surgery.

Those are just a few of the Twins' more serious and, in some cases, sad injuries through the years. Here are four more:

Bernie Allen

When Bernie Allen, fresh off the Purdue campus as the Boilermakers' quarterback, signed with the Twins in June 1961, he received the biggest bonus ($50,000) ever given to that point by the franchise. Though technically a "bonus baby," which meant he was required to stay on the major league roster, Allen earned his keep with an outstanding season in 1962. In 159 games, the Twins' new second baseman batted .269, hit 12 home runs, scored 79 runs, drove in 64, and banged 27 doubles and seven triples. He placed third in Rookie of the Year balloting behind the Yankees' Tom Tresh and the Angels' Buck Rodgers.

In 1963 Allen, 24, had another solid season and teamed again with shortstop Zoilo Versalles, 23, in what figured to be Minnesota's double-play tandem into the 1970s. Then, in a game at Washington on June 13, 1964, Don Zimmer walked for the Senators in the fifth inning and barreled toward second on a ground ball. He collided with Allen, forcing an error on the second baseman's relay to first and forever altering the infielder's career.

Allen played only 22 more games that season, getting 14 hits in 70 at-bats before shutting down entirely on September 1. He spent less than a month with the team in the middle of the 1965 season, rehabbing most of that year with the Twins' Class AAA affiliate in Denver. His average in those 41 minor league games was .246, and when Allen returned to Minnesota in 1966, he batted .238 in 101 games. In December Allen was packaged with Camilo Pascual to Washington for pitcher Ron Kline (who went 7–1 in 1967).

Allen never got close to his rookie production again. In his first season with the Senators, he hit .193, more or less banishing himself to a backup role. Over his final six seasons, spent with the Senators, the Yankees, and the Expos, Allen never scored more than 33 runs and only once hit better than .247.

Years later, on the Internet site baseball-reference.com, where players are compared statistically across generations, one of the guys whose career hitting stats are most similar to Allen's is Zimmer—whose own career was diminished by a pair of beanings in the 1950s.

Jimmie Hall

Hall was a big, strong kid with a classic 1963 crew cut when he burst on the scene in Bloomington by hitting 33 home runs that season. It was the most in American League history by a player with no previous major league experience. When the 1964 season began with Hall in center field, Harmon Killebrew in left, and new guy Tony Oliva in right, the Twins' outfield—and heart of their batting order—seemed set for years.

But on May 27, 1964, in the fifth inning of the first game of a twi-night doubleheader in Anaheim, Angels starter Bo Belinsky unleashed a pitch that smashed into the left-handed-hitting Hall's face, just under his left eye as he spun back.

"You couldn't see the ball at all," Hall said many years later. "I didn't move until the last instant. Tried to turn away, and it got me in the face."

Bad as it was, Hall managed to pinch-hit against Boston four days later and then returned to his starting role four days after that. There was no obvious drop-off in his game—Hall hit .285 the rest of that season, with 15 home runs and 46 RBIs in the 112 games he played after the beaning and was named to the AL All-Star team. In 1965 he was chosen again for the All-Star Game, played right at Met Stadium, and helped the Twins to the World

Series with a .285 average, 20 homers, 86 RBIs, and 14 stolen bases, furthering some public comparisons to Mickey Mantle.

But those closest to him, and those who noticed the details, felt Hall did carry some internal baggage after Belinsky's left-handed pitch hammered into him.

"Jimmie still was dangerous," pitcher Jim Kaat said, "but he wasn't quite the same against lefties. He was a little gun-shy after that."

Tom Mee, the Twins' longtime media relations director, felt Hall grew tentative even in the field after his brush with a potentially career-ending injury. "He was gun-shy from that time on," Mee said in 2007. "He wouldn't even go near the fences in center field. When his feet would hit the warning track, he would pull up, not like the guy [Torii Hunter] they have out there [this season]."

In what might have been a self-fulfilling strategy, Twins manager Sam Mele began using Hall more as a platoon player—in essence, telling him that he wasn't going to be effective against left-handed pitchers. He ended up playing in 120 games and batting only 356 times in 1966, hitting .239 with 20 home runs and 47 RBIs.

Before the 1967 season, Minnesota packaged Hall in the trade to California that delivered right-hander Dean Chance, a move that almost put the Twins back in the World Series. Hall gave the Angels 16 homers, 55 RBIs, and a .249 average, but they traded him the following June. From 1968 through 1970, Hall played for five teams, hitting .208 in 562 at-bats with seven home runs and 48 RBIs.

After baseball, Hall moved home to North Carolina, raised a family, and worked a variety of jobs. He dusted off some carpentry skills and spent a number of years making long hauls as a truck driver. When the Twins held a 40th reunion for the 1965 Series team, Hall declined to participate. A rumor circulated that he had become reclusive, but he made it clear to a reporter that he simply was not interested. Too much time had passed, Hall said, with too little contact. He said the Yankees, for whom he played just 80 games in 1969, made him feel more like an alumnus of that ballclub that Minnesota ever had.

Tony Oliva

Had Tony Oliva pulled up just a little, had he played a bit less hard, had he dwelled on his plate appearances even when he was patrolling the outfield—a trait that Ted Williams was proud of, even if it dampened his glove work—the Twins' line-drive machine from Pinar Del Rio, Cuba, probably would have a little place of his own in upstate New York. Think bronze plaque. Think Cooperstown.

Instead, Oliva dived for Joe Rudi's line drive in the ninth inning of his team's game at Oakland on June 29, 1971. His right knee took the worst of it, damaging Oliva's career and dealing a pretty harsh blow to the Twins, too, all for the right fielder's attempt to keep a 5–3 victory at 5–2.

Oliva didn't play the outfield again for three weeks, making only two failed pinch-hit appearances in early July. At the time of his injury—which cost him a trip to the All-Star Game in Detroit (Reggie Jackson took Oliva's place and hit his famous home run off the right-field roof)—Oliva had been batting .375 with 18 homers and 49 RBIs. After his return, he hit .289 with four home runs and 32 RBIs, but his average had enough cushion to win his third batting title at .337.

After the season, Oliva had the first of what would be 11 surgeries on that knee. He tested it in 10 games in June 1972 but had to shut down after 28 at-bats. "The only people who knew how much I was hurt were my wife [Gordette] and Rod Carew, because he was my roomie," Oliva said. "You don't want to leave your room in the middle of the night to get ice. [Carew] would get some ice for me."

The designated hitter rule, adopted by the American League in 1973 as a grab for more offense, had the side benefit of new life for some gimpy veterans such as Orlando Cepeda, Rico Carty, and Oliva. The Twins' new DH batted 571 times in 146 games, banged 16 homers (including the first in history by a DH), and drove in 92 runs while hitting .291. Freed from the physical demands of playing the field, Oliva hit .285 in 1974 and .270 the next season, with 13 home runs each year.

But the pain from his knee and the side effects it had on his overall condition and ability got to be too much. Before long, even the base paths and the batter's boxes became problems. Oliva batted .211 in 67 appearances in 1976, hitting his lone home run as a pinch-hitter at Yankee Stadium on August 24. He called it quits that fall.

"At the time, he was really depressed. I told him that life goes on without baseball, and you have to be thankful for your accomplishments," Gordette Oliva told the *Minneapolis Star Tribune* in 2000. "There were times I would think he was ready to give it up. He would just work a little harder and go on."

Ironically, if getting hurt derailed Oliva's passage into baseball's Hall of Fame, playing hobbled for those five extra years after the initial injury might have damaged his case, too. Had his playing days ended abruptly—like his pal Kirby Puckett or like old Cleveland pitcher Addie Joss, who died of meningitis at age 30 after just nine seasons—Oliva might have had sentiment on his side and caused some baseball writers to lobby for an exception to the 10-year rule.

Over his first eight seasons in the majors—up to the point of his knee injury in Oakland—Oliva averaged almost 22 home runs and 86 RBIs while batting .315. He was chosen as an All-Star and received MVP votes in each of those eight years.

John Castino

Baseball players historically have not been required to run the fastest, jump the highest, or clean-and-jerk the heaviest weights. They don't have to be especially tall, big, or strong or, for that matter, tiny, lean, or lithe. The game has had room for shortstops built like jockeys, first basemen shaped like offensive tackles, outfielders who look like sprinters, and pitchers who range in appearance from point guards to power forwards. As long as a guy has tremendous hand-eye coordination and an abundance of fast-twitch muscles, he has a shot in the big leagues.

Oh, and it helps to have a healthy back. Something to do with all that torque swinging a bat. And running. And, if you're an infielder, bending over to handle a ground ball. And a hundred other things.

John Castino thought he had a strong, healthy back, from his teen years as a high school sports star, through his selection by the Twins in the 1976 amateur draft to the 1979 season in which Castino shared the AL Rookie of the Year Award with Toronto's Alfredo Griffin. Fact is, Minnesota's promising third baseman believed in his back right to the instant he lunged at a line drive by Dave Winfield in a 1981 game at Met Stadium. The discomfort from that play sent Castino off to get an X-ray.

"The doctors said it showed there was a hairline fracture in the vertebra and also that I had been born with a defect called 'spondylolysis,'" he recalled in 2007. "But it hadn't surfaced until this injury. This had exacerbated it and made the crack larger."

Castino wrapped up that year hitting .268, a drop of 34 points from his sophomore season in the big leagues. He had spinal-fusion surgery that winter, spent much of the off-season in a body cast, and then probably came back too soon. The Twins had made plans for Castino to switch to second base—to make room at third for Gary Gaetti—and Castino was antsy to get back on the field anyway. But he had lost muscle while wearing the cast and batted a piddling .241.

With more prep time and a real workout regimen, Castino thrived in 1983, making just seven errors in 132 games at second base while contributing 11 home runs, 30 doubles, and a .277 average. Some talent from the crop of 15 rookies the Twins fielded in 1982 was beginning to jell, so 1984 looked bright for all of them.

Until, that is, Castino was involved in a collision at home plate in spring training, damaging his spine again. He tried all manner of treatments to ease his pain, missed the first three weeks of the season, and then gritted his teeth through eight games. He was batting .391 when he stepped in against California on May 7. After going 2-for-3 through the first seven innings, Castino singled off Curt Kaufman in the top of the ninth, driving home Gaetti to put the Twins up 9–1. Three batters later, after another Minnesota run, Castino tagged at third on Darrell Brown's sacrifice fly. To beat the throw, with a needless run, he went headfirst into home plate. *Ouch!*

"That's something I shouldn't have done," Castino said. "That was the last game I played."

Forced into retirement at age 29, Castino eventually underwent four more spinal fusions. He successfully switched fields, becoming a partner in a financial-planning firm based in the Twin Cities. But he still has back pain, a nagging reminder of what once was and what might have been. Castino still would have been in his prime, probably still manning second base for the Twins when they won the World Series in 1987, if not for that aching back.

"When I was 24 and in the majors, I felt invincible," he said. "I thought I could play until I was 45. All your life your identity is centered on sports. On the field, I thought I could beat anybody."

SAVING REARDON

The math alone suggested that former Twins reliever Jeff Reardon either was participating in some sort of goofball reality TV show stunt or really, truly was suffering from something far more serious and personal.

Those seemed to be the only two explanations possible after Reardon, late in December 2005, walked into the Hamilton Jewelers store in a Palm Beach Gardens, Florida, shopping mall and handed the saleswoman a note, claiming he had a gun and informing her that the store was being robbed.

She gave $170 to a man who already had $600 in his wallet, after a pitching career in the big leagues that had earned him more than $11 million over 16 seasons.

See? This either had to be a goof or a sign that something was seriously wrong.

Unfortunately for Reardon and his family, it was the latter.

In logging 367 saves for seven different clubs—most memorably, 31 in 1987 and three more in the postseason to help Minnesota win the World Series for the first time—Reardon's personality was a little at odds with his image as a late-inning "Terminator." Soft-spoken and thoughtful away from the field, Reardon's primary tools of intimidation were a full dark beard and

Jeff Reardon was the foundation for the Twins' championship bullpen in 1987, but his life took a dark and tragic turn after he retired in 1994.

steely glare that made him look menacing and, of course, some serious velocity on his pitches. He survived a rocky start after joining the Twins via trade before that 1987 season, but then, that squad was so eager for a lockdown closer that teammates patiently waited for the right-hander to find his groove.

A four-time All-Star, Reardon had three seasons of at least 40 saves and four more ringing up 30 or more. He left Minnesota for Boston after the 1989 season and then worked for Atlanta, Cincinnati, and the Yankees before retiring in 1994, at age 38, settling into what figured to be an idyllic post-baseball retirement.

Idyllic, admittedly, is something most often perceived from the outside, with the ordinary challenges of everyday living present even for the most comfortable families. And sometimes, extraordinary challenges, as Reardon, wife Phebe, and their three kids—Jay, Kristi, and Shane—sadly found out.

In February 2004, Shane Reardon, 20, was found dead of a drug overdose in his Orlando apartment. He apparently had relapsed into the drinking and drug abuse that had reared up during high school.

"When I heard what happened to his son, I was just shocked," said Al Newman, the utility infielder who had played with Reardon in both Montreal and Minnesota. "I knew Jeff was going to take it hard. You could tell it was a tight-knit family."

The tragic news sent both Jeff and Phebe into a downward spiral of despair, grief, and depression. Reardon went on a prescription for antidepressants, evidently requiring heavy doses. When he encountered symptoms of heart problems, he underwent an emergency angioplasty and was put on more medication. That was just days before he passed the hold-up note to the saleswoman.

"I just walked out casually, started going to my car," Reardon recalled. "[Then] I walked right up to a security guard and said, 'I think I did something stupid.' He said, 'What do you mean?' I said, 'There's money in this bag.' I said, 'Maybe I robbed a store or something.' I didn't know."

Reardon was arrested and spent a night in jail, explaining to police about the possible side effects of his prescriptions. The news made national headlines, with most assuming that, well, Reardon sure had hit rock bottom. Except that robbing a jewelry store wasn't as low as he would go. The former big-leaguer already had tried to commit suicide at least once by stepping into the path of an oncoming truck (it swerved), and he had contemplated it on other occasions. He sought help at a mental health hospital, checked back in shortly after his arrest, and underwent electroshock therapy. The evidence of his condition was overwhelming, and in August 2006 Reardon was acquitted of the robbery charge by reason of insanity.

Reflecting on that rough three- to four-year period in his family's life, Reardon told a Twin Cities reporter in 2007: "I would like the people in Minnesota to know, everyone needs to know, that I was actually crazy to do that."

The loss of their son Shane was nothing that Jeff and Phebe Reardon likely will ever get over. The challenge was to learn to live with it, or through it, or in spite of it, as best they could.

That's why old Twins teammates saw it as such an encouraging sign when the Reardons took part in a 20th reunion of that '87 championship team. Many fans did, too, giving the pitcher a warm round of applause when he was introduced before an August 2007 game. His old employer, the Twins, announced that a $100,000 contribution (from commemorative bobblehead sales, of course) would be made to the Shane Reardon Memorial Fund, set up to aid the families of drug abusers.

Said Reardon: "It's the nicest thing that's ever been done for our family. We only had $18,000 in the account for the foundation. You can't help many kids with $18,000, but we can do some good work now."

The Twins and their fans remembered all the good work Reardon had done for them. Which, in the end, was only a game.

DON'T CALL HIM "ZORRO!"

No Twins player ever had a flame that burned brighter, then flickered out more quickly, than shortstop Zoilo Versalles. In 1965 Versalles had a magical season, leading the Twins to the World Series in only their fifth year after moving to Minnesota and earning the American League's Most Valuable Player Award at age 25.

Versalles was in his seventh major league season, after breaking in at 19 with the Washington Senators, but he had his career year, averaging .273, hitting 19 home runs with 77 RBIs, scoring 126 runs, and stealing 27 bases. His defense was strong, though he did lead the league in errors that season. And while a nickname of "Zorro" never stuck or was appreciated, his given name—Zoilo Casanova Versalles—already was special enough.

A native of Vedado, Cuba, Versalles was part of the franchise's famous Latin pipeline, dating back to the 1910s and '20s in Washington. Eventual manager and owner Clark Griffith, during a three-season stint with the Cincinnati Reds, had used a pair of Cuban players on his 1911 roster: Armando Marsans and Rafael Almeida.

Shortstop Zoilo Versalles was the improbable winner of the AL MVP Award in 1965 for the pennant-winning Twins.

Later, during World War II, the status of foreign-born players as exempt from the U.S. military draft appealed to Griffith as a businessman and a competitor. He also made of habit of signing top prospects to very cheap contracts, another brick in the Senators/Twins tradition.

The influx of Cuban players, in particular, took off in the '40s under the supervision of talent scout Joe "Papa Joe" Cambria. "When I was coming up in the minor leagues, sometimes I felt like I was home in Cuba because we had so many Cuban players," said first baseman Julio Becquer, who spent most of his seven big-league seasons with the franchise and settled in Minneapolis.

Cambria's top discoveries included Pedro Ramos, Camilo Pascual, Versalles, and his gem, Tony Oliva. Oliva in 1964 and

1965 became the first player to win batting titles in his first two seasons. But Versalles did Cambria proud in '65 as well, giving that Series team its heart and surpassing Oliva's second-place point total for MVP by more than 100.

After becoming the first Latin player to win an MVP award—beating his idol Luis Aparicio, who had finished second in helping the White Sox to the 1959 pennant—Versalles never approached that level of play again. Though he thrived with coach Billy Martin as his mentor, Versalles never again hit more than seven home runs in a season, drove in more than 50, or stole more than 10 bases. The Twins shipped him to the Dodgers after the 1967 season, and he rapidly slipped through the Cleveland, Washington, and Atlanta systems before washing out in 1971 at age 31.

Some who knew him claim that Versalles, in achieving such team and individual glory all at once in 1965, lost his ambition and focus. Despite having a lovely wife and six beautiful daughters, Versalles's post-playing days proved difficult. Money always was tight, and he sold off his MVP trophy and All-Star ring while drifting through odd jobs. He sought out former Twins owner Calvin Griffith for "loans" and then relied on Social Security and disability payments.

By the time the Twins made it to the Series again in 1987, Versalles had no interest in the team. "When I got traded, that was it," he told a reporter. "I wasn't part of the Twins anymore. I think they'll win the World Series, but I don't care."

On June 9, 1995, Versalles, just 55, was found dead at his home in Bloomington, Minnesota.

THE COMEBACK KID

Jim Eisenreich, professional baseball player, lasted 15 seasons in the major leagues. He batted .290 in his career on 1,160 hits, hitting 52 home runs and driving in 477 runs in 1,422 games. The teams for which he played made it to two World Series, with the outfielder hitting .294 in 11 games, with two homers and 10 RBIs.

It has been estimated that Eisenreich earned more than $10 million in his career. As his playing days wound down, in 1998, he was an elder statesman of sorts, the oldest player in the National League with his 40th birthday fast approaching.

And to think, there were days in his rookie season with the Twins when Jim Eisenreich wasn't able to make it through one whole ballgame.

A native of St. Cloud, Minnesota, it seemed part storybook when the hard-hitting outfielder took the big step from Class A ball to the Twins' major league roster. Not just hanging onto a spot but penciled in as the center fielder. Batting leadoff. Club owner Calvin Griffith called Eisenreich the best player ever to come up through his farm system and predicted star status.

For a few weeks, there was ample evidence that the owner was right. After a season-opening homestand of nine games, Eisenreich was batting .344. He got 10 hits and seven walks on the Twins' eight-game trip that followed, and he was starting his 20th game when Minnesota opened a three-game weekend series against Milwaukee at the new indoor Metrodome.

Eisenreich went 1-for-3 through the first five innings, but as he took his position for the top of the sixth, he was in obvious distress. And it was getting worse. "Jim seemed to be taking quick, short, stiff-legged steps between each pitch," Twins manager Billy Gardner described later. "He would step first to his left and then to his right. Also, between pitches, Jim was turning his back to the infield. His movements seemed machine-like. When he bent to anticipate the pitch, his body was rigid. It seemed to hinge 90 degrees from the waist."

Eisenreich's teammates were as confused as the visiting Brewers when the center fielder began to twitch and shake uncontrollably. He struggled to catch his breath, called "Time!" and ran to the dugout. The team's trainer urged him to drink some water and head back onto the field, but Eisenreich refused. The whole sequence played itself out again on Saturday and Sunday, the leadoff man bailing out and needing a sudden replacement for, well, a condition that Twins management simply didn't understand.

In two games at Boston, Eisenreich took verbal abuse from fans in the Fenway Park bleachers, which only made his condition worse. Then, in Milwaukee for three games, Eisenreich never stepped across the lines. He scratched himself from the series opener, scared the trainer enough with his sporadic breathing and belching to send the player to a downtown hospital, and didn't even go to the ballpark for the last two games.

From there, Eisenreich's situation got worse. The Twins' medical staff, trying to diagnose his condition, settled on three possible maladies: performance anxiety (or "stage fright"), agoraphobia (the fear of vast open spaces), or Tourette's syndrome. After numerous tests, the team focused more on the first two

Despite his best efforts, outfielder Jim Eisenreich's battle with Tourette's syndrome forced him to leave the field on several occasions. Photo courtesy of AP/Wide World Photos.

possibilities than the third. Eisenreich went the other way. He learned through family that he had shown symptoms of Tourette's by the age of six, developing tics and spastic muscle movements in his face, neck, and arms. Also, that diagnosis held some appeal for Eisenreich because, if there was something wrong with him, he preferred that it be a physical problem rather than something psychological.

It was, to be sure, a baseball problem. Eisenreich came back for 1983 but lasted only two games with the Twins before the behavior returned. In 1984 he made it through 12 games. When the player continued to take medication for Tourette's rather than accede to their diagnoses, the Twins negotiated a buyout of his contract. Eisenreich went back home to St. Cloud, presumably to retire.

An odd thing happened there, however. Still in love with the game, Eisenreich played for the semipro St. Cloud Saints. And the symptoms that had forced him out of Minneapolis dramatically lessened.

Next came a lucky connection—Bob Hegman, an old college teammate at St. Cloud State, happened to be working in the Kansas City Royals' scouting and development office. So Eisenreich, after all those lost seasons, went to spring training with the Royals, a low-cost gamble for the ballclub.

His tics and gyrations weren't completely gone, but they were seemingly under control. Eisenreich, working again for a familiar face (Gardner was by now managing the Royals), batted .238 in 44 games, appeared in 82 in 1988, and then, at age 30, hit .293 with 33 doubles, nine homers, 59 RBIs, and 27 stolen bases for Kansas City in 1989.

He was, however belatedly, on his way. After six seasons with the Royals—during which he met and married his wife Leann—he signed with Philadelphia, where his extreme shyness became just another personality quirk on a free-spirited team that made it to the 1993 World Series. After the 1996 season, Eisenreich signed with the Florida Marlins, participating as the underdogs beat Atlanta for the pennant and then Cleveland in the 1997 Series.

Retiring after the 1998 season, Eisenreich became comfortable enough with his story and condition to become a spokesperson about Tourette's, both to seek donations to continue the medical fight and to put at ease others who suffer from it. And while he doesn't look back with regret, he does occasionally think about his time with the Twins.

"I don't want to brag, but if I had been able to play, Kirby [Puckett] would've been in right field when he came up," Eisenreich said. "I could go get the ball, and I could always catch it."

NOTES

THE GOOD

Kirby Puckett

"But personality...," Patrick Reusse, "A Plaque Preview," *Minneapolis Star Tribune*, May 4, 2001.

"In so many ways, professional athletes...," Dan Barreiro, "Puckett's Election Makes Revisiting Past Worthwhile," *Minneapolis Star Tribune*, Jan. 17, 2001.

"I just played baseball like every game...," Dan Barreiro, "Puckett's Election Makes Revisiting Past Worthwhile," *Minneapolis Star Tribune*, Jan. 17, 2001.

"He's just a down-to-earth nice guy...," Paula Parrish, "Killebrew Sings Praise of Robinson, Puckett," *Minneapolis Star Tribune*, May 24, 1997.

"Sixteen-story buildings with 10 apartments...," Patrick Reusse, "Puckett Brings Smile to Cooperstown," *Minneapolis Star Tribune*, August 5, 2001.

"I found out Hack was only...," Patrick Reusse, "A Plaque Preview," *Minneapolis Star Tribune*, May 4, 2001.

"This was the phenom we've been waiting for?...," Jim Souhan, "Decade of Fun," *Minneapolis Star Tribune*, September 6, 1996.

"I was unconscious...," Jim Souhan, "Decade of Fun," *Minneapolis Star Tribune*, September 6, 1996.

"If I had written it up myself...," Jim Souhan, "Decade of Fun," *Minneapolis Star Tribune*, September 6, 1996.

"My God, you have a guy struck down...," Dan Barreiro, "Puckett's Election Makes Revisiting Past Worthwhile," *Minneapolis Star Tribune*, Jan. 17, 2001.

"He handled it better than anybody...," John Henderson, "Where Are They Now?" *Baseball Digest,* Nov. 1, 2000.

"What else am I supposed to do?" John Henderson, "Where Are They Now?" *Baseball Digest,* Nov. 1, 2000.

"Baseball owes me nothing," Dan Barreiro, "Puckett's Election Makes Revisiting Past Worthwhile," *Minneapolis Star Tribune*, Jan. 17, 2001.

1987 World Champions

"I talk more about '87, I think...," Kelsie Smith, "Days of Thunder," *St. Paul Pioneer Press*, August 16, 2007.

"I couldn't wait to get out there...," Patrick Reusse, "Something Great Was in the Air," *Minneapolis Star Tribune*, August 9, 1997.

"Even if we had won those...," Jay Weiner, "Twins Are the Underdogs," *Minneapolis Star Tribune*, Oct. 6, 1987.

"It is, isn't it?...," Doug Grow, "Hugs, Emotions and the American League Pennant," *Minneapolis Star Tribune*, Oct. 12, 1987.

"After we beat Detroit...," Kelsie Smith, "Days of Thunder," *St. Paul Pioneer Press*, August 16, 2007.

"Things that I remember most...," Alan Ross, *Twins Pride,* Cumberland House, 2006.

"We never feel down in this place...," Mark Vancil, "Hrbek Brings Twins to Their Knees, Then Brings Crowd to Its Feet," *Minneapolis Star Tribune*, Oct. 25, 1987.

"I remember catching the throw...," Leslie Parker, "Twins Won It as a Team in '87," MLB.com, July 26, 2007.

"I was trying to get to the pile...," Leslie Parker, "Twins Won It as a Team in '87," MLB.com, July 26, 2007.

1991 World Champions

"After Game 6, people started...," Dan Bickley, "Magic, Michael and More," *Chicago Sun-Times*, Dec. 29, 1991.

"I think it's ridiculous for us...," Jeff Lenihan, "Twins Hit Bottom, Bounce Back to the Top of AL West," *The Washington Post,* August 5, 1991.

"We had a much better ballclub this year...," Don Burke, "Twins Ready To Take On World," *The Record (Bergen County, NJ),* Oct. 14, 1991.

"So many things happened...," Steve Adamek, "Talkin' Classic Baseball," *The Record (Bergen County, NJ),* Oct. 24, 1991.

"Ten, 30, 50 years from now, when I look at it...," Steve Rushin, "A Series to Savor," *Sports Illustrated,* Nov. 4, 1991.

"I'm a lousy loser...," Thomas Boswell, "Series of Special Events," *The Washington Post,* Oct. 29, 1991.

"This was the greatest game...," Steve Rushin, "A Series to Savor," *Sports Illustrated,* Nov. 4, 1991.

"Days like this...," Mark Maske, "World Series '91: Playing Baseball on Razor's Edge," *The Washington Post,* Oct. 29, 1991.

THE BAD

The Great Race of 1967

"There are a few things you can laugh at now...," Patrick Reusse, "Anniversary Summer: The Great Race The 1967 Season," *Minneapolis Star Tribune,* July 21, 2007.

"Sam had been around awhile...," Patrick Reusse, "Anniversary Summer: The Great Race The 1967 Season," *Minneapolis Star Tribune,* July 21, 2007.

"I've never seen a perfect player...," Dan Schlossberg, "When Carl Yastrzemski Became a Star," *Baseball Digest,* July 1, 2002.

The Hard-Luck Kid

"Through the entire losing streak...," Staff report, "Hen's Felton Snaps Skid," *Toledo Blade,* June 16, 1983.

"I was 0–9 in the big leagues...," Staff report, "Hen's Felton Snaps Skid," *Toledo Blade,* June 16, 1983.

"Everybody really has been pulling for Terry...," Staff report, "Hen's Felton Snaps Skid," *Toledo Blade,* June 16, 1983.

The Lost Years (1993–2000)

"It was trying because you started to question...," Jack Etkin, "Twins Grow Up," *Rocky Mountain News,* June 9, 2003.

"The goal on my watch, or whatever...," Jack Etkin, "Putting the Win Back in Twins," *Rocky Mountain News,* August 30, 2004.

"There isn't a better feeling for us...," Jack Etkin, "Twins Grow Up," *Rocky Mountain News,* June 9, 2003.

THE UGLY

Fighting Mad

"He was beat to a pulp...," Patrick Reusse, "Site of Martin-Boswell Fracas Closes Up Shop," *Minneapolis Star Tribune,* Dec. 12, 2002.

"If I feel like I can't help the team...," LaVelle E. Neal III, "Morneau Back in Lineup," *Minneapolis Star Tribune,* June 9, 2005.

"Everybody's got to be tightly knit...," LaVelle E. Neal III, "Infighting Continues as Season Plays Out," *Minneapolis Star Tribune,* Oct. 1, 2005.

"When that stuff all happens at the same time...," LaVelle E. Neal III, "Infighting Continues as Season Plays Out," *Minneapolis Star Tribune,* Oct. 1, 2005.

Ron Davis

"There were enough games that got away...," Patrick Reusse, "Ron Davis' 9th Inning Adventures," *Minneapolis Star Tribune,* August 13, 2006.

"Ron Davis was a very hyper guy...," Alan Ross, *Twins Pride,* Cumberland House Publishing, 2006.

"The tension disappeared...," Patrick Reusse, "Ron Davis' 9th Inning Adventures," *Minneapolis Star Tribune,* August 13, 2006.

"It's a nice feeling to have it over with...," Patrick Reusse, "Ron Davis' 9th Inning Adventures," *Minneapolis Star Tribune,* August 13, 2006.

"People ask me, if I had my choice...," Patrick Reusse, "Ron Davis' 9th Inning Adventures," *Minneapolis Star Tribune,* August 13, 2006.

The Metrodome

"I think the main thing...," Steve Aschburner, "Home Sweet Dome," *Minneapolis Star Tribune*, August 16, 1987.

"The best home-field advantage ever...," Alan Ross, *Twins Pride*, Cumberland House Publishing, 2006.

"The play was a disgrace to baseball...," Alan Ross, *Twins Pride*, Cumberland House Publishing, 2006.

TWINS PITCHERS WHO BATTED

"I'm playing for right now...," Steve Adamek and Mike Celizic, "Aguilera Is Center of Attention At the Plate," *The Record (Bergen County NJ)*, Oct. 24, 1991.

"It's not something where you can just...," Steve Adamek and Mike Celizic, "Aguilera Is Center of Attention At the Plate," *The Record (Bergen County NJ)*, Oct. 24, 1991.

"I wasn't going to pitch Aggie...," Steve Adamek and Mike Celizic, "Aguilera Is Center of Attention At the Plate," *The Record (Bergen County NJ)*, Oct. 24, 1991.

"They [the Braves] don't have a book on me...," Steve Adamek and Mike Celizic, "Aguilera Is Center of Attention At the Plate," *The Record (Bergen County NJ)*, Oct. 24, 1991.

IN THE CLUTCH

Allison's Catch in 1965

"My coordination is gone...," Bob Cohn, "Loss of Power: Former Twins Slugger Battling Rare Illness," *Arizona Republic*, October 1991.

"This guy had the ideal body...," Bob Cohn, "Loss of Power: Former Twins Slugger Battling Rare Illness," *Arizona Republic*, October 1991.

You Can Go Home

"I felt awful...," Patrick Reusse, "Something Great Was in the Air," *Minneapolis Star Tribune*, August 9, 1997.

"I can't believe I threw home...," Patrick Reusse, "Something Great Was in the Air," *Minneapolis Star Tribune*, August 9, 1997.

Nabbing Darrell Napping

"Gary and I have a...," Joe Goddard, "Twins Cash in As Tigers Falter," *Chicago Sun-Times*, Oct. 12, 1987.

"I just got too far off...," Richard Justice, "Tigers' Sloppy Play Results in 5-3 Loss," *The Washington Post*, Oct. 12, 1987.

"I think the pickoff...," Richard Justice, "Tigers' Sloppy Play Results in 5-3 Loss," *The Washington Post*, Oct. 12, 1987.

"T. Rex" Wrecks Gant

"When I was a kid, six, seven, eight years old...," Steve Adamek, "Hrbek an Unlikely Villain," *The Record (Bergen County N.J.)*, Oct. 22, 1991.

"In my judgment, his momentum carried him...," Steve Adamek, "Twins Pull One Out," *The Record (Bergen County N.J.)*, Oct. 21, 1991.

"He [Gant] knocked me over...," Steve Adamek, "Twins Pull One Out," *The Record (Bergen County N.J.)*, Oct. 21, 1991.

"I didn't know you could pull people...," Steve Adamek, "Twins Pull One Out," *The Record (Bergen County N.J.)*, Oct. 21, 1991.

"Gant gets a single to put guys...," Thomas Boswell, "Time to Put on Brave Face," *The Washington Post*, Oct. 21, 1991.

"I'm not that scared...," Mark Maske, "Minnesota's Hrbek Wrestles with Complaints," *The Washington Post*, Oct. 23, 1991.

"I'd want to be a good guy...," Steve Adamek, "Hrbek an Unlikely Villain," *The Record (Bergen County N.J.)*, Oct. 22, 1991.

Lonnie Smith Joins Club

"We still should have scored...," Bob Nightengale, "Smith Still Feeling Blame," *Chicago Sun-Times*, Oct. 18, 1992.

"I knew right there what everyone...," Bob Nightengale, "Smith Still Feeling Blame," *Chicago Sun-Times*, Oct. 18, 1992.

"I never saw that damn ball...," Bob Nightengale, "Smith Still Feeling Blame," *Chicago Sun-Times*, Oct. 18, 1992.

"I knew when we didn't score in that game...," Bob Nightengale, "Smith Still Feeling Blame," *Chicago Sun-Times,* Oct. 18, 1992.

"I think people really thought...," Bob Nightengale, "Smith Still Feeling Blame," *Chicago Sun-Times,* Oct. 18, 1992.

The Hitless Wonders

"I wish I was still in baseball...," www.baseball-almanac.com.

NUMBERS DON'T LIE (OR DO THEY?)

Flirting with .400

"You wear down when you swing...," Jim Souhan, "The Final Frontier," *Minneapolis Star Tribune,* September 24, 1997.

"I've never had a game like this...," Joel Rippel, "75 Memorable Moments in Minnesota Sports," Minnesota Historical Society, 2003.

Let's Play Nine!

"He's probably the best utility player we've ever had...," Juan C. Rodriguez, "Cesar Tovar, Twins Outfielder from 1965–72, Is Dead at 54," *Minneapolis Star Tribune,* July 15, 1994.

IT AIN'T OVER 'TIL IT'S OVER

Rollin' Ryan

"This has been creeping in and creeping in...," Bob Nightengale, "Stress Leads Ryan to Resign as Twins GM," *USA Today,* September 14, 2007.

The Leather Experts

"I'm suicidal...," Stan McNeal, "Hello, Walls: Twins Gold Glove Center Fielder Torii Hunter Will Run through Walls to Make a Catch," *The Sporting News,* September 2, 2002.

"I have to do it for my pitchers...," Stan McNeal, "Hello, Walls: Twins Gold Glove Center Fielder Torii Hunter Will Run through Walls to Make a Catch," *The Sporting News,* September 2, 2002.

HR Feats
"Schaaf reported Oliva's home run as it happened...," Alan Ross, *Twins Pride,* Cumberland House Publishing, 2006.

Calvin Griffith
"You talk about somebody standing up...," Jason Wolf, "Former Twins Owner Dies," Associated Press, Oct. 21, 1999.

"This really is the completion of...," Jay Weiner, "Calvin Griffith, 1911–1999: A Big League Legend Dies," *Minneapolis Star Tribune,* Oct. 21, 1999.

"I haven't been in the clubhouse...," Alan Ross, *Twins Pride,* Cumberland House Publishing, 2006.

"I said, 'Calvin, I agree...," Phil Pepe, *Talkin' Baseball: An Oral History of Baseball in the 1970s,* Ballantine Books, 1998, page 163.

"After every [game], we would go home...," Max Nichols, "The Last of His League," *The (Oklahoma City) Journal Record,* August 22, 1996.

"Those first few years at the Met...," Alan Ross, *Twins Pride,* Cumberland House Publishing, 2006.

"The interesting thing is that the organization...," Jay Weiner, "Calvin Griffith, 1911–1999: A Big League Legend Dies," *Minneapolis Star Tribune,* Oct. 21, 1999.

"I think I'm a person...," Alan Ross, *Twins Pride,* Cumberland House Publishing, 2006.

"I was so mad...," Jay Weiner, "Calvin Griffith, 1911–1999: A Big League Legend Dies," *Minneapolis Star Tribune,* Oct. 21, 1999.

"From now on, baseball owners...," Jay Weiner, "Calvin Griffith, 1911–1999: A Big League Legend Dies," *Minneapolis Star Tribune,* Oct. 21, 1999.

"You know the people who don't like Calvin Griffith...," Jay Weiner, "Calvin Griffith, 1911–1999: A Big League Legend Dies," *Minneapolis Star Tribune,* Oct. 21, 1999.

Home Invaders
"After I got into it, I really enjoyed...," Paul Post, "Stealing Home: A Lost Art," *Baseball Digest,* August 2002.

"It was high-emotion time...," Paul Post, "Stealing Home: A Lost Art," *Baseball Digest,* August 2002.

"He'd jump up on the top step and yell...," Paul Post, "Stealing Home: A Lost Art," *Baseball Digest,* August 2002.

KIDS IN THE HALL (OR NOT)

"The Killer," Harmon Killebrew

"He told me that I should be hitting...," Jim Souhan, "MVP: Justin Morneau," *Minneapolis Star Tribune,* Nov. 22, 2006.

"He hit line drives that put the opposition...," Alan Ross, *Twins Pride,* Cumberland House Publishing, 2006.

"I got the book on how to pitch...," Alan Ross, *Twins Pride,* Cumberland House Publishing, 2006.

"It's so hard for the average fan...," Paul Post, "Former Pitcher Jim Kaat... Recalls His Storied Career," *Baseball Digest,* August 1, 2005.

"Killebrew gives us class...," Alan Ross, *Twins Pride,* Cumberland House Publishing, 2006.

"Dad used to work with my brother...," Adam Schefter, "Hall of Fame Slugger: Harmon Killebrew (Interview)," *Baseball Digest,* Dec. 1, 2004.

Hall of Famers

"The injuries were frustrating...," Larry Stone, "Mariners Hitting Coach Molitor Emerges as One of the All-Time Greats," *Seattle Times,* July 24, 2004.

"In my mind, if Paulie hadn't gotten hurt...," Larry Stone, "Mariners Hitting Coach Molitor Emerges as One of the All-Time Greats," *Seattle Times,* July 24, 2004.

"I remember the Minnesota media...," Larry Stone, "Mariners Hitting Coach Molitor Emerges as One of the All-Time Greats," *Seattle Times,* July 24, 2004.

"It's pretty incredible to imagine...," Jim Souhan, "3,000 the Molitor Way," *Minneapolis Star Tribune,* September 17, 1996.

"I didn't have an easy, smooth career...," Jim Souhan, "Dave Winfield's Numbers Add Up," *Minneapolis Star Tribune,* Jan. 17, 2001.

"Killebrew, Zoilo Versalles—my first glove...," Jim Souhan, "Dave Winfield's Numbers Add Up," *Minneapolis Star Tribune,* Jan. 17, 2001.

"I left Minnesota and went out...," Patrick Reusse, "Winfield Enjoys Special Time," *Minneapolis Star Tribune,* June 9, 2001.

Hall of the Very Good

"Tony Oliva was critical in teaching...," Alan Ross, *Twins Pride,* Cumberland House Publishing, 2006.

"It's better to go into the Hall...," LaVelle E. Neal III, "On the Brink... Again," *Minneapolis Star Tribune,* Feb. 27, 2000.

"Without baseball, I would have stayed...," Alan Ross, *Twins Pride,* Cumberland House Publishing, 2006.

"I was a little guy as a kid...," Paul Post, "Former Pitcher Jim Kaat... Recalls His Storied Career," *Baseball Digest,* August 1, 2005.

"I remember warming up next to him...," Paul Post, "Former Pitcher Jim Kaat... Recalls His Storied Career," *Baseball Digest,* August 1, 2005.

"Jim threw what we call a 'heavy' ball...," Alan Ross, *Twins Pride,* Cumberland House Publishing, 2006.

"He was as good as there was for a long time...," thebaseballpage.com, "Bert Blyleven."

"If you vote for me one year...," LaVelle E. Neal III, "Blyleven, Morris Miss Hall Election," *Minneapolis Star Tribune,* Jan. 10, 2007.

"I would love to have all...," Britt Robson, "King of the Hill," *City Pages,* April 6, 2005.

"He is, without a doubt, one of the nastiest...," Patrick Reusse, "Hall Should Have a Plaque for Jack Morris," *Minneapolis Star Tribune,* July 23, 2004.

"I've got to do the best I can for my future...," Thomas Boswell, "Can't Call Morris a Pussycat," *The Washington Post,* Dec. 20, 1991.

SCREWBALLS, ODDBALLS, AND OTHER FAVORITES

A Cast of Characters

"I said, 'My gosh, I'm rebuilding from scratch again...,'" Mike Downey, "Hatcher a Most Unlikely Hero in Dodger Blue," *Chicago Sun-Times,* Jan. 15, 1989.

"What's happened to me the last couple of months...," Mike Downey, "Hatcher a Most Unlikely Hero in Dodger Blue," *Chicago Sun-Times,* Jan. 15, 1989.

"Sometimes you've got to dig a little deeper...," Jerry Zgoda, "No Clowning Around Now for Hatcher," *Minneapolis Star Tribune,* Oct. 11, 2002.

"I told them, 'Any one of you right here...," Jerry Zgoda, "No Clowning Around Now for Hatcher," *Minneapolis Star Tribune,* Oct. 11, 2002.

"I didn't go out to argue with the umpire...," Patrick Reusse, "One More Year to Remember the Good Ol' Days," *Minneapolis Star Tribune,* Nov. 16, 1997.

"The first thing you want is just to be part...," Richard Justice, "At Last, Niekro in The Series," *The Washington Post,* Oct. 22, 1987.

"There was magic to that season...," Patrick Reusse, "'65 in '05: A Twins Reunion," *Minneapolis Star Tribune,* August 20, 2005.

"Teams always want pitching...," Patrick Reusse, "'65 in '05: A Twins Reunion," *Minneapolis Star Tribune,* August 20, 2005.

"You lose something every year you throw...," Jim Thielman, *Cool of the Evening: The 1965 Minnesota Twins,* Kirk House Publishers (January 15, 2005).

"Look at my guy out there," Doug Grow, "Norm Coleman is Pitching but There's Nothing to Throw," *Minneapolis Star Tribune,* August 4, 1999.

"When they draft you into the Army...," Jay Weiner, "New Twin Ends up Playing for Time," *Minneapolis Star Tribune,* May 9, 1984.

"I manage the Twins...," Patrick Reusse, "One More Year to Remember the Good Ol' Days," *Minneapolis Star Tribune,* Nov. 16, 1997.

"I'm glad of the days Bert is pitching...," Thomas Boswell, "Blyleven: Now the Joker Has a Starring Role," *The Washington Post*, July 16, 1989.

"Want to know why morale's...," Thomas Boswell, "Blyleven: Now the Joker Has a Starring Role," *The Washington Post*, July 16, 1989.

"My friends from Panama said, 'What's wrong...," Patrick Reusse, "The Heat is Off for Berenguer," *Minneapolis Star Tribune*, August 7, 1997.

"A lot of people want to know what was in there...," Ben Goessling, "Twin Enjoys Chaotic, Happy Retirement," *Minneapolis Star Tribune*, March 22, 2006.

Infinity and Beyond

"I don't give a [bleep] about it...," Charley Walters, "Vikings' Peterson a Quick Study," *St. Paul Pioneer Press*, August 21, 2007.

The Voice: Herb Carneal

"If she was out in the backyard...," Judd Zulgad, "Goodbye to an Old Friend," *Minneapolis Star Tribune*, April 2, 2007.

"He never had a great...," Judd Zulgad, "Goodbye to an Old Friend," *Minneapolis Star Tribune*, April 2, 2007.

The Voice: Bob Casey

"Sometimes I do it on purpose...," "Casey at the Mike: a Twins Legend," Associated Press, June 1, 2003.

"As a kid from Miami...," LaVelle E. Neal III, "Bob Casey, 1925-2005; A Trademark Voice with a Unique Flair," *Minneapolis Star Tribune*, March 28, 2005.

"Man, that's cool...," Jerry Zgoda, "Casey at the Mike," *Minneapolis Star Tribune*, August 9, 1998.

TRADING PLACES

Met Stadium

"In the early years before they put a double deck...," Paul Post, "Former Pitcher Jim Kaat...Recalls His Storied Career," *Baseball Digest,* August 1, 2005.

"We played in some brutally cold weather...," Paul Post, "Former Pitcher Jim Kaat...Recalls His Storied Career," *Baseball Digest,* August 1, 2005.

"I tell you, there's been a lot of feeling...," Jim Thielman, www.cooloftheevening.com, "Calvin Griffith Says Goodbye to Metropolitan Stadium," Oct. 1, 1981.

PAIN AND SUFFERING

Danny Thompson

"Desire. That's the thing...," Maury Allen, "Remembering Danny," *New York Post,* Dec. 13, 1976.

"I didn't want the world knowing...,"Alan Ross, *Twins Pride / For the Love of Kirby, Kent and Killebrew,* Cumberland House Publishing, 2006.

"I can't understand what's wrong with Thompson...," Patrick Reusse, "Leukemia Once Again Creeping into Kusick's Life," *Minneapolis Star Tribune,* Jan. 22, 2005.

"I was asleep and my wife woke me up...," Phil Pepe, "Hisle Makes Spirit of Christmas Live for His Pal," *New York Daily News,* Dec. 24, 1976.

"I talked to him on the phone...," Maury Allen, "Remembering Danny," *New York Post,* Dec. 13, 1976.

Devastating Injuries

"If it's deemed that he can't play catcher...," Joe Christensen, "Mauer, Gardenhire Firing Back," *Minneapolis Star Tribune,* September 4, 2007.

"Guys in here know that I play hard...," Joe Christensen, "Mauer, Gardenhire Firing Back," *Minneapolis Star Tribune,* September 4, 2007.

"You couldn't see the ball at all...," Patrick Reusse, "Keeping His Distance," *Minneapolis Star Tribune,* July 17, 2005.

"Jimmie still was dangerous...," Patrick Reusse, "Keeping His Distance," *Minneapolis Star Tribune,* July 17, 2005.

"The only people who knew how much...," LaVelle E. Neal III, "On the Brink...Again," *Minneapolis Star Tribune,* Feb. 27, 2000.

"At the time, he was really depressed...," LaVelle E. Neal III, "On the Brink...Again," *Minneapolis Star Tribune,* Feb. 27, 2000.

"The doctors said it showed there...," Bob Vanderberg, "Castino Provides a Cautionary Tale," *Chicago Tribune,* June 27, 2007.

"That's something I shouldn't have done...," Bob Vanderberg, "Castino Provides a Cautionary Tale," *Chicago Tribune,* June 27, 2007.

"When I was 24 and in the majors...," Alan Gersten, "A Rookie of the Year, a World-Class Adviser," *Financial Planning,* March 1, 2005.

Saving Reardon

"When I heard what happened...," Joe Christensen, "Reardon's Arrest Stuns Some Former Teammates," *Minneapolis Star Tribune,* Dec. 28, 2005.

"I just walked out casually, started...," Kelsie Smith, "Former Twins Reliever Reardon Seeking Relief," *St. Paul Pioneer Press,* August 12, 2007.

"I would like the people in Minnesota...," Kelsie Smith, "Former Twins Reliever Reardon Seeking Relief," *St. Paul Pioneer Press,* August 12, 2007.

"It's the nicest thing that's ever been done...," Patrick Reusse, "Twins' Actions Says Thanks to Reardon," *Minneapolis Star Tribune,* 2007.

Don't Call Him "Zorro!"

"When I was coming up...," William Gildea, "Once There Was a Pipeline From Cuba to D.C.," *The Washington Post,* March 28, 2003.

"When I got traded...," *Chicago Sun-Times* wire report, Oct. 21, 1987.

The Comeback Kid

"Jim seemed to be taking quick...," Rick Swaine, *Beating the Breaks: Major League Ballplayers Who Overcame Disabilities,* McFarland & Company, 2004.

"I don't want to brag, but...," Patrick Reusse, "Safe at Home: Eisenreich Overcame Tourette's," *Minneapolis Star Tribune,* Dec. 25, 1999.